A CIRCLE OF WITCHES

By the same author

THE GENTLEWOMEN OF EVIL
THE SATANIST

A CIRCLE
OF WITCHES

An Anthology of
Victorian Witchcraft Stories

SELECTED AND INTRODUCED **BY**

PETER HAINING

ILLUSTRATED

TAPLINGER PUBLISHING COMPANY
NEW YORK

First published in the United States in 1971 by

TAPLINGER PUBLISHING CO., INC.

New York, New York

Copyright © Collection copyright by Peter Haining 1971

ISBN 0-8008-1590-4

Library of Congress Catalog Card Number 79-126286

PRINTED IN GREAT BRITAIN

"She thought only of the moment when sudden darkness had fallen upon her and all because of this woman—this witch; this Enchantress who trapped victim after victim in her evil power; this Sorceress of whom all poems and stories spoke."

"The Sorceress"
(1893)

CONTENTS

CONTENTS

ILLUSTRATIONS

PICTURE CREDITS

The author: 1, 4, 9, 10, 11, 13, 14, 15, 16; Radio Times
Hulton Picture Library: 2, 3; Mary Evans Picture
Library: 5, 6, 7, 8, 12, 17.

INTRODUCTION

Most of us born in the twentieth century probably think of the Victorian era as one of hansom cabs and gas lighting; of extravagant wealth and crushing poverty. An era when manners dominated and the right kind of birth was essential for success in business or social life. Our grandparents, indeed, lived at a time when the British Empire really *was* an empire and the Bulldog still had teeth which could strike fear into the heart of any truculent nation.

However, while there was much to keep our grandfathers busy in commerce or society, our grandmothers lived a simple, closeted life within strict boundaries and even stricter morals. While little was permitted to them outside their homes, their freedom within the sitting room and parlour was almost unlimited and they used it for the holding of social gatherings to both reflect their tastes and enable them to indulge their desire for fashionable gossip. These were the Ladies' Circles.

If we could step back a century we would see that the Circle was a mixture of lace curtains and crinolins, of severe furniture and silent, dutiful servants; of tea, cakes and talk, talk, talk. It was a meeting of mutual interests, of minds directed on the unimportant, the trivial and the scandalous. Good ladies though most of the members were, their circle represented an almost terrible power: to be excluded meant disgrace, to find yourself the subject of their conversation a stigma of grave significance. Nonetheless the ladies loved every minute, for it was the nearest they had to the business world of their husbands, the clubs and schools of their sons.

Surprising as it may seem, however, the Circles did enable certain abilities to flower; some ladies were responsible for the most exquisite and detailed needlework, others developed skills at design, painting, poetry and writing. And it was in this last category that we find some of the most extraordinary developments—for the ladies were in no way inhibited by their surroundings and produced stories of mystery, intrigue, romance and *evil*.

Those readers of my earlier anthology, *The Gentlewomen of Evil* will recall there how I selected from the work of Victorian ladies tales of the weird and the occult. The book enjoyed more than a modest success and hence I decided to study further the literature of this period—and its lady writers in particular—to see if there was any one subject amongst all those covered by the heading 'macabre' which most fascinated the women. And there was: witchcraft.

Writing these words in Nice, one of the corners of the world which seems—from an architectural view point—almost a monument to Victorian England, it is hard to believe that those demure, sheltered gentlewomen could have been *interested* in—let alone know anything about—such a subject as witchcraft. Yet they certainly were and pursued their interest into the realms of detailed research with considerable enthusiasm. Bear this point well in mind, too, for this collection presents, like its predecessor, a contrast between what one *might* expect a lady of leisure and substance to do with her time and what she actually did! Whether the power of those seemingly innocent ladies circles played any part in directing their interest into the dark areas of Satanism and traffic with the Fiend I leave to you to decide!

During my research the one point which has emerged most strongly is how carefully the ladies rooted all their stories in *fact*. While there are many contemporary witchcraft tales by men full of wild flights of fancy (judge, for instance, W. Harrison Ainsworth's *The Lancashire Witches*) most female authors put conviction as their keynote and objectivity as their by-word. It makes for absorbing and authentic reading as you will see. (To underline this very pertinent fact I have provided an entire section by ladies devoted to British witchcraft history.)

In leaving you to the stories, then, please allow me just to add that I have received help and assistance from a great many people while working on this book, but I must record my particular thanks to Mr A. H. Waysencraft of the University of London Library, whose help and guidance made my task so much easier. Also to the staffs of the Mary Evans Picture Library and the Radio Times Hulton

Picture Library for help in locating many of the pictures contained herein. Finally a word of gratitude to my wife, Philippa, who has willingly shared me with other women (again) and been, as always, my best adviser and critic.

PETER HAINING

Nice, 1969.

PART ONE

Fact

"I am not a fanciful woman, but there are some things that wake one's imagination. On such a dark night as this I always think of something uncomfortable happening. Misfortune seems to lie in wait about those black corners; and I think of witches pondering in the dark vile schemes against the innocent. . . ."

Mrs Margaret Oliphant
("Salem Chapel")

WITCHCRAFT IN ENGLAND

Mrs E. Lynn Linton

Mrs Eliza Lynn Linton (1822-1898) rightly earns her place at
the beginning of this collection as her book *Witch Stories* is certainly the most distinguished work on the subject of witchcraft to
have been written by a Victorian gentlewoman. Mrs Linton,
who was the wife of the outstanding wood-engraver, William
James Linton, was born the daughter of a Cumberland vicar and
became interested in writing at 11, her first novel, *Azeth, the
Egyptian*, being published when she was 23. Nevertheless, it was
reportage that mainly attracted her during these early years and in
1851 she began contributing to several daily papers and magazines—laying claim to the title of the first woman journalist.
Some of her articles such as "The Shrieking Sisterhood" and
"Mature Sirens" became famous dinner-table topics of conversation throughout the land and brought her name to public
attention. However, it was her interest in the supernatural which
was to finally establish her reputation with the publication of
Witch Stories in 1861. The result of considerable enquiry, the
book describes most of the important English and Scottish witchcraft cases, and in the following two extracts I have selected a
cross-section of stories from the two countries. In prefacing the
stories, Mrs Linton gives us a guideline to witchcraft which
might well be borne in mind as you read each item in the book:
"As a general rule, I think we may apply four conditions to every
case reported; in what proportion, each reader must judge for
himself. Those who believe in direct and personal intercourse
between the spirit-world and man, will probably accept every
account with the unquestioning belief of the sixteenth and seventeenth centuries; those who have faith in the calm and uniform
operations of nature, will hold chiefly to the doctrine of fraud;
those who have seen much of disease and that strange condition
called 'mesmerism' or 'sensitiveness', will allow the presence of
absolute nervous derangement, mixed up with a vast amount of

B

conscious deception, which the insane credulity and marvellous ignorance of the time rendered easy to practise; and those who have been accustomed to sift evidence and examine witnesses, will be utterly dissatisfied with the loose statements and wild distortion of every instance on record."

"Every old woman with a wrinkled face, a furr'd brow, a hairy lip, a gobber tooth, a squint eye, a squeaking voice, or a scolding tongue, having a ragged coate on her back, a skull-cap on her head, a spindle in her hand, and a Dog or Cat by her side, is not only suspected but pronounced for a witch," says John Gaule author of "Select Cases of Conscience"; while Reginald Scot in his "Discoverie of Witchcraft" (1584) puts forth as his experience:— "One sort of such as are said to be witches, are women which be commonly old, lame, blear-eyed, pale, fowle, and full of wrinckles; poor, sullen, superstitious, and Papists; or such as know no religion; in whose drousie minds the devill hath gotten a fine seat; so as, what mischief, mischance, calamity or slaughter is brought to passe, they are easily persuaded the same is done by themselves; imprinting in their minds an earnest and constant imagination thereof."

These are the sentiments of two somewhat wise and sane men, who lived in a time of universal madness, and gave their minds to the task of stemming the raging torrent. For the whole world was overrun with witches. From every town came crowds of these lost and damned souls; from every hovel peered out the cursing witch, or cried aloud for help the stricken victims. These poor and old and wretched beings, upon whose heads lighted the wrath of a world, and against whom every idle lad had a curse and a stone to fling at his will, were held capable of all but omnipotence. They could destroy the babe in the womb and make "the mother of many children childless among women;" they could kill with a look and disable with a curse; bring storms or sunshine as they listed; by their "witch-ropes," artfully woven, draw to themselves all the profit of their neighbours' barns and breweries; yet ever remained poor and miserable, glad to beg a mouthful of meat, or a can of sour milk from the hands of those whom they could ruin by half a dozen mutered words; they could take on themselves what shapes they would, and transport themselves wither they would; no bolt or bar kept them out, no distance by land or sea was too great for them to accomplish; a straw—a broomstick—the serviceable imp ever at hand—was enough for them; and with a pot of magic ointment, and a charm of spoken gibberish, they might visit the king on his throne, or the lady in her bower, to do what ill was in their hearts against them, or to gather to themselves what gain and store they would. Yet with all this power the superstitious world of the time saw nothing doubtful or illogical in the fact of their exceeding poverty, and never stayed to think that if they could transport themselves through the air to any distance they chose, they would be but slippery holding in prison, and not very likely to remain there for the pleasure of being tortured and burnt at the end. But neither reason nor logic had anything to do with the matter. The whole thing rested on fear, and that practical atheism of fear, which denies the power of God and the wholesome beauty of Nature, to exalt in their stead the supremacy of the Devil. This belief in the Devil's material presence and power over men was the dark chain that bound them all. Even the boldest opponent of the Witchcraft Delusion dared not fling it off; not the bravest man or freest thinker could shake his mind clear of this terrible trammel, this bugbear, this mere phantasm of human fear and ignorance, this ghastly lie and morbid delusion, or abandon the slavish worship of Satan for the glad freedom of God and Nature. It was much when such men as Reginald Scot, Gaule of Straughton, Sir Robert Filmer, and a dozen more shining lights could bring themselves to deny the supernatural power of a few half-crazed old beggar-women, and plead for humanity and mercy towards them, instead of cruelty and condemnation; but not one dare take the wider step beyond, and deny the existence of that phantom fiend, belief in whom wrought all this misery and despair. Even the very best of the time gave in to this delusion, and discussed gravely the properties and proportions of what we know now were mere lies. In the Church and amongst the more notoriously "religious" men of the time it was worse. In Archbishop Cranmer's 'Articles of Visitation' (1549) is this clause:— "You shall enquire whether you know of any that use Charms, Sorcery, Enchantments, Soothsaying, or any like Craft invented by the Devil"; and Bishop Jewel, preaching before Queen Elizabeth (1558), informed her how that "witches and sorcerers within these last few years are marvellously increased in your Grace's realm. Your Grace's subjects pine away even unto their death, their colour fadeth, their flesh rotteth, their speech is benumbed, their senses are bereft; I pray God they never practise further than upon the subject . . . . These eyes have seen most evident and manifest marks of their wickedness". At the next Parliament the new Bill against the detestable sin of witchcraft was passed, and Strype says, partly on account of the Lord Bishop's earnest objurgation. Dalton's 'Country Justice' (1655)* shows to what a pass, a century later, witchcraft had come in credulous England. Truly Scot was right when he said that his greatest adversaries were "young ignorance and old customs." They have always been the greatest adversaries of all truth. Of late, thank God, the march of humanity has been steadily, if slowly, towards the daylight; but at present you and I, my reader, have to do with the most debasing superstition that ever afflicted history, in the matter of those poor wretched servants of the devil—those witches and wizards, who somehow managed to lose on all sides—to suffer in time and be ruined for eternity, and to get only ill-will and ill-usage from man and fiend alike.

---

* Conjuration or invocation of any evil spirit was felony without benefit of clergy; so also to consult, covenant with, entertain, feed, or reward any evil spirit, or to take up any dead body for charms or spells; to use or practise witchcrafts, enchantment, charm, or sorcery, so that any one was lamed, killed, or pined, was felony without benefit of clergy, to be followed up by burning. Then 'The Country Justice' goes on to give the legal signs of a witch, and those on which a magistrate might safely act, as legal "discoveries." She was to be found and proved by insensible marks; by teats; by imps in various shapes, such as toads, mice, flies, spiders, cats, dogs, &c.; by pictures of wax or clay; by the accusations of the afflicted; by her apparition seen by the afflicted as coming to torment them; by her own sudden or frequent inquiries at the house of the sick; by common report; by the accusations of the dying; and the bleeding of the corpse at her touch; by the testimony of children; by the afflicted vomiting pins, needles, straw, &c.; in short, by all the foolery, gravely formularized, to be found in the lies and deceptions hereafter related.

THE WITCH OF BERKELEY

One of our earliest English witches, so early indeed that she becomes mythical and misty and out of all possible proportion, was the celebrated Witch of Berkeley, who got the reward of her sins in the middle of the ninth century, leaving behind her a tremendous lesson, by which, however, after generations did not much profit. The witch had been rich and the witch had been gay, but the moment of reckoning had to come in the morning; the feast had been noble and well enjoyed, but the terrible account had to be paid when all was over; and the poor witch found her ruddy-cheeked apple, now that the rind was off and eaten, filled with nothing but dust and ashes—which she must digest as best she may. As the moment of her death approached, she called for the monks and the nuns of the neighbouring monasteries, and sent for her children to hear her confession; and then she told them of the compact she had made, and how the Devil was to come for her body as well as her soul. "But," said she, "sew me in the hide of a stag, then place me in a stone coffin, and fasten in the covering lead and iron. Upon this place another stone, and chain the whole down with heavy chains of iron. Let fifty psalms be sung each night, and fifty masses be said by day, to break the power of the demons. If you can thus keep my body for three nights safe, on the fourth day you may bury it—the Devil will have sought and not found." The monks and the nuns did as they were desired; and on the first night, though the demons kept up a loud howling and wailing outside the church, the 'priests conquered, and the old witch slept undisturbed.' On the second night the demons were more fierce and clamorous, and the monks and the nuns told their beads faster and faster; but the fiends were getting more powerful as time went on, and at last broke open the gates of the monastery, in spite of prayer and bolt and bar; and two chains of the coffin burst asunder, but the middle one held firm. On the third night the fiends raged sore and wild. The monastery was shaken to its foundations, and the monks and the nuns almost forgot their paters and their aves in the uproar that drowned their voices and quailed their hearts; but they still went on, until, with an awful crash, and a yell from all the smaller demons about, a Devil,

larger and more terrible than any that had come yet, stalked into
the church and up to the foot of the altar, where the old woman and
coffin lay. Here he stopped, and bade the witch rise and follow him.
Piteously she answered that she could not—she was kept down by
the chain in the middle: but the Devil soon settled that difficulty;
for he put his foot to the coffin, and broke the iron chain like a bit
of burnt thread. Then off flew the covering of lead and iron, and
there lay the witch, pale and horrible to see. Slowly she uprose, blue,
dead, stark, as she was; and then the Devil took her by the hand, and
led her to the door where stood a gigantic black horse, whose back
was all studded with iron spikes, and whose nostrils, breathing fire,
told of his infernal manger below. The Devil vaulted into the saddle,
flung the witch on before him, and off and away they rode—the yells
of the clamouring demons, and the shrieks of the tortured soul,
sounding for hours, far and wide, in the ears of the monks and the
nuns. So here too, in this legend, as in all the rest, the Devil is
greater than God, and prayer and penitence inefficacious to redeem
iniquity.

o

A rare and curious black-letter pamphlet* gives a marvellous
account of a woman's possession, as it happened in Somersetshire;
which perchance we of the light-minded and sceptical ninteeenth
century might interpret differently to what the believing sixteenth
held likely.

THE WOMAN AND THE BEAR

One Stephen Cooper, of Ditchet, a yeoman of honest reputation,
good wealth, and well beloved by his neighbours, being sick and
weak, sent his wife Margaret to a farm of his at Rockington,
Gloucestershire, where she remained a few days—not finding all

* 'A true and most dreadfull discourse of a Woman possessed with the Deuill;
who, in the likenesse of a headlesse Beare, fetched her oute of her Bedde, in the
presence of seven persons, most straungely roulled her thorow three Chambers,
and downe a high paire of stairres on the fower and twentie of May last, 1584. At
Ditchet, in Somersetshire. A matter as miraculous as ever was seen in our time.
Imprinted at London for Thomas Nelson.'

to her liking, she said. When she returned she found her husband somewhat better, but she herself was strange and wild, using much idle talk to him concerning an old coin which her little son had found and which she wanted to see, and raving about the farm in Gloucestershire, as if she had been bewitched, and knew not what she said. Then she began to change in very face, and to look on her husband with "a sad and staring countenance;" and, one night, things came to a climax, for she got very wild and bad, and shook so frightfully that they could scarce keep her down in the bed; and then she began talking of a headless bear, which, she said, she had been into the town to beat away during the time of her fit, and which had followed her from Rockington: as the sequel proved was true. Her friends and husband exhorted her to prayer and patience, but she still continued marvellously holden, the Devil getting quite the better of her until Sunday night, when she seemed to come to her worst. Suddenly the candle, which they had not been noticing, went out, and she set up a lamentable cry; they lighted another, but it burnt so dim it was almost useless, and the friends and neighbours themselves began to be disquieted. Wildly and hurriedly cried Margaret, "Look! do you not see the Devil?" herself all terrified and disturbed. They bade her be still and pray. Then said Margaret, "Well, if you see nothing now, you shall see something by and bye;" and "forthwith they heard a noise in the streete, as it had been the coming of two or three carts, and presently they in the chamber cried out, "Lord helpe us, what manner of thing is this that commeth here!" For up to the bedside where the woman lay with heaving breasts and dilated eyes, came a thing like a bear, only that it had no head and no tail; a thing "half a yard in height and half a yard in length" (no bigger, Margaret? not so big as a well-trussed man on all-fours?) which, when her husband saw, he took a joyn'd stool, and "stroke" at it, and the blow sounded as though it had fallen on a feather bed. But the creature took no notice of the man: it wanted only Margaret. Slowly it paddled round the bed, then smote her thrice on the feet, took her out of bed, and rolled her to and fro in the chamber, round about the floor and under the bed; the husband and friends, sore amazed and affrighted, only calling on God to assist them, not daring to lift a hand for themselves or her. And all the while the candle grew dimmer and dimmer, so that they could scarce see each other: which was what Margaret and the head-less bear, no doubt, desired. Then the creature took her in its arms, thrust her head between her legs so that he made her into a round ball, and "so roulled her in a rounde compasse like an Hoope through each other Chambers, downe an highe paire of staires, in the Hall, where he kept her for the space of a quarter of an hour." The people above durst not come down, but remained above, weeping pitifully and praying with loud and fervent prayer. And there was such a terrible stench in the hall, and such fiery flames darting hither and thither, that they were fain to stop their noses with clothes and napkins, expecting every moment to find that hell was opening beneath their feet, and that they would be no longer able to keep out of harm's way and the Devil's. Then Margaret cried out, "He is gone. Now he is gone!" and her husband joyfully bade her come up to him again; which she did, but so quickly that they greatly marvelled at it, and thought to be sure the Devil had helped her. Yet she proved to be none the worse for the encounter: which was singular, as times went. They then put her in bed, and four of them kept down the clothes, praying fervently. Suddenly the woman was got out of bed: she did not move herself by nerves, muscles, or will, of course; but she was carried out by a supernatural power, and taken to the window at the head of the bed. But whether the devil or she opened the window, the pamphlet does not determine. Then her legs were thrust out of the window, and the people heard a thing knock at her feet as if it had been upon a tub; and they saw a great fire, and they smelt a grievous smell; and then, by the help of their prayers, they pulled Margaret into the room again, and set her upon her feet. After a few moments she cried out, "O Lord, methinks I see a little childe!" But they paid no heed to her. Twice or thrice she said this, and ever more earnestly; and at last they all looked out at the window, for they thought to be sure she must have some meaning for her raving. And "loe, they espied a thing like unto a little child, with a bright shining countenaunce casting a greate light in the chamber." And then the candle, which had hitherto burnt blue and dim, gave out its natural light so that they could all see each other. Whereupon they fell to joyful prayer, and gave thanks to God for the deliver-ance. And Margaret Cooper was laid in her bed again, calm, smiling, and collected, never more to be troubled by a Headless Bear which rolled her about like a ball, or by a bright shining child looking out for the chinks of a rude magic lantern. As for the bear, I confess I think he was nearer akin to man than devil; that he was known about Rockington in Gloucestershire; and that Margaret Cooper understood the conduct of the plot from first to last. But then this is the sceptical nineteenth century, wherein the wiles of human cunning are more believed in than the power of the devil, or the miracles of supernaturalism. Yet this was a case which, in spite of all its fraud and folly so patently displayed, was cited as one of the most notorious and striking instances of the power of Satan over the bodies as well as the souls of those who gave themselves up to the things of the world.

◌

THE WITCHES OF LANCASHIRE

In Pendle Forest, a wild tract of land on the borders of Yorkshire, lived an old woman about the age of fourscore, who had been a witch for fifty years, and had brought up her own children, and instructed her grandchildren to be witches. "She was a generall agent for the Deuill in all these partes;" her name was Elizabeth Southernes, usually called Mother Demdike; the date of her arraignment 1612. She was the first tried of this celebrated "coven", twenty of whom stood before Sir James Altham and Sir Edward Bromley, charged with all the crimes lying in sorcery, magic, and witchcraft. Old Mother Demdike died in prison before her trial, but on her being taken before the magistrate who convicted them all, Roger Nowell, Esq., she made such a confession as effectually insured her due share of execration, and hedged in the consciences of all who had assailed her from any possible pangs of self-reproach or doubt.

About fifty years ago, she said, she was returning home from begging, when, near a stone pit in the Pendle Forest, she met a spirit or devil in the shape of a boy, with one half of his coat brown and the other half black, who said to her, if she would give him her soul, she should have all that she might desire. After a little further talk, during which he told her that his name was Tibb, he vanished away, and she saw him no more for this time. For five or six years

Mother Demdike never asked any kind of help or harm of Tibb, who always came to her at "daylight gate" (twilight); but one Sabbath morning, she having her little child on her knee, and being in a light slumber, Tibb came to her in the likeness of a brown dog, and forced himself on her knee, trying to get blood from under her left arm. Mother Demdike awoke sore troubled and amazed, and strove to say, "Jesus, save my child," but could not, neither could she say, "Jesus, save myself." In a short time the brown dog vanished away, and she was "almost starke madde for the space of eight weekes." She and Tibb had never done much harm, she said; not even to Richard Baldwin, for all that he had put them off his land, and taken her daughter's day's work at his mill without fee or reward, and when she, led by her grandchild Alison (for she was quite blind), went to ask for pay, gave them only hard words and insolence for their pains, saying, "he would burn the one, and hang the other," and bidding them begone for a couple of witches—and worse. She confessed though, after a little pressing, that at that moment Tibb called out to her, "Revenge thee of him!" to whom she answered, "Revenge thou either of him or his!" on which he vanished away, and she saw him no more. She would not say what was the vengeance done, or if any. But if she was silent, and not prone to confession, there were others, and those of her own blood, not so reticent. Elizabeth Device her daughter, and Alison and James and Jennet Device, her grandchildren, testified against her and each other in a wonderful manner, and filled up all the blanks in the most masterly and graphic style.

Alison said that her grandmother had seduced her to the service of the devil, by giving her a great black dog as her imp or spirit, with which dog she had lamed one John Law, a petit chapman or pedlar, as he was going through Colnefield with his pack at his back. Alison wanted to buy pins off him, but John Law refused to loose his pack or sell them to her; so Alison in a rage called for her black dog, to see if revenge could not do what fair words had failed in. When the black dog came he said, "What wouldst thou have me to do with yonder man?" To whom she answered, "What canst thou do at him?" and the dog answered again, "I can lame him." "Lame him," says Alison Device; and before the pedlar went forty yards he fell lame. When questioned, he, on his side, said, that as he was going through Colnefield he met a big black dog with very fearful fiery eyes, great teeth, and a terrible countenance, which looked at him steadily then passed away; and immediately after he was bewitched into lameness and deformity. And this took place after having met Alison Device and refused to sell her any pins. Then Alison fell to weeping and praying, beseeching God and that worshipful company to pardon her sins. She said further that her grandmother had bewitched John Nutter's cow to death, and Richard Baldwin's woman-child on account of the quarrel before reported, saying that she would pray for Baldwin himself, "both still and loud," and that she was always after some matter of devilry and enchantment, if not for the bad of others then for the good of herself. For once, Alison got a piggin* full of blue milk by begging, and when she came to look into it she found a quarter of a pound of butter there, which was not there before, and which she verily believed old Mother Demdike had procured by her enchantments. Then Alison turned against the rival Hecate, Anne Whittle, *alias* Chattox, between whom and her family raged a deadly feud with Mother Demdike and her family; accusing her of having bewitched her father, John Device, to death, because he had neglected to pay her the yearly tax of an aghen dole (eight pounds) of meal, which he had covenanted to give her on consideration that she would not harm him. For they had been robbed, these poor people, of a quarter of a peck of cut oatmeal and linens worth some twenty shillings, and they had found a coif and band belonging to them on Anne Whittle's daughter; so John Device was afraid that old Chattox would do them some grievous injury by her sorceries if they cried out about it, therefore made that covenant for the aghen dole of meal, the non-payment of which for one year set Chattox free from her side of the bargain and cost John's life. She said, too, that Chattox had bewitched sundry persons and cattle, killing John Nutter's cow because he, John Nutter, had kicked over her canfull of milk, misliking her devilish way of placing two sticks across it; and slaying Anne Nutter because she laughed and mocked at her; slaying John Morris' child, too, by a picture of clay—with other misdeeds to be hereafter verified and substantiated. So Alison Device was hanged, weeping bitterly, and very penitent.

James Device, her brother, testified to meeting a brown dog

* An earthenware swine trough.

coming from his grandmother's about a month ago, and to hearing a
noise as of a number of children shrieking and crying, "near daylight
gate." Another time he heard a foul yelling as of a multitude of cats,
and soon after this there came into his bed a thing like a cat or a hare,
and coloured black; which lay heavily on him for about an hour. He
said that his sister Alison had bewitched Bullock's child, and that old
Mother Chattox had dug up three skulls, and taken out eight teeth,
four of which she kept for herself and gave four to Mother Demdike;
and that Demdike had made a picture of clay of Anne Nutter, and
had burned it, by which the said Anne had been bewitched to death.
Also she had bewitched to death one Mitton, because he would not
give her a penny; with other iniquities of the same sort. He said that
his mother, Elizabeth Device, had a spirit like a brown dog called
Ball, and that they all met at Malking Tower; all the witches of
Pendle—and they were not a few—going out in their own shapes, and
finding foals of different colours ready for their riding when they got
out: Jennet Preston was the last: when they all vanished. He then
confessed, for his own part, that his grandmother Demdike told him
not to eat the communion bread one day when he went to church, but
to give it to the first thing he met on the road on his way homewards.
He did not obey her, but ate the bread as a good Christian should;
and on the way he met with a thing like a hare which asked him for
the bread; but he said he had not got it; whereupon the hare got very
angry and threatened to tear him in pieces, but James "sained*" himself, and the devil vanished. This, repeated in various forms, was
about the pith of what James Device confessed, his confession not
including any remarkable betrayal of himself, or admission of any
practical and positive evil. His young sister Jennet, a little lassie of
nine, supplied the deficiencies. She had evidently been suborned,
says Wright, and gave evidence enough to have hanged half Lancashire. She said that James had sold himself to the devil, and that his
spirit was a black dog called Dandy, by whom he had bewitched
many people to death; and she confirmed what he had said of Jennet
Preston's spirit, which was a white foal with a black spot in its forehead. And then she said that she had seen the witches' meetings, but
had taken no part in them; and that on Good Friday they had all
dined off a roasted wether which James had stolen from Christian

* Made the sign of the cross.

Swyers; and that John Bulcocke turned the spit. She said that her mother Elizabeth had taught her two prayers, the one to get drink and the other to cure the bewitched. The one to get drink was a very short one, simply—"Crucifixus, hoc signum vitam eternam, Amen:" but this would bring good drink into the house in a very strange manner. The other, the prayer to cure the bewitched, was longer:—

" Vpon Good Friday, I will fast while I may,
Vntill I heare them knell,
Our Lord's owne Bell,
Lord in his messe
With his twelve Apostles good,
What hath he in his hand?
Ligh in* Leath † wand:
What hath he in his other hand?
Heauen's doore key.
Open, open, Heauen doore keyes,
Steck, steck, hell doore.
Let Crizum ‡ child
Go to it Mother mild.
What is yonder that casts a light so farrandly? §
Mine owne deare Sone that's nail'd to the Tree,
He is nail'd sore by the heart and hand,
And holy harne Panne.||
Well is that man
That Fryday spell can,
His Childe to learne
A Crosse of Blewe, and another of Red,
As good Lord was to the Roode.
Gabriel laid him downe to sleepe
Vpon the grounde ¶ of holy weepe;
Good Lord came walking by,
Sleep'st thou, wak'st thou, Gabriel?
No, Lord, I am sted with stick and stake,
That I can neither sleepe nor wake:

* "Ligh in," lusty.
† "Leath," flexible.
‡ The chrism was the white cloth placed over the brow of a newly-baptized child in the Roman Catholic service. When children died within the month they were called chrisoms.
§ "Farrandly," fair, handsome.
|| "Harne panne," brain case, cranium.
¶ Gethsemane.

Rise vp, Gabriel, and goe with me,
The stick nor the stake shall neuer deere* thee,
Sweete Jesus our Lorde.   Amen."

On such conclusive testimony as this, and for such fearful crimes, James Device was condemned for "as dangerous and malicious a witch as ever lived in these parts of Lancashire, of his time, and spotted with as much Innocent bloud as euer any witch of his yeares." Poor lad!

"O Barbarous and inhumane Monster, beyond example; so farre from sensible vnderstanding of thy owne miserie as to bring thy owne naturall children into mischiefe and bondage, and thyselfe to be a witnesse vpone the gallowes, to see thy owne children, by thy deuillish instructions, hatcht vp in villanie and witchcraft, to suffer with thee, euen in he beginning of their time, a shamefull and untimely Death!" These are the words which Thomas Potts addresses to Elizabeth Device, widow of John the bewitched, daughter to old Demdike the "rankest hag that ever troubled daylight," and mother of Alison and James the confessing witches; mother, also, of young Jennet on nine, their accuser and hers, by whose testimony she was mainly condemned. Elizabeth was charged with having bewitched sundry people to death, by means and aid of her spirit, the brown dog Ball, spoken of by James; also she had gone to the Sabbath held at Malking Tower, where they had assembled to consult how they could get old Mother Demdike, their leader, out of prison, by killing her gaoler and blowing up the castle, and where they had beef and bacon and roasted mutton—the mutton that same wether of Christopher Swyers' of Barley, which James had stolen and killed; with other things as damnable and insignificant. So Elizabeth Device, "this odious witch, who was branded with a preposterous marke in Nature even from her Birth, which was her left Eye standing lower than the other, the one looking down the other looking up," was condemned to die because she was poor and ugly, and had a little lying jade for a daughter, who made up fine stories for the gentlefolks.

Anne Whittle, *alias* Chattox, was next in influence, power, and age to Mother Demdike, and she began her confession by saying that old Demdike had originally seduced her by giving her the devil in the

* "Deere," hurt.

shape and proportion of a man, who got her, body and soul, and sucked on her left ribs, and was called Fancie. Afterwards she had another spirit like a spotted bitch, called Tibbe, who gave them all to eat and to drink, and said they should have gold and silver as much as they wanted. But they never got the gold and silver at all, and what they ate and drank did not satisfy them. "This Anne Whittle, *alias* Chattox, was a very old withered, spent, decrepid creature, her Sight almost gone; A dangerous Witch of very long continuance; always opposite to old Demdike; For whom the one fauoured the other hated deadly: and how they curse and accuse one an other in their Examinations may appear. In her Witchcraft always more ready to doe mischiefe to men's goods than themselves; Her lippes ever chattering and talking; but no man knew what. She lived in the Forest of Pendle amongst this wicked Company of dangerous Witches. Yet in her Examination and Confession she dealt always very plainely and truely; for vpon a speciall occasion, being oftentimes examined in open Court, she was neuer found to vary, but alwayes to agree in one and the selfe same thing. I place her in order next to that wicked Firebrand of mischiefe, old Demdike, because from these two sprung all the rest in order; and even the Children and Friendes of these two notorious Witches."

Nothing special or very graphic was elicited about old Chattox. She had certainly bewitched to death sundry of the neighbourhood, lately deceased; but then they all did that; and her devil, Fancie, came to her in various shapes—sometimes like a bear, gaping as though he would worry her, which was not a pleasant manner of fulfilling his contract—but generally as a man, in whom she took great delight. She confessed to a charm for blessing forespoken drink; which she had chanted for John Moore's wife, she said, whose beer had been spoilt by Mother Demdike or some of her crew:—

> " Three Biters hast thou bitten,
>   The Hart, ill Eye, ill Tonge;
> Three Bitter shall be thy boote,
>   Father, Sonne, and Holy Ghost.
>   a God's Name
> Fiue Paternosters, fiue Auies,
>   and a Creede,
> For worship of flue woundes
>   of our Lord."

Of course there was no help or hope for old Chattox if she said such wicked things as these. The righteous justice of England must be satisfied, and Anne Whittle was hung—one of the twelve who sorrowed the sunlight in Lancaster on that bloody assize.

Her daughter, Ann Redfearne, was then taken, accused of making pictures of clay and other maleficent arts; and she, too, was hanged; and then well-born, well-bred, but unfortunate Alice Nutter—a gentlewoman of fortune living at Rough Lee, whose relatives were anxious for her death that they might come into some property, out of which she kept them while living, and between whom and Mr. Justice Nowell there was a long-standing grudge on the question of a boundary-line between their several properties—Alice Nutter, whom one would have thought far removed from any such possibility was accused by young Jennet of complicity and companionship, and put upon her trial with but a faint chance of escape behind her. For Elizabeth Device swore that she had joined with her and old Demdike in bewitching the man Mitton, because of that twopence so fatally refused; and young Jennet swore that she was one of the party who went on many-coloured foals to the great witch meeting at Malking Tower; and so poor Alice Nutter, of Rough Lee, the well-bred gentlewoman, was hanged with the rest of that ragged crew; and her relations stood in her place, quite satisfied with their dexterity.

Then there was Katherine Hewitt, *alias* Mouldheels, accused by James Device, who seemed to think that if he had to be hanged for nothing he would be hanged in brave company, and, by sharing with as many as could be found, lessen the obloquy he could not escape; and John Bulcocke, who turned the spit, and Jane his mother, for the same crimes and on the same testimony; for the added crime, too, of helping in the bewitching of Master Leslie, about which nefarious deed other hands were also busy; and Margaret Pearson, delated by Chattox as entertaining a man spirit cloven-footed, with whom she went by a loophole into Dodson's stable, and sat all night, on his mare until it died. She was also accused by Jennet Booth, who went into her house and begged some milk for her child; Margaret goodnaturedly gave her some, and boiled it in a pan, but all her reward was, that Jennet accused her of witchcraft, for there was, said she, a toad, or something very like a toad, at the bottom of the pan when the milk was boiled, which Margaret took up with a pair of tongs and carried out of the house. Of course the toad was an imp, and Jennet Booth was quite right to repay an act of neighbourly generosity by accusation and slander. Margaret got off with standing in the pillory in open market, at four market towns on four market days, bearing a paper on her head setting forth her offence written in great letters, about which there could be no mistake; after which she was to confess, and afterwards be taken to prison, where she was to lie for a year, and then be only released when good and responsible sureties would come forward to answer for her good behaviour.

And there was Isabel Roby, who bewitched Peter Chaddock for jilting her, and in the spirit pinched and buffeted Jane Williams, so that she fell sick with the impression of a thumb and four fingers on her thigh; and Jennet Preston, she who had the white foal spirit, and who was afterwards hung at York for the murder of Master Thomas Lister—for Master Thomas in his last illness had been for ever crying out that Jennet Preston was lying on him, and when she was brought to see the body it gushed out fresh blood on her, which settled all doubts, if haply there had been any. So the famous trial of the Pendle Witches came to an end; and of the twenty who were accused twelve were hanged while the rest escaped only for the present, many of them meeting with their doom a few years afterwards.

∽

THE WITCH ON A PLANK

"Many are in a belief that this silly sex of women can by no means attaine to that so vile and damned a practise of Sorcery and Witch-craft, in regard of their illiterateness and want of learning, which many men have by great learning done;" nevertheless the Earl of Essex and his army, marching through Newberry, saw a feat done by a woman which not the most learned man of them all could have accomplished by natural means.* Two soldiers were loitering behind the main body, gathering nuts, blackberries, and the like, when one

* 'A most Certain Strange and true Discovery of a witch, being taken by some Parliamentary Forces as she was standing on a small planck-board and sayling on it over the River of Newberry. 1643.' The author believes that politics were at the back of this story and there may have been no truth in it at all.

climbed up a tree for sport, and the other followed him, jesting. From their vantage place, looking on the river, they there espied a "tall, lean, slender woman treading of the water with her feet with as much ease and firmnesse as if one should walk or trample on the earth." The soldier called to his companion, and he to the rest; and soon they all—captains, privates, and commanders alike—saw this marvellous lean woman, who now they perceived was standing on a thin plank, "which she pushed this way and that at her pleasure, making it a pastime to her, little perceiving who was on her tracks.' Then she crossed the river, and the army after her; but there they lost her for a time, and when they found her all were too cowardly to seize her. At last one dare-devil went up and boldly caught her, demanding what she was. The poor wretch was dumb—perhaps with terror— and spoke nothing; so they dragged her before the commanders, "to whom, though she was mightily urged, she did reply as little." As they could bethink themselves of nothing better to do with her, they set her upright against a mud bank or wall, and two of the soldiers, at their captain's command, made ready and fired. "But with a deriding and loud laughter at them, she caught their bullets in her hands and chew'd them, which was a stronger testimony then her treading water that she was the same that their imagination thought her for to be." Then one of the men set his carbine against her breast and fired; but the bullet rebounded like a ball, and narrowly missed the face of the shooter, which "so enraged the Gentleman, that one drew out his sword and manfully run at her with all the force his strength had power to make, but it prevailed no more than did the shot, the woman though still speechlesse, yet in a most contemptible way of Scorn still laughing at them, which did the more exhaust their furie against her life; yet one amongst the rest had heard that piercing or drawing bloud from forth the veines that crosse the temples of the head, it would prevail against the strongest sorcery, and quell the force of Witchcraft, which was allowed for Triall: the woman, hearing this, knew then the Devil had left her, and her power was gone; wherefore she began alowd to cry and roare, tearing her haire, and making pitious moan, which in these words expressed were: And is it come to passe that I must dye indeed? Why then his Excellency the Earle of Essex shall be fortunate and win the field. After which no more words could be got from her; wherewith they immediately discharged a Pistoll underneath her eare at which she straight sunk down and dyed, leaving her legacy of a detested carcasse to the wormes, her soul we ought not to judge of, though the euills of her wicked life and death can scape no censure. Finis. This Book is not Printed according to order."

∽

DOLL BILBY AND HER COMPEER

Burton Agnes, in the county of York, was troubled; for Faith Corbet, the young daughter of Henry Corbet, was taken violently ill, and Alice Huson and Doll Bilby had bewitched her. Good Mrs Corbet—beyond her age in generous unbelief—refused to entertain her daughter's suspicions; indeed she had chidden her some years ago for calling old Alice a witch, for she had a liking to the poor widow, and kept her about the house, looking after her young turkeys, &c., and was kind and liberal to her, and sought to make her wasting life pass as easily as might be. But Miss Faith hated the old woman and cried out against her as a witch; and when she lost her gloves, swore that Alice had taken them to play cantrips with, and that she should never be well again. Then she began to fall into fits, when she would be so terribly tormented that it took two or three to hold her; and she would screech and cry out vehemently, and bite and scratch anything she could lay hold of, all the while exclaiming, "Ah, Alice, old witch, have I gotten thee!" And sometimes she would lie down, all drawn together in a round, and be speechless and half swooning for days together; and then she would be wildly merry, and as full of antics as a monkey. Physicians were consulted, but none came near to her disorder; and though her father carried her about hither and thither, for change of air, nothing would cure her, she said, so long as Alice Huson and Doll Bilby remained at liberty. Still the father and mother held out, until, one day, before a whole concourse of people come to look at her in her fits, she cried out, "O Faithless and incredulous People! shall I never be believed till it be past Time? For I am as near Death as possibly may be, and when they have got my Life you will repent when it is past Time." On hearing this the father went to the minister of Burton Agnes, Mr Wellfet, and he,

Sir. Fr. Boynton—a justice of the peace—and Mr Corbet himself at last dragged the old woman Huson into Faith's chamber. At which Miss Faith gave a great screech, but presently called for toast and beer; then for cordials; and having taken a somewhat large quantity of both, she got up, dressed herself, and came down stairs. This, too, after she had been so weak that she could not turn herself in bed: which proved that Mother Huson had some extraordinary influence over the girl—an influence more potent than holy said the bystanders. This happy state did not continue. Faith said she should never be well while the two women were at liberty; and so it proved; for when at last arrested, and held in strict security and durance, the young lady pronounced herself healed, and gave no one any more trouble. Then Alice Huson was got to make confession to Mr. Wellfet, the minister, and thus sealed her own doom, and saved the prosecution the pain of conviction.

She said that for three years she had had intercourse with the devil, who, one day as she was on the moor, appeared to her in the form of a black man riding on horseback. He told her she should never want if she would follow his ways and give herself up to him: which Alice promised to. Then he sealed the bargain by giving her five shillings; at another time he gave her seven; and often—indeed six or seven times—repeating his gifts to the like munificent extent. He was like a black man with cloven feet, riding on a black horse, and Alice fell down and worshipped him, as she had covenanted. And she had hurt Faith Corbet by her evil spirit, for she did, in her apprehension, ride her; and when Mr Wellfet examined her once before, the devil stood by, and gave her answers; and she was under the Corbets' window as a cat when Mrs Corbet said she was—for even her kindly faith was shaken at last; and Doll Bilby had a hand in all this evil too; for Doll wanted to kill Faith outright, but old Alice interposed thinking they had done enough harm already. She confessed to killing Dick Warmers "by my wicked heart and wicked eyes;" and to having lent Lancelot Harrison eight shillings of the ten which the devil had given her at Baxter's door, a fortnight ago, "about twilight or daygate;" and she had a bigge, or witch mark, where the devil sucked from supper-time till after cock-crowing, twitching at her heart as if it was drawn with pincers the while; and she meant to practise witchcraft four years ago, when she begged old clothes of

Mrs Corbet, and the children refused her; and the devil told her not to tell of Doll Bilby. And to all this raving Timothy Wellfet, minister of Burton Agnes, set his name, and so hanged Alice Huson and Doll Bilby at the next York assizes: after which Miss Faith Corbet was for ever rid of her fits and fancies.

∽

JULIAN'S TOADS

At the Taunton assizes, in 1663, Julian Cox, about seventy years old, was indicted before Judge Archer for practising her arts of witchcraft upon a "young Maid, whereby her Body languished, and was impaired of Health." And first were taken proofs of her witchcraft. One witness, a huntsman, swore that one day, as he was hunting not far from Julian's house, he started a hare, which the dogs ran very close till it came to a bush; when, going round to the other side to keep it from the dogs, he perceived Julian Cox grovelling on the ground, panting and out of breath. She was the hare, and had had just time enough to say the magic stave which changed her back to woman's form again, ere the dogs had caught her. Another man swore that one day, passing her house as "she was taking a Pipe of Tobacco upon the Threshold of the Door," she invited him to come in and join her; which he did; when presently she cried out, "Neighbour, look what a pretty thing there is!" and there was a "monstrous great Toad betwixt his Legs, staring him in the Face." He tried to hit it, but could not, whereupon Julian told him to desist striking it and it would do him no hurt; but he was frightened, and went off to his family, telling them that he had seen one of Julian Cox's devils. Yet even when he was at home this same toad appeared again betwixt his legs, and though he took it out, and cut it in several pieces, still, when he returned to his pipe, there was the toad. He tried to burn it, but could not; then to beat it with a switch, but the toad ran about the room to escape him; presently it gave a cry and vanished, and he was never after troubled with it. A third witness swore that one day, when milking, Julian Cox passed by the yard where he was and "stooping down scored upon the ground for some small time during which time his Cattle ran Mad, and some of them ran their Heads against the Trees, and most of them died speedily." Concluding by which signs that they were bewitched, he cut off their ears to burn them and, while they were on the fire, Julian Cox came in a great heat and rage, crying out that they abused her without cause; but, going slily up to the fire, she took off the ears, and then was quiet. By the laws of witchcraft it was she who was burning, not the beasts' ears. A fourth, as veracious as the former, swore to having seen her "fly into her own Chamber-window in her full proportion;" all of which testimony gave weight and substance to the maid's charge.

The maid was servant at a certain house, where Julian came one day to ask for alms; but the maid gave her a cross answer, and said she should have none; so Julian told the maid she should repent her incivility before night. And she did; for she was taken with convulsions, and cried out to the people of the house to save her from Julian, for she saw her following her. In the night she became worse, saying that she saw Julian Cox and the black man by her bedside, and that they tempted her to drink, but "she defy'd the Devil's Drenches." The next night, expecting the same kind of conflict, she took up a knife and laid it at the head of her bed. In the middle of the night came the spiritual Julian and the black man, as before, so the maid took the knife, and stabbed at Julian, whom she said she had wounded in the leg. The people, riding out to see, found Julian in her own house with a fresh wound on her leg, and blood was also on the maid's bed. The next day Julian appeared to the maid and forced her to eat pins. Her apparition was on the house wall; and "all the Day the Maid was observ'd to convey her Hand to the House wall, and from the Wall to her Mouth, and she seem'd by the motion of her Mouth as if she did eat something." So towards night, still crying out on Julian, she was undressed, and all over her body were seen great swellings and bunches in which were huge pins—as many as thirty or more—which she said Julian Cox, when in the house wall, had forced her to eat. Was not all this enough to hang a dozen Julian Coxes? Judge Archer thought so; especially when was added to this testimony Julian's own enforced confession, of how she had been tempted by the devil to become a witch, but would never consent; yet how one evening, walking about a mile from her house, she met three persons riding on broom-staves, borne up about a yard and a half from the ground, two of whom she knew—a witch and a wizard, hanged for witchcraft several years ago—but the third, a black man, she did not then know. He however tempted her to give up her soul, which she did by pricking her finger and signing her name with her blood. So that, by her own showing, as well as by the unimpeachable testimony of reputable witnesses, she was a witch and one coming under the provisions of the Awful Verse. And further, as she could not repeat the Lord's Prayer, but stumbled over the clause "And lead us not into Temptation," which she made into "And lead us into temptation," or "And lead us not into no temptation," but could in no manner repeat correctly, the judge and jury had one conclusion to come to, which was that she be hanged four days after her trial. But some of the less blind and besotted spoke harsh words of Judge Archer for his zeal and precipitancy, and openly declared poor Julian's innocence when advocacy could do her strangled corpse no good.

◦

We come now (1712) to the last authentic trial for witchcraft where the accused was condemned to death for an impossible crime by a jury of sane, decent, respectable Englishmen. Jane Wenham was this latest offshoot of the old tree of judicial bigotry; not the latest fruit, but the last instance of the law and judgment. There is a report current in most witch books of a case at a later period—but I can find no *authentic* account of it—that, in 1716, of a Mrs Hicks and her little daughter of nine, hanged at Huntingdon for selling their souls to the devil, bewitching their neighbours to death and their crops to ruin, and, as a climax to all, taking off their stockings to raise a storm. It may well be so, but I have not met with it in any reliable shape, so meanwhile we must accept Jane Wenham as the last officially condemned.

THE WITCH OF WALKERNE

Jane Wenham was the witch of Walkerne, a little village in the north of Hertford. She had long lived under ill fame, and her neighbours were resolved to get rid of her at the earliest opportunity. That opportunity presented itself in the person of John Chapman's man, one Matthew Gilson, whom Jane sent into a daft state by asking him for a pennyworth of straw, which he refused to give her. The old woman went away, muttering and complaining, whereupon Matthew, impelled by he knew not what impulse, ran out of the barn for a distance of three miles, asking as he went for pennyworths of straw. Not getting any, he went on to some dirt heaps, and gathered up straw from them, which he put in his shirt and brought home. A witness testified that he had seen Gilson come back with his shirt stuffed full of straw, that he moved along quickly, and walked straight through the water, instead of passing over the bridge like any other decent man. For this odd behaviour of his servant, John Chapman, who had all along suspected Jane of more cunning than was good for him or her, called her a witch the next time he saw her; and Jane took him before the magistrate, Sir Herbert Chauncey, to answer to the charge of defamation. But the magistrate recommended them to go to Mr Gardiner the minister, and a great believer in witchcraft, and get their matter settled without more trouble or vexation. Mr Gardiner was too zealous to be just. He scolded poor old Jane roundly, and advised her to live more peaceably with her neighbours— which was just what she wanted to do—and gave as his award that Chapman do pay the fine of one shilling. While this bit of one-sided justice was going on, Anne Thorne, Mr Gardiner's servant, was sitting by the fire with a dislocated knee. Jane, not able to compass her wicked will on Chapman, and angry that Mr. Gardiner had spoken so harshly to her, turned her malice on the girl, and bewitched her, so that as soon as they all left the kitchen Anne felt a strange "Roaming in her Head, and she thought she must of Necessity run somewhere." In spite then of her dislocated knee, she started off and ran up the close, and away over a five-barred gate "as nimbly as a greyhound," along the highway and up a hill. And there she met two of John Chapman's men, who wanted her to go home with them; and one took her hand; but she was forced away from them, speechless, and not of her own volition, and so was driven on, on, towards Cromer, where the great sea would have either stopped or received her. But when she came to Hockney Lane, she met there a "little Old Woman muffled up in a Riding-Hood," who asked her whither she was going. "To Cromer," says Anne, "for sticks to make me a fire." "There be no sticks at Cromer," says the little old woman in the riding hood: "here be sticks enow; go to that oak tree and pluck them there." Which Anne did, laying them on the ground as they were gathered. Then the old woman bade her pull off her gown and apron, and wrap the sticks in them; asking her if she had ne'er a pin about her; but finding that she had not, she gave her a large crooked pin, with which she bade her pin her bundle, then vanished away. So Anne Thorne ran home half-naked, with her bundle of leaves and sticks in her hand, and sat down in the kitchen, crying out "I am ruined and undone!"

When Mrs Gardiner had opened the bundle, and seen all the twigs and leaves, she said they would burn the witch, and not wait long about it; so they flung the twigs and leaves into the fire; and while they were burning in came Jane Wenham, asking for Anne's mother, for she had, she said, a message to her, how that she was to go and wash next day at Ardley Bury, Sir Herbert Chauncey's place: which on inquiry turned out to be a falsehood: consequently Jane Wenham was set down doubly as a witch, the charm of burning her in the sticks having proved so effectual. John Chapman and his men then told their tale. Mr Gardiner was not slow in fanning the flame into a fire, and poor old Jane was examined, searched for marks but none found, and committed to gaol, there to wait her trial at the next assizes. She earnestly entreated not to go to prison; protested her innocence, and appealed to Mrs Gardiner to help her, woman-like, and not to swear against her; offering to submit to be swum—anything they would—so that she might be kept free of jail. But Sir Herbert Chauncey was just manly and rational enough not to allow of this test, though the Vicar of Ardeley tried her with the Lord's Prayer, which she could not repeat: and terrified and tortured her into a kind of confession, wherein she implicated three other women, who were immediately put under arrest, though they came to no harm in the end. When she was brought to trial, sixteen witnesses, including three clergymen, were standing there ready to testify against her, how that she had bewitched this one's cattle, and that one's sheep; and taken all the power from this one's body, and all the good from that one's gear; and slaughtered this child, and that man, by her evil eye and her curses; and in fact how that she had done all the mischief that had happened in the neighbourhood for years past. And there was Matthew Gilson, who had been sent mad,

and forced to wander about the country with his shirt stuffed full of
straw like a scare-crow; and Anne Thorne, who had had fits ever
since her marvellous journey with the dislocated knee; and another
Anne, very nearly as hardly holden as the first; and others beside,
whom her malice had rendered sick and lame, and unfit for decent
life: moreover, two veracious witnesses deposed positively to her
taking the form of a cat when she would, and to hearing her converse
with the devil when under the form of a cat, he also as a cat; together
with Anne Thorne's distinct accusation that she was beset with cats—
tormented exceedingly—and that all the cats had the face and the
voice of Jane Wenham.

The lawyers, who believed little in the devil and less in witchcraft,
refused to draw up the indictment on any other charge save that of
"conversing familiarly with the devil in the form of a cat." But in
spite of Mr Bragge's earnest appeals against such profanation, and
the ridicule which it threw over the whole matter, the jury found the
poor old creature guilty, and the judge passed sentence of death
against her. The evidence was too strong. Even one of the Mr
Chaunceys deposed that a cat came knocking at his door, and that
he killed it—when it vanished away, for it was no other than one of
Jane Wenham's imps; and all Mr Gardiner's house went mad, some
in one way and some in another: and credible witnesses deposed that
they had seen pins come jumping through the air into Anne Thorne's
mouth, and when George Chapman clapped his hand before her
mouth to prevent them skipping in, he felt one stick against his hand,
as sharp as might be; and every night Anne's pincushion was left full,
and every morning found empty, and who but Jane could have conveyed them all from the pincushion into her mouth, where they were
to be found all crooked and bent? But though the jury could not
resist the tremendous weight of all this evidence, and the judge could
not resist the jury, he managed to get a reprieve which left the people
time to cool and reflect, and then he got a pardon for her—quietly
and kindly done. And Colonel Plummer, of Gilston, took her under
his protection, and gave her a small cottage near his house, where she
lived, poor soul, in peace and safety to the end of her days, doing
harm to no one and feared by none. As for Anne Thorne, the doctor,
who had ordered her, as part of his remedy, to wash her hands and
face twice a day in fair water, and who, as another part, had her

watched and sat with by a "lusty young fellow" who asked nothing better, managed matters so well, that in a short time Anne and her brisk bachelor were married; and from that time we hear no more of her vomiting crooked pins, or being tormented with visions of cats wearing Jane Wenham's face, and speaking with Jane Wenham's voice. But though all the rest got well off with their frights and follies, no public compensation was given to poor old Jane for the brutal attacks of the mob upon her, for the hauling and maiming and scratching and tearing, by which they proved to their own satisfaction that she was a witch, and deserved only the treatment accorded to witches.

૦

OUR LATEST

But if the last officially condemned, Jane was not the last actually destroyed, for a curious MS. letter to be found in the British Museum "From Mr Manning, Dissenting Teacher, at Halstead, in Essex, to John Morley, Esq., Halstead," gives us a strange garbled account of a reputed sacrifice; and the sadder and more brutal story of Ruth Osborne follows a few years after.

"Halstead, August 2, 1732.

"Sir—The narrative which I gave you in relation to witchcraft, and which you are pleased to lay your commands upon me to repeat, is as follows:—There was one Master Collett, a smith by trade, of Haveningham, in the county of Suffolk, who, as 'twas customary with him, assisting the maide to churne, and not being able (as the phrase is) to make the butter come, threw a hot iron into the churn, under the notion of witchcraft in the case, upon which a poore labourer, then employed in carrying of dung in the yard, cried out in a terrible manner, 'They have killed me, they have killed me;' still keeping his hand upon his back, intimating where the pain was, and died upon the spot.

"Mr Collett, with the rest of the servants then present, took off the poor man's clothes, and found to their great surprise, the mark of the iron that was heated and thrown into the churn, deeply impressed upon his back. This account I had from Mr Collett's own mouth, who being a man of unblemished character, I verily believe to be matter of fact.

"I am, Sir, your obliged humble Servant,

"SAM. MANNING."

The only falsehood, probably, in the history is the manner of the poor fellow's death, for either he was foully murdered on a wild suspicion of being concerned in the witching of a dirty milk vessel, or he died suddenly of some ordinary organic complaint, and the circumstances of the horse-shoe and the scarred back were purely imaginary. But again in 1751 was witch blood actually poured out on English soil, and the cry of the innocent murdered sent up to heaven in vain for mercy. At Tring, in Hertfordshire, lived an old man, one Osborne, and his wife; poor as witches always were; old—past seventy both of them—and obliged to beg from door to door for what, if the popular superstition was true, the devil had given them power to possess at any moment for themselves. But this was a point of view no one ever took. In the rebellion of '45, just six years ago, old Mother Osborne had gone to one Butterfield, a dairyman living at Gubble-cot, to beg for buttermilk. Butterfield was a churlish fellow, and told her roughly that he had not enough for his hogs, still less for her. Says old Mother Osborne, grumbling, "The Pretender will soon have thee and thy hogs too." Now the Pretender and the devil were in league together, according to the belief of many, and old Mother Osborne might just as well have told the dairyman at once that he was going to the devil, or that she would send her imps to bewitch him; for soon Butterfield's calves became distempered, and soon his cows died, and his affairs went so far to the bad that he left his diary and took a public-house, in hopes that the imps which could bewitch the one might be powerless against the other. But he reckoned without his host, for in 1751 he himself was bewitched; he had fits—bad fits— and sent for a white witch all the way from Northamptonshire to tell him what ailed him. The white witch told him he was bewitched, and bade six men, with staves and pitchforks hanging round their necks as counter charms for their own safety, watch his house night and day. Doubtless they discovered all they were set there to seek.

Suddenly there appeared a notice that certain and various witches were to be ducked at Longmarston the 22nd day of April. A crowd assembled at Tring to watch the sport; and but one thought went through that crowd—the Osbornes were to be the ducked witches, and the sport they would have would be rare. The parish officers had taken the old couple into the workhouse for safety, but the mob broke through the gates, and crushed down the doors, and searched the whole place through, from end to end, even to the salt box, "lest the witch should have made herself little," and have hidden in the corners. But they could not find her, not even there; so, in a rage, they broke the windows, smashed the furniture, and then heaped up straw high against the house, threatening to burn it down, and every living soul within it, if the Osbornes were not given up to them. The master was frightened he had never faced such a scene before, and his nerve forsook him—not unreasonably. He brought the old people from their hiding place, and gave them up to that wild, tossing, furious mob. In a moment they were stripped stark naked, then cross-bound in the prescribed manner, wrapped loosely in a sheet, and dragged two miles along the road to a small pond or river, where with many a curse and many a kick they were thrown in, to prove whether they were witches or not. A chimney sweeper, called Colley, was the most active of the crew. Seeing that Mother Osborne did not sink, he waded into the water and turned her over with his stick. She slipped out of the sheet, and thus lay exposed, naked, and half choked with mud, before the brutal crowd, who saw nothing pitiful, and nothing shameful, in her state. After a time they dragged her out, flung her on the bank, and kicked and beat her till she died. Her husband died also, but not on the spot. The man who had arranged this rare diversion then went round among the crowd collecting money in return for his amusement. But government took the matter up. A coroner's inquest was held, and a verdict of wilful murder returned against Colley, the chimney sweep, who, much to his own surprise and the indignation of the people—many ranking him as a martyr—was hanged by the neck till he was dead, for the murder of the witch of Tring, poor old Ruth Osborne. The act against witchcraft, under colour and favour of which all the judicial murders had been done, had been repealed a few years before, namely, in 1736, and Colley's comrades bewailed piteously the degenerate times that were at hand, when a witch was no longer held fit sport for the public, but was protected and defended like ordinary folk, and let to live on to work her wicked will unchecked.

But the snake is scotched, not killed. So far are we in advance of the men of the ruder past, inasmuch as our superstitions, though quite as silly, are less cruel than theirs, and hurt no one but ourselves. Yet still we have our wizards and witches lurking round area gates and prowling through the lanes and yards of the remoter country districts; still we have our necromancers, who call up the dead from their graves to talk to us more trivial nonsense than ever they talked while living, and who reconcile us with earth and humanity by showing us how infinitely inferior are heaven and spirituality; still we have the unknown mapped out in clear lines sharp and firm; and still the impossible is asserted as existing, and men are ready to give their lives in attestation of what contravenes every law of reason and of nature; still we are not content to watch and wait and collect and fathom before deciding, but for every new group of facts or appearances must at once draw up a code of laws and reasons, and prove, to a mathematical certainity, the properties of a chimera, and the divine life and beauty—of a lie. Even the mere vulgar belief in witchcraft remains among the lower classes; as witness the old gentleman who died at Polstead not so long ago, and who, when a boy, had seen a witch swum in Polstead Ponds, "and she went over the water like a cork;" who had also watched another witch feeding her three imps like blackbirds; and who only wanted five pounds to have seen all the witches in the parish dance on a knoll together: as witness also the strange letter of the magistrate, in the 'Times' of April 7, 1857; and the stranger trial at Stafford, concerning the bewitched condition of the Charlesworths, small farmers living at Rugeley, which trial is to be found in the 'Times' of March 28, 1857; the case reported by the clergyman of East Thorpe, Essex, who had actually to mount guard against the door of an old Trot accused of witchcraft; while the instances of silly servant maids, and fortune tellers, whose hands are to be crossed with silver, and the stars propitiated with cast off dresses and broken meat, are as numerous as ever. And, indeed, so long as conviction without examination, and belief without proof, pass as the righteous operations of faith, so long will superstition and credulity reign supreme over the mind, and the functions of critical reason be abandoned and foresworn.

THE WITCHES OF SCOTLAND

Mrs E. Lynn Linton

Mrs Lynn Linton continues her study of witchcraft in Britain
with this report of the activities of witches—both real and alleged
—in Scotland.

∽∽∽∽∽∽∽∽∽∽∽∽∽∽∽∽∽∽∽∽∽∽∽∽∽∽∽∽∽∽∽∽

Scotland was always foremost in superstition. Her wild hills and
lonely fells seemed the fit haunting-places for all mysterious powers;
and long after spirits had fled, and ghosts had been laid in the level
plains of the South, they were to be found lingering about the glens
and glades of Scotland. Very little of graceful fancy lighted up the
gloom of those popular superstitions. Even Elfame, or Faërie, was a
place of dread and anguish, where the devil ruled heavy-handed and
Hell claimed its yearly tithe, rather than the home of fun and beauty
and petulant gaiety as with other nations: and the beautiful White
Ladies, like the German Elle-women, had more of bale than bliss as
their portion to scatter among the sons of men. Spirits like the goblin
Gilpin Horner, full of malice and unholy cunning,—like grewsome
brownies, at times unutterably terrific, at times grotesque and rude,
but then more satyr-like than elfish,—like May Moulachs, lean and
hairy-armed, watching over the fortunes of a family, but prophetic
only of woe, not of well,—like the cruel Kelpie, hiding behind the
river sedges to rush out on unwary passers-by, and strangle them
beneath the waters,—like the unsained laidly* Elf, who came tempt-

* Loathsome.

ing Christian women, to their souls' eternal perdition if they yielded to the desires of their bodies,—like the fatal Banshee, harbinger of death and ruin,—were the popular forms of the Scottish spirit-world; and in none of them do we find either love or gentleness, but only fierceness and crime, enmity to man and rebellion to God. But saddest and darkest and unholiest of all was the belief in witchcraft, which infested society for centuries like a sore eating through to the very heart of humanity, and which was nowhere more bitter and destructive than among the godly children of our Northern sister. Strange that the land of the Lord should have been the favourite camping-ground of Satan, that the hill of Zion should have had its roots in the depths of Tophet!

The formulas of the faith were as gloomy as the persons. The power of the evil eye; the faculty of second sight, which always saw the hearse plumes, and never the bridal roses; the supremacy of the devil in this God-governed world of ours, and the actual and practical covenant into which men and women daily entered with him; the unlimited influence of the curse, and the sin and mischief to be wrought by charm and spell; the power of casting sickness on whomsoever one would, and the ease with which a blight could be sent on the corn, and a murrain to the beasts, by those who had not wherewithal to stay their hunger for a day, these were the chief signs of that fatal power with which Satan endowed his chosen ones—those silly, luckless chapmen who bartered away their immortal souls for no mess of pottage even, and no earthly good to breath or body, but only that they might harm their neighbours and revenge themselves on those who crossed them. Sometimes, indeed, they had no need to chaffer with the devil for such faculties: as in the matter of the evil eye; for Kirk, of Aberfoyle, tells us that "some are of so venomous a Constitution, by being radiated in Envy and Malice, that they pierce and kill (like a Cockatrice) whatever Creature they first set their Eyes on in the Morning: so was it with Walter G ahame, some Time living in the Parock wherein now I am, who killed his own Cow after commending its Fatness, and shot a Hair with his Eyes, having praised its Swiftness (such was the Infection of ane Evill Eye); albeit this was unusual, yet he saw no Object but what was obvious to other Men as well as to himselfe." And a certain woman looking over the door of a byre or cowhouse, where a neighbour sat milking, shot the calf dead and dried up and sickened the cow, "by the venomous glance of her evill eye." But perhaps she had got that venom by covenant with the devil; for this was one of the prescriptive possessions of a witch, and ever the first dole from the Satanic treasury. When Janet Irving was brought to trial (1616) for unholy dealings with the foul fiend, it was proved—for was it not sworn to? and that was quite sufficient legal proof in all witchcraft cases—that he had told her "ye schoe bure ill-will to onie bodie, to look on them with opin eyis, and pray evill for thame in his name, and schoe sould get hir hartis desyre;" and in almost every witch trial in Scotland the "evil eye" formed part of the counts of indictment against the accused. The curse was as efficacious. Did a foul-mouthed old dame give a neighbour a handful of words more forcible than courteous, and did terror, or revenge, induce, or simulate, a nervous seizure in consequence, the old dame was at once carried off to the lock-up, and but few chances of escape lay between her and the stake beyond. To be skilful in healing, too, was just as dangerous as to be powerful in sickening; and to the godly and unclean of the period all sorts of devilish cantrips lay in "south-running waters" and herb drinks, and salves made of simples; while the use of bored stones, of prayers said thrice or backwards, of "mwildis" powders, or any other more patent form of witchcraft, though it might restore the sick to health, yet was fatally sure to land the user thereof at the foot of the gallows, and the testimony of the healed friend was the strongest strand in the hangman's cord. This, indeed, was the saddest feature in the whole matter—the total want of all gratitude, reliance, trustiness, or affection between a "witch" and her friends. The dearest intimate she had gave evidence against her frankly, and without a second thought of the long years of mutual help and kindliness that had gone before; the neighbour whom she had nursed night and day with all imaginable tenderness and self-devotion, if he took a craze and dreamed of witchcraft, came forward to distort and exaggerate every remedy she had used, and every art she had employed; her very children turned against her without pity or remorse, and little lips, scarce dry from the milk of her own breasts, lisped out the glibbest lies of all. Most pitiful, most sad, was the state of these poor wretches; but instructive to us, as evidencing the strength of superstition, and the weakness of every human virtue when brought into contact and collision with it.

D

What other gifts and powers belonged to the witches will be best gathered from the stories themselves; for varied as they are, there is a strange thread of likeness running through them all; specially is there a likeness in all of a time or district, as might be expected in a matter which belonged so much to mere imitation.

Scotland played an unenviable part in the great witch panic that swept like an epidemic over Europe during the sixteenth and seventeenth centuries. It suited with the stern, uncompromising, Puritan temper, to tear this accursed thing from the heart of the nation, and offer it, bleeding and palpitating, as a sacrifice to the Lord; and accordingly we find the witch trials of Scotland conducted with more severity than elsewhere, and with a more gloomy and savage fanaticism of faith. Those who dared question the truth of even the most unreliable witnesses and the most monstrous statements were accused of atheism and infidelity—they were Sadducees and sinners —men given over to corruption and uncleanness, with whom no righteous servant could hold any terms. And then the ministers mingled themselves in the fray; and the Kirk like the Church, the presbyter like the priest, proved to be on the side of intolerance and superstition, where, unfortunately, priests of all creeds have ever been. And when James VI came with his narrow brain and selfish heart, to formularize the witch-lie into a distinct canon of arbitrary faith, and give it increased political significance and social power, the reign of humanity and common sense was at an end, and the autocracy of cruelty and superstition began. It is a dreary page in human history; but so long as a spark of superstition lingers in the world it will have its special and direct uses.

The first time we hear of Scottish witches was when St Patrick offended them and the devil alike by his uncompromising rigour against them: so they tore off a piece of a rock as he was crossing the sea and hurled it after him; which rock became the fortress of Dumbarton in the days which knew not St Patrick. Then there was the story of King Duff (968), who pined away in mortal sickness, by reason of the waxen image which had been made to destroy him; but by the fortunate discovery of a young maiden who could not bear torture silently, he was enabled to find the witches—whom he burnt at Forres in Murray, the mother of the poor maiden who could not bear torture among them: enabled, too, to save himself by breaking the wasting waxen image roasting at the "soft" fire, when almost at its last turn. Then we come to Thomas of Ercildoune, whom the Queen of Faërie loved and kept; and then to Sir Michael Scot of Balweary, that famous wizard, second to none in power; while a little further removed from those legendary times we see the dark figure of William Lord Soulis, who was boiled to death at Nine Stane Brig, in fitting punishment for his crimes. And then in 1479 twelve mean women and several wizards were burnt at Edinburgh for roasting the king in wax, and so endangering the life of the sovereign liege in a manner which no human aid could remedy; and the Earl of Mar was at their head, and very properly burnt too. And in 1480 Incubi and Succubi held the land between them, and even the young lady of Mar gave herself up to the embraces of an Incubus—a hideous monster, utterly loathsome and deadly to behold; and if the young ladies of the nobility could do such things, what might not be expected from the commonalty? But now we come out into the light of written history, and the story of "The Devil's Secretary."

◇

THE DEVIL'S SECRETARY

On the 26th of December, 1590, John Fian, *alias* Cuningham ('spelt Johanne Feane, *alias* Cwninghame), master of the school at Saltpans, Lothian, and contemptuously recorded as "Secretar and Register to the Devil," was arrainged for witchcraft and high treason. There were twenty counts against him, the least of which would have been enough to have lighted up a witch-fire on that fatal Castle Hill, for the bravest and best in the land. First, he was accused of entering into a covenant with Satan, who appeared to him in white, as he lay in bed, musing and thinking ("mwsand and pansand," says the dittay in its quaint language) how he should be revenged on Thomas Trumbill, for not having whitewashed his room, according to agreement. After promising his Satanic majesty allegiance and homage, he received his mark, which later was found under his tongue, with two pins therein thrust up to their heads. Again, he was found guilty— "fylit" is the old legal term—of "feigning himself to be sick in the said Thomas Trumbill's chamber, where he was stricken in great ecstacies and trances, lying by the space of two or three hours dead, his spirit taken, and suffered himself to be carried and transported to many mountains, as he thought through all the world, according to his depositions." Note, that these depositions were made in the midst of fearful torture, and recanted the instant after. Also, he was found guilty of suffering himself to be carried to North Berwick church, where, together with many others, he did homage to Satan, as he stood in the pulpit, making doubtful speeches, saying, "Many come to the fair, and all buy not wares;" and desired him "not to fear though he was grim, for he had many servants who should never want, or ail nothing, so long as their hair was on, and should never let one tear fall from their eyes so long as they served him;" and he gave them lessons, and said, "Spare not to do evil, and to eat and drink and be blithe, taking rest and ease, for he should raise them up at the latter day gloriously." But the pith of the indictment was that he, Fian, and sundry others to be spoken of hereafter, entered into a league with Satan to wreck the king on his way to Denmark, whither, in a fit of clumsy gallantry, he had set out to visit his future queen. While he was sailing to Denmark, Fian and a whole crew of witches and wizards met Satan at sea, and the master, giving an enchanted cat into Robert Grierson's hand, bade him "cast the same into the sea, holà," which was accordingly done; and a pretty capful of wind the consequence. Then, when the king was returning from Denmark, the devil promised to raise a mist which should wreck him on English ground. To perform which feat he took something like a football—it seemed to Dr. Fian like a wisp—and cast it into the sea, whereupon arose the great mist which nearly drove the cumbrous old pedant on to English ground, where our strong-fisted queen would have made him pay for his footing in a manner not quite congenial to his tastes. But, being a Man of God, none of these charms and devilries prevailed against him. A further count was, that once again he consorted with Satan and his crew, still in North Berwick church, where they paced round the church wider shins (wider scheins?), that is, contrary to the way of the sun. Fian blew into the lock—a favourite trick of his—to open the door, and blew in the lights which burned blue, and were like big black candles held in an old man's hand round about the pulpit. Here Satan as a "mekill blak man, with ane blak baird stikand out lyke ane gettis (goat's) baird; and ane hie ribbit neise, falland doun scharp lyke the beik of ane halk; with ane lang rumpill (tail); cled in ane blak tatie goune, and ane ewill favorit scull bonnett on his heid; haifand ane blak buik in his hand," preached to them, commanding them to be good servants to him, and he would be a good master to them, and never let them want. But he made them all very angry by calling Robert Grierson by his Christian name. He ought to have been called "Ro" the Comptroller, or "Rob the Rower." This slip of the master's displeased them sorely, and they ran "hirdie girdie" in great excitement, for it was against all etiquette to be named by their earthly names; indeed, they always received new names when the devil gave them their infernal christening, and they made themselves over to him and denied their holy baptism. It was at this meeting that John Fian was specially accused of rifling the graves of the dead, and dismembering their bodies for charms. And many other things did this Secretar and Register to the devil. Once, at the house of David Seaton's mother, he breathed into the hand of a woman sitting by the fire, and opened a lock at the other end of the kitchen. Once he raised up four candles on his horse's two ears, and a fifth on the staff which a man riding with him carried in his hand. These magic candles gave as much light as the sun at noonday, and the man was so terrified that he fell dead on his own threshold. He sent an evil spirit, who tormented a man for twenty weeks; and he was seen to chase a cat, and in the chase to be carried so high over a hedge that he could not touch her head. The dittay says he flew through the air —a not infrequent mode of progression with such people. When asked why he hunted the cat, he said that Satan had need of her, and that he wanted all the cats he could lay hands on, to cast into the sea, and cause storms and shipwrecks. He was further accused of endeavouring to bewitch a young maiden by his devilish cantrips* and horrid charms, but by a wile of the girl's mother, up to men's arts, he practised on a heifer's hairs instead of the girl's, and the result was that a luckless young cow went lowing after him everywhere—even into his school-room—rubbing herself against him, and exhibiting all the languish and desire of a love-sick young lady. A curious old plate represents John Fian and the heifer in grotesque attitudes; the heifer with large, drooping, amorous eyes, intensely ridiculous—the schoolmaster with his magic wand drawing circles in the sand. These, with

* Spells.

divers smaller charges, such as casting horoscopes, and wearing modewart's (mole's) feet upon him, amounting in all to twenty counts, formed the sum of the indictment against him. He was put to the torture. First, his head was "thrawed* with a rope" for about an hour, but still he would not confess; then they tried fair words and coaxed him, but with no better success; and then they put him to the "most severe and cruell pains in the worlde," namely, the boots, till his legs were completely crushed, and the blood and marrow spouted out. After the third stroke he became speechless; and they, supposing it to be the devil's mark which kept him silent, searched for that mark, that by its discovery the spell might be broken. So they found it, as stated before, under his tongue, with two charmed pins stuck up to their heads therein. When they were drawn out—that is, after some further torture—he confessed anything which it pleased his tormentors to demand of him, saying how, just now, the devil had been to him all in black, but with a white wand in his hand; and how, on his, Fian's, renouncing him, he had broke his wand, and disappeared. The next day he recanted this confession. He was then somewhat restored to himself, and had mastered the weakness of his agony. Whereupon it was assumed that the devil had visited him through the night, and had marked him afresh. They searched him— pulling off every nail with a turkas, or smith's pincers, and then thrusting in needles up to their heads; but finding nothing more satanic than blood and nerves, they put him to worse tortures, as a revenge. He made no other relapse, but remained constant now to the end; bearing his grievous pains with patience and fortitude, and dying as a brave man always knows how to die, whatever the occasion. Finding that nothing more could be made of him, they mercifully came to an end. He was strangled and burnt "in the Castle Hill of Edinburgh, on a Saterdaie, in the ende of Januarie last past 1591;" ending a may be loose and not over-heroic life in a manner worthy of the most glorious martyr of history. John Fian, schoolmaster of Saltpans with no great idea to support him, and no admiring friends to cheer him on, bore himself as nobly as any hero of them all, and vindicated the honour of manhood and natural strength in a way that exalts our common human nature into something godlike and divine.

* Twisted or wrenched.

ELSPETH CURSETTER AND HER FRIENDS

Elspeth Cursetter was tried, May 29, 1602, for all sorts of bad actions. She bade one of her victims "get the bones of ane tequhyt (linnet), and carry thame in your claithes"; and she gave herself out as knowing evil, and able to do it too, when and to whomsoever she would; and she sat down before the house of a man who refused her admittance—for she was an ill-famed old witch, and every one dreaded her—saying "Ill might they all thrive, and ill may they speed,"whereby in fourteen days' time the man's horse fell just where she had sat, and was killed most lamentably. But she cured a neighbour's cow by drawing a cog of water out of the burn that ran before William Anderson's door, coming back and taking three straws—one for William Anderson's wife, and one for William Coitt's wife, and one for William Bichen's wife—which she threw into the pail with the water, then put the same on the cow's back; by which charm the three straws danced in the water, and the water bubbled as it had been boiling. Then Elspeth took a little quantity of this charmed water, and thrust her arm up to the elbow into the cow's throat, and on the instant the cow rose up as well as she had ever been; but William Anderson's ox, which was on the hill, dropped down dead. Likewise she worked unholy cantrips for a sick friend with a paddock (toad), in the mouth of a pail of water, which toad was too large to get down the mouth, and when it was cast forth another man sickened and died immediately: and she spake dangerous words to a child, saying, "Wally fall that quhyt head of thine, but the pox will tak the away frae thy mother." As it proved, for the little white head was laid low a short time after, when the small-pox raged through the land. "Thow can tell eneough yf thow lyke," said the mother to her afterwards, "that could tell that my bairne wold die so long befoir the tyme." "I can tell eneugh if I durst," replied Elspeth, over proud of her safety. But in spite of all this testimony, Elspeth got off with "arbitrary punishment," which did not include burning or strangling, so was luckier than her neighbours. Luckier than poor Jonet Rendall was, who, on the 11th of November (1629), was proved a witch by the bleeding of the corpse of the poor wretch whom she had "enchanted" to his death. For "as soon as she came in the corpse having lain a good space, and not having bled any, immediately bled much blood, as a sure token that she was the author of his death." And had she not said, too, when a certain man refused her a Christmas lodging, "that it wald be weill if the gude man of that hous sould make ane other yule banket" (Christmas banquet); by which curse had he not died in fifteen days after? Wherefore was she a proved murderess as well as witch, and received the doom appointed to both alike. Alexander Drummond was a warlock who cured all kinds of horrid diseases, the very names of which are enough to make one ill; and he had a familiar, which had attended him for "neir this fifty yeiris:" so he was convicted and burnt.

Then came Jonet Forsyth, great in her art. She could cast sickness on any one at sea, and cure him again by a salt-water bath; she could transfer any disease from man to beast, so that when the beast died and was opened, nothing could be found where its heart should have been but "a blob of water;" she knew how to charm and sain* all kinds of cattle by taking three drops of a beastie's blood on All Hallow E'en, and sprinkling the same in the fire within the innermost chamber; she went at seed time and bewitched a stack of barley belonging to Michael Reid, so that for many years he could never make it into wholesome malt; and this she did for the gain of Robert Reid, changing the "profit" of the grain backwards and forwards between the two, according as they challenged or displeased her. All this did Jonet Forsyth of Birsay, to the terror of her neighbours and the ultimate ruin of herself, both in soul and body. Then came Catherine Oswald, spouse to Robert Aitcheson, in Niddrie, who was brought to trial for being "habite and repute" a witch—defamed by Elizabeth Toppock herself a witch and, as is so often the case, a dear friend of Katie's. Elizabeth need not have been so eager to get rid of her dear friend and gossip, for she was burnt afterwards for the same crimes as those for which poor Catherine suffered the halter and the stake. It seems that Katie was bad for her enemies. She was offended at Adam Fairbairn and his wife, so she made their "twa kye run mad and rammish† to died," and also made a gentleman's bairn that they had a-fostering run wood (mad) and die. And she fired William Heriot's kiln, full of grain; and burnt all his goods before his eyes;

* Shield from evil influence.
† To go about under the influence of strong passion.

and made his wife, in a "frantick humour," drown herself; and she cursed John Clark's ground, so that for four years after "by hir sorceries, naether kaill, lint, hempe, nor any other graine" would grow thereon, though doubly "laboured and sowen." She bewitched Thomas Scott by telling him that he looked as well as when Bessie Dobie was living, whereby he immediately fell so deadly sick that he could not proceed further, but was carried on a horse to Newbiggin, where he lay until the morrow, when "a wife" came in and told him he was forespoken. And other things as mischievous—and as true— did Catherine Oswald, as the Record testifies. She was well defended, and might have got off, but that a witness deposed to having seen Mr John Aird the minister, and a most zealous witch-finder, prick her in the shoulder with a pin, and that no blood followed thereafter, nor did she shrink as with pain or feeling. And as there was no gainsaying the evidence of the witch-mark, Satan and Mr John Aird claimed their own. Was Catherine's brand like a "blew spot, or a little tate, or reid spots, like flea-biting?" or with "the flesh sunk in and hallow?" according to the description of such places, published by Mr John Bell, minister of the gospel in Gladsmuir. We are seldom told of what precise character the marks were, only that they were found, pricked, and tested, and the witch hung or burnt on their testimony.

◇

SANDIE AND THE DEVIL

Soon after Catherine Oswald's execution, one of her crew or coven, who had been with her on the great storm in "the borrowing days (in anno 1625), on the Brae of the Saltpans," a noted warlock, by name Alexander Hunter, or Hamilton, *alias* Hatteraick, which last name he had gotten from the devil, was brought to execution on the Castle Hill. It was in 1629 that he was taken. It was proved that on Kingston hills he had met with the devil as a black man, or, as Sinclair says, as a mediciner; and often afterwards he would meet him riding on a black horse, or he would appear as a corbie, cat, or dog. When Alexander wanted him he would beat the ground with a fir stick lustily, crying, "Rise up, foul thief!" for the master got but hard names at times from his servants. This fir stick, and four shillings sterling, the devil gave to him when the compact was first made between them; and he confessed, moreover, that when raised in this manner he could only be got rid of by sacrificing to him a cat or dog, or such like, "quick." Also he set on fire Provost Cockburn's mill of corn, by taking three stalks from his stacks, and burning them on Garleton Hills; and he owned to a deadly hatred against Lady Ormiston, because she once refused him "ane almous," and called him "ane custroune carle." So, to punish her, he and some witches raised the devil in Salton Wood, where he appeared like a man in gray clothes, and gave him the bottom of a blue clew, telling him to lay it at the lady's door: "which he and the women having done, 'the lady and her daughter were soon thereafter bereft of their naturall lyfe.' " But Sinclair's account is the most graphic. I will give it in his own words:—

"Anent Hattaraick, an old Warlock.

"This man's name was Sandie Hunter, who called himself Sandie Hamilton, and it seems so called Hattaraik by the devil, and so by others as a Nickname. He was first a Neatherd in East Lothian, to a gentleman there. He was much given to charming and cureing of men and Beasts, by words and spels. His charms sometimes succeeded and sometimes not. On a day, herding his kine upon a Hill side in the summer time, the Devil came to him in form of a Mediciner, and said, 'Sandie, you have too long followed my trade, and never acknowledged me for your master. You must not take on with me, and I will make you more perfect in your calling. Whereupon the man gave up himself to the devil and received his Mark with this new name. After this he grew very famous throw the countrey for his charming cureing of diseases in men and beasts, and turned a vagrant fellow like a Jockie, gaining Meat, Flesh, and Money by his Charms, such was the ignorance of many at that time.

"Whatever House he came to, none durst refuse Hattaraik any alms, rather for his ill than his good. One day he came to the yait of Samuelstown, when some Friends after dinner were going to Horse. A young Gentleman, Brother to the Lady, seeing him, switcht him about the ears, saying, 'You Warlok Cairle, what have you to do here?' whereupon the Fellow goes away grumbling, and was overheard to say, 'You shall dear buy this, ere it be long.' This was *Damnum Minatum*. The young Gentleman conveyed his Friends a far way off, and came home that way again, where he slept. After supper, taking his horse and crossing Tine-water to go home, he rides throw a shadowy piece of a Haugh, commonly called the Allers, and the evening being somewhat dark he met with some Persons there that begat a dreadful consternation in him, which for the most part he would never reveal. This was *malum secutum.* When he came home, the Servants observed terror and fear in his countenance. The next day he became distracted, and was bound for several days. His sister, the Lady Samuelstoun, hearing of it, was heard to say, 'Surely that knave Hattaraik is the cause of his Trouble. Call for him in all haste.' When he had come to her, 'Sandie,' says she, 'what is this you have done to my brother William?' 'I told him,' says he, 'I should make him repent his striking of me at the Yait lately.' She gave the Rogue fair words, and promising him his Pock full of Meal with Beef and Cheese, persuaded the Fellow to cure him again. He undertook the business; 'but I must first,' says he, 'have one of his Sarks,' which was soon gotten. What pranks he plaid with it cannot be known. But within a short while the gentleman recovered his health. When Hatteraik came to receive his wages, he told the Lady, 'Your Brother William shal quickly goe off the Countrey but shall never return.' She, knowing the Fellow's prophecies to hold true, caused her Brother to make a Disposition to her of all his patrimony, to the defrauding of his younger brother George. After that this Warlock had abused the Countrey for a long time, he was at last apprehended at Dunbar, and brought into Edinburgh, and burnt upon the Castle Hill. But not until he had delated several others of hitherto good repute, so that for the next few months the witchfinder's hands were full."

⌒

One of the most extraordinary tales I have to relate was that wonderful bit of knavery and credulity called

THE DEVIL OF GLENLUCE

when Master Tom Campbell set the whole country in a flame, and brought no end of notice and sympathy upon his house and family.

In 1654 one Gilbert Campbell was a weaver in Glenluce, a small village not far from Newton Stewart. Tom, his eldest son, and the most important personage in the drama, was a student at Glasgow College; and there was a certain old blaspheming beggar, called Andrew Agnew—afterwards hanged at Dumfries for his atheism, having said, in the hearing of credible witnesses, that "there was no God but salt, meal, and water"—who every now and then came to Glenluce to ask alms. One day old Andrew visited the Campbells as usual, but got nothing; at which he cursed and swore roundly, and forthwith sent a devil to haunt the house, for it was soon after this refusal that the stirs began, and the connection was too apparent to be denied. For what could they be but the malice of the devil sent by old Andrew in revenge? Young Tom Campbell was the worst beset of all, the demon perpetually whistling and rioting about him, and playing him all sorts of diabolical and malevolent tricks. Once, too, Jennet, the young daughter, going to the well, heard a whistling behind her like that produced by "the small slender glass whistles of children," and a voice like the damsel's, saying, "I'll cast thee, Jennet, into the well! I'll cast thee, Jennet, into the well!" About the middle of November, when the days were dark and the nights long, things got very bad. The foul fiend threw stones in at the doors and windows, and down the chimney head; cut the warp and threads of Campbell's loom; slit the family coats and bonnets and hose and shoon into ribbons; pulled off the bed-clothes from the sleeping children, and left them cold and naked, besides administering sounding slaps on those parts of their little round rosy persons usually held sacred to the sacrifices of the rod; opened chests and trunks, and strewed the contents over the floor; knocked everything about, and ill-treated bairn and brother; and, in fact, persecuted the whole family in the most merciless manner. The weaver sent his children away, thinking their lives but barely safe, and *in their absence there were no assaults whatever*—a thing to be specially noted. But on the minister's representing to him that he had done a grievous sin in thus withdrawing them from God's punishments, they were brought back again in contrition. Only Tom was left behind, and nothing ensued until Tom appeared; but unlucky Tom brought back the devil with him, and then there was no more peace to be had.

On the Sunday following Master Tom's return, the house was set on fire—the devil's doing: but the neighbours put the flames out again before much damage had ensued. Monday was spent in prayer; but on Tuesday the place was again set on fire, to be again saved by the neighbours' help. The weaver, in much trouble, went to the minister, and besought him to take back that unlucky Tom, whom the devil so cruelly followed and molested; which request he, after a time, "condescended to," though assuring the weaver that he would find himself deceived if he thought that the devil would quit with the boy. And so it proved; for Tom, having now indoctrinated some of his juniors with the same amount of mechanics and legerdemain as he himself possessed, managed that they should be still sore troubled— the demon cutting their clothes, throwing peats down the chimney, pulling off turf and "feal" from the roof and walls, stealing their coats, pricking their poor bodies with pins, and raising such a clam- our that there was no peace or rest to be had.

The case was becoming serious. Glenluce objected to be made the head-quarters of the devil; and the ministers convened a solemn meeting for fast and humiliation; the upshot of which was that weaver Campbell was led to take back his unlucky Tom, with the devil or without him. For this was the point at issue in the beginning; the motive of which is not hard to be discoverd. Whereupon Tom returned; but as he crossed the threshold he heard a voice "for- bidding him to enter that house, or any other place where his father's calling was exercised." Was Tom, the Glasgow student, afraid of being made a weaver, consent or none demanded? In spite of the warning voice he valiantly entered, and his persecutions began at once. Of course they did. They were tremendous, unheard of, barbarous; in fact, so bad that he was forced to return once more for a time to the minister's house; but his imitator or disciple left behind carried on business in his absence. On Monday, the 12th day of February, the demon began to speak to the family, who, nothing afraid, answered quite cheerily: so they and the devil had long con- fidential chats together, to the great improvement of mind and morals. The ministers, hearing of this, convened again, and met at weaver Campbell's to see what they could do. As soon as they entered, Satan began: "Quum literatum is good Latin," quoth he. These were the first words of the Latin rudiments, as taught in the grammar- school. Tom's classical knowledge was coming into play.

After a while he cried out, "A dog! a dog!" The minister, thinking he was alluded to, answered, "He thought it no evil to be reviled of him;" to which Satan replied civilly, "It was not you, sir, I spoke to: I meant the dog there;" for there was a dog standing behind backs. They then went to prayer, during which time Tom—or the devil— remained reverently silent; his education being not yet carried out to the point of scoffing. Immediately after prayer was ended, a counterfeit voice cried out, "Would you know the witches of Glenluce? I will tell of them," naming four of five persons of indifferent repute, but one of whom was dead. The weaver told the devil this, thinking to have caught him tripping; but the foul fiend answered promptly, "It is true she is dead long ago, but her spirit is living with us in the world."

The minister replied, saying, "Though it was not convenient to speak to such an excommunicated and intercommuned person, 'the Lord rebuke thee, Satan, and put thee to silence. We are not to receive information from thee, whatsoever fame any person goes under. Thou art seeking but to seduce this family, for Satan's kingdom is not divided against itself.'" After which little sparring there was prayer again; so Tom did not take much by this move.

All the while the young Glasgow student was very hardly holden, so that there was more prayer on his special behalf. The devil then said, on their rising, "Give me a spade and a shovel, and depart from the house for seven days, and I will make a grave and lie down in it, and shall trouble you no more."

The good man Campbell answered, "Not so much as a straw shall be given thee, through God's assistance, even though that would do it. God shall remove thee in due time." Satan cried out, impudently, "I shall not remove for you. I have my commission from Christ to tarry and vex this family." Says the minister, coming to the weaver's assistance, "A permission thou hast, indeed; but God will stop it in due time." Says the demon, respectfully, "I have, sir, a commission which perhaps will last longer than yours." And the minister died in the December of that year, says Sinclair. Furthermore, the demon said he had given Tom his commission to keep. Interrogated, that young gentleman replied in an off-hand way, that "he had had something put into his pocket, but it did not tarry." They then began to search about for the foul fiend, and one gentleman said, "We think this voice speaks out of the children." The foul fiend, very angry at this—or Master Tom frightened—cries out, "You lie! God shall judge you for your lying; and I and my father will come and fetch you to hell with warlock thieves." So the devil discharged (forbade) the gentleman to speak anything, saying, "Let him that hath a commission speak (meaning the minister), for he is the servant of God." The minister then had a little religious controversy with the devil, who answered at last, simply, "I knew not these scriptures till my father taught me them." Nothing of all this disturbing the easy faith of the audience, they, through the minister, whom alone he would obey, conjured him to tell them who he was; whereupon he said that he was an evil spirit come from the bottomless pit of hell, to vex this house, and that Satan was his father. And then there appeared a naked hand, and an arm from the elbow downward, beating on the floor till the house did shake again, and a loud and fearful crying, "Come up, father! come up, father! I will send my father among ye! See! there he is behind your backs!"

Says the minister, "I saw, indeed, a hand and an arm, when the stroke was given and heard."

Says the devil, "Saw ye that? It was not my hand, it was my father's; my hand is more black in the loof."

"Oh!" said Gilbert Campbell, in an ecstacy, "that I might see thee as well as I hear thee!"

"Would ye see me?" says the foul thief. "Put out the candle, and I shall come but* the house among you like fire-balls; I shall let ye see me indeed."

Alexander Bailie of Dunraget said to the minister, "Let us go ben,† and see if there is any hand to be seen." But the demon exclaimed, "No! let him (the minister) come ben alone: he is a good honest man: his single word may be believed." He then abused Mr. Robert Hay, a very honest gentleman, very ill with his tongue, calling him witch and warlock: and a little while after, cried out, "A witch! a witch! there's a witch sitting upon the ruist! take her away." He meant that there was a hen sitting on one of the rafters. They then went to prayer again, and, when ended, the devil cried out, "If the good man's son's prayers at the College of Glasgow did not prevail

* To the outer room.
† To the inner room.

with God, my father and I had wrought a mischief here ere now."
Ah, Master Tom, did you then know so much of prayer and the
inclining of the counsels of God?

Alexander Bailie said, "Well, I see you acknowledge a God, and
that prayer prevails with him, and therefore we must pray to God,
and commit the event to him." To whom the devil replied, having an
evident spite against Alexander Bailie, "Yea, sir, you speak of
prayer, with your broad-lipped hat" (for the gentleman had lately
gotten a hat in the fashion with broad lips); "I'll bring a pair of
shears from my father's which shall clip the lips of it a little." And
Alexander Bailie presently heard a pair of shears go clipping round
his hat, "which he lifted, to see if the foul thief had meddled with it."

Then the fiend fell to prophesying. "Tom was to be a merchant,
Bob a smith, John a minister, and Hugh a lawyer," all of which came
to pass. Turning to Jennet, the good man's daughter, he cried,
"Jennet Campbell, Jennet Campbell, wilt thou cast me thy belt?"

Quoth she, "What a widdy would thou do with my belt?"

"I would fain," says he, "fasten my loose bones together."

A younger daughter was sitting "busking her puppies" (dressing
her puppets, dolls), as young girls are used to do. He threatens to
"ding out her harns," that is, to brain her; but says she quietly, "No,
if God be to the fore," and so falls to her work again. The good wife
having brought out some bread, was breaking it, so that every one of
the company should have a piece. Cries he, "Grissel Wyllie! Grissel
Wyllie! give me a piece of that haver bread.* I have gotten nothing
this day but a bit from Marritt," that is, as they speak in the country,
Margaret. The minister said to them all, "Beware of that! for it is
sacrificing to the devil!" Marritt was then called, and inquired if she
had given the foul fiend any of her haver bread. "No," says she;
"but when I was eating my due piece this morning, something came
and clicked it out of my hands."

The evening had now come, and the company prepared to depart;
the minister, and the minister's wife, Alexander Bailie of Dunraget,
with his broad-lipped hat, and the rest. But the devil cried out in
a kind of agony—

"Let not the minister go! I shall burn the house if he goes."
Weaver Campbell, desperately frightened, besought the minister to

---

* A common type of country bread made with water.

Four distinguished Victorian witchcraft writers: Mrs E. Lynn Linton,
Lady Lucie Duff-Gordon, Amelia Edwards, Pauline Bradford Mackie

Dr Fian and his coven at North Berwick. See the story entitled "The Devil's Secretary" by Mrs Lynn Linton

A nineteenth-century illustration of a witches' coven. Note the devil figure at the rear providing the music for the ritual dance

stay; and he, not willing to see them come to mischief, at last consented. As he turned back into the house, the devil gave a great gaff of laughing, saying, "Now, sir! you have done my bidding!" which was unhandsome of Tom—very.

"Not thine, but in obedience to God, have I returned to bear this man company whom thou dost afflict," says the minister, nowise discomposed, and not disdaining to argue matters clearly with the devil.

Then the minister "discharged" all from speaking to the demon, saying, "that when it spoke to them they must only kneel and pray to God." This did not suit the demon at all. He roared mightily, and cried, "What! will ye not speak to me? I shall strike the bairns, and do all manner of mischief!" No answer was returned; and again the children were slapped and beaten on their rosy parts—where children are accustomed to be whipped. After a while this ended too, and then the fiend called out to the good-wife, "Grissel, put out the candle!"

"Shall I do it?" says she to the minister's wife.

"No," says that discreet person, "for then you shall obey the devil."

Upon which the devil shouted, with a louder voice, "Put out the candle!" No one obeyed, and the candle continued burning. "Put out the candle, I say!" cries he, more terribly than before. Grissel, not caring to continue the uproar, put it out. "And now," says he, "I will trouble you no more this night." For by this time I should suppose that Master Tom was sleepy, and tired, and hoarse.

Once again the ministers and gentlemen met for prayer and exorcism; when it is to be presumed that Tom was not with them, for everything was quiet; but soon after the stirs began again, and Tom and the rest were sore molested. Gilbert Campbell made an appeal to the Synod of Presbyters, a committee of whom appointed a special day of humiliation in February, 1656, for the freeing of the weaver's house from this affliction. In consequence whereof, from April to August, the devil was perfectly quiet, and the family lived together in peace. But after this the mischief broke out again afresh. Perhaps Tom had come home from college, or his father had renewed his talk of settling him firmly to his own trade: whatever the cause, the effect was certain, the devil had come back to Glenluce.

One day, as the good-wife was standing by the fire, making the porridge for the children, the demon came and snatched the "tree-

E

plate," on which was the oat-meal, out of her hand, and spilt all the meal. "Let me have the tree-plate again," says Grissel Wyllie, very humbly; and it came flying back to her. "It is like if she had sought the meal too she might have got it, such is his civility when he is entreated," says Sinclair. But this would have been rather beyond even Master Tom's power of legerdemain. Things after this went very ill. The children were daily thrashed with heavy staves, and every one in the family underwent much personal damage; until, as a climax, on the eighteenth of September, the demon said he would burn the house down, and did, in fact, set it on fire. But it was put out again, before much damage was done.

After a time—probably by Tom's going away, or becoming afraid of being found out—the devil was quieted and laid for ever; and Master Tom employed his intellect and energies in other ways than terrifying his father's family to death, and making stirs which went by the name of demoniac.

This account is taken almost verbatim from an article of mine in "All the Year Round;" and if a larger space has been given to this than to many other stories, it is because there was more colouring, and more distinctness in the drawing, than in anything else that I have read. Though scarcely belonging to a book on witches, there is yet a hook and eye, if a very slender one, in the fact that the old beggar, Andrew Agnew, was hanged; and we may be sure that it was not only his atheism, but also his naughty tricks with Satan, and his connection with the devil of Glenluce, that helped to fit the hangman's rope round his neck. There are many other stories of haunted houses, notably, Mr Monpesson's at Tedworth caused by the Demon Drummer, and the Woodstock Devil who harried the Parliamentary Commissioners to within an inch of their lives, and others to the full as interesting; but there is no hook and eye with them—nothing by which they can be hung on to the sad string of witches, or witchcraft murders. Baxter has two or three such stories; and the curious in such matters will find a large amount of interesting matter in the various works referred to at the foot of the pages; matter which could not be introduced here, because of its not belonging strictly to the subject in hand. I do not think that any candid or unprejudiced person will fail in seeing the dark shadow of fraud and deceit flung over every such account remaining. The importance of which, to me, is the evident and distinct likeness between these stories and the marvels going on now in modern society. And now to our next account.

∽

THE WITCHES OF AULDEARNE:

and Isobel Gowdie's marvellous confessions in A.D. 1662. Isobell was neither pricked nor tortured before she entered on her singular history of circumstantial lies. She was probably a mere lunatic, whose ravings ran in the popular groove, and who was not so much deceiving, as self-deceived by insanity. The assize which tried her was composed of highly respectable people, and she seems to have been only encouraged to rave, not forced to lie. She began by stating that one day, fifteen years ago, as she was going between "the towns" or farmsteads of Drumdewin and the Heads, she met the devil, who spoke to her and invited her to meet him that night at the parish church of Auldearne. She promised that she would, and accordingly she went, and he baptized her by the name of "Janet", and accepted her service. Margaret Brodie held her while she denied her Christian baptism; and then the devil marked her on the shoulder, sucking out the blood which he "spouted" into his hand, then sprinkled it on her head, saying, "I baptize thee, Janet, in my own name!" But first he had put one hand on the crown of her head, and the other on the soles of her feet, while she made over to him all that lay betwixt, giving herself body and soul into his keeping. He was in the Reader's desk while all this took place, appearing as a "mickle, black, hairy man" reading out of a black book; so Isobell was henceforth Janet in the witch world, and was one of the most devoted of her coven; for they were divided into covens or bands, she said, and placed under the leadership of proper officers. John Young was the officer of her coven and the number composing it was thirteen. She and others of her band took Breadley's corn from off his land. They took an unchristened child which they had raised out of its grave, parings of their nails, ears of all sorts of grain, and cole-wort leaves, all chopped very fine and small, and mixed up well together; and this charm they buried on his land, whereby they got all the strength of his corn and goods to themselves, and parted them among the coven. Another time they yoked a plough of paddocks (toads). The devil held it, and John Young drove it: it was drawn by toads instead of oxen, the traces were of quickens (dog-grass), the coulter was a riglen's horn (ram's horn), so was the sock; and they went two several times about the field, all the coven following and praying to the devil to give them the fruit of that land, and that only thistles and briars might grow on it for the master's use. So Breadley had trouble enough to work his land, and when it was worked he got no good out of it, but only weeds and thorns, while the coven made their bread of his labour.

When asked how she and her sister witches managed to leave their husbands o' nights, she said that, when it was their Sabbath nights, they used to put besoms or three-legged stools in bed beside their husbands; so that if these deluded men should wake before their return, they might believe they had their wives safe as usual. The besoms and three-legged stools took the right form of the women, and prevented a too early discovery. To go to these Sabbaths they put a straw between their feet, crying "Horse and Hattock in the Devil's name!" and then they would fly away, just as straws in the wind. Any kind of straw would do, and they who saw them floating about in the whirlwind, and did not sanctify themselves, could be shot dead at the witches' pleasure, and their bodies remained with them as horses, and small as straws.

These night meetings always ended with a supper; the Maiden of the Coven being placed next to the devil, as he was partial to young, plump, blooming witches, and did not care much for the "rigwoodie hags," save to beat and belabour them. And after they had gotten their meat they would say as a grace—

> "We eat this meat in the devil's name,
> With sorrow and *sich* (sighs) and mickle shame;
> We shall destroy both house and hald;
> Both sheep and nolt intil the fauld,
> Little good shall come to the fore,
> Of all the rest of the little store."

And when supper was done, each witch would look steadily upon their "grisly" president and say, bowing low, "We thank thee, our

Lord, for this!" But it was not much to thank him for in general; for the old adage seems to have been pretty nearly kept to, and the cooks, at least, not to speak of the meat, to be of the very lowest description. The poor witches never got more from the devil than what they might have had at home; which was one more added to the many proofs that the mind cannot travel beyond its own sphere of knowledge, and that even hallucinations are bounded by experience, and clairvoyance by the past actual vision.

Then Isobell went to the Downie Hills, to see the "gude wichtis" who had wrought Bessie Dunlop and Alesoun Peirsoun such sad mishap. The hill side opened and she went in. Here she got meat more than she could eat, which was a rare thing for her to do in those days, and seemed to her one of the most noticeable things of the visit. The Queen of Faërie was bravely clothed in white linen, and white and brown clothes, but she was nothing like the glorious creature who bewitched Thomas of Ercildoun with her winsom looks and golden hair; and the king was a braw man, well favoured and broad faced; just an ordinary man and woman of the better classes, buxom, brave, and comely, as Isobell Gowdie and her like would naturally take to be the ultimate perfection of humanity. But it was not all sunshine and delight even in the hill of Faërie, for there were "elf bullis rowting and skoylling" up and down, which frightened poor Isobell, as well as her auditory: for here she was interrupted and bidden on another track. She then went on to say that when they took away any cow's milk they did so by twining and platting a rope the wrong way and in the devil's name, drawing the tether in between the cow's hinder feet, and out between her fore feet. The only way to get back the milk was to cut the rope. When they took away the strength of any one's ale in favour of themselves or others, they used to take a little quantity out of each barrel, in the devil's name (they never forgot this formula), and then put it into the ale they wished to strengthen; and no one had power to keep their ale from them, save those who had well sanctified the brewing. Also she and others made a clay picture of a little child, which was to represent all the male children of the Laird of Parkis. John Taylor brought home the clay in his "plaid newk" (corner), his wife brake it very small like meal, and sifted it, and poured water in among it in the devil's name, and worked it about like rye porridge ("vrought it werie sore, lyk ryebowt") and made it into a picture of the Laird of Parkis' son. "It haid all the pairtis and merkis of a child, such as heid, eyes, nose, handis, foot, mowth, and little lippes. It wanted no mark of a child; and the handis of it folded down by its sydes." This precious image, which was like a lump of dough or a skinned sucking pig, was put to the fire till it shrivelled and became red as a coal; they put it to the fire every other day, and by the wicked power enclosed in this charm all the male children of the Laird of Parkis would suffer, unless it were broken up. She and the rest went in and out their neighbours' houses, sometimes as jackdaws, sometimes as hares, cats, &c., and ate and drank of the best; and they took away the virtue of all things left "unsained;" and each had their own powers. "Bot," said Isobell, sorrowfully, "now I haw no power at all." In another confession she told all about her Coven. There were thirteen in each, and every person had a nickname, and a spirit to wait on her. She could not remember the names of all, but she gave what she could. Swein clothed in grass green waited on Margaret Wilson called Pickel-nearest-the-wind: Rorie in yellow waited on Bessie Wilson, or Throw-the-corn-yard: the Roaring Lion in seagreen waited on Isobell Nichol, or Bessie Rule: Mak Hector, a young-like devil, clothed in grass green, was appropriated by Jean Martin, daughter to Margaret Wilson (Pickle-nearest-the-wind), the Maiden of the Coven and called Over-the-Dyke-with-it; this name given to her because the devil always takes the maiden in his hand next him, and when he would leap they both cry out, "Over the dyke with it!" Robert the Rule in sad dun, a commander of the spirits, waited on Margaret Brodie, Thief-of-hell-wait-upon-herself: he waited also on Bessie Wilson, otherwise Throw-the-corn-yard: Isobell's own spirit was the Red Riever, and he was ever clothed in black; the eighth spirit was Robert the Jakes, aged, and clothed in dun, "ane glaiked gowked spirit," and he waited on Bessie Hay, otherwise Able-and-Stout: the ninth was Laing, serving Elspet Nishie, re-named Bessie Bauld; the tenth was Thomas, a faerie:—but there Isobell's questioners stopped her, afraid to hear aught of the "guide wychtis," who might be then among them, injuring those who offended them to death. So no more information was given of the spirits of the Coven. She then told them that to raise a wind they took a rag of cloth which they wetted, then knocked on a stone with a beetle (a flat piece of wood) saying thrice—

"I knok this ragg wpon this stane,
To raise the wind in the Divelle's name;
It sall not lye, vntil I please againe!"

When the wind was to be laid, they dried the rag, and said thrice—

"We lay the wind in the divellis name,
It sall not rise quhill we lyk to raise it again!"

And if the wind would not cease the instant after they said this, they called to their spirit: "Thieffe! thieffe! conjure the wind and caws it to lye!" As for elf-arrow heads, the devil shapes them with his own hand, and then delivers them to elf boys who sharpen and trim them with a thing like a packing-needle: and when Isobell was in elf-land she saw the boys sharpening and trimming them. Those who trimmed them, she said, are little ones, hollow and hump-backed, and speak gruffly like. When the devil gave the arrows to the witches he used to say—

"Shoot these in my name,
And they sall not goe heall hame."

And when the witches shoot them, which they do by "spanging" them from their thumb nails, they say—

"I shoot yon man in the devillis name,
He sall nott win heall hame!
And this salbe alswa trw,
Thair sall not be an bitt of him on liew."*

Isobell had great talent for rhymes. She told the court how, when the witches wanted to transform themselves into the shape of hare or cat, they said thrice over—always thrice—

"I sall goe intill ane haire,
With sorrow, and sych, and mickle caire;
And I sall goe in the divellis name,
Ay whill I com hom againe."

Once Isobell said this rhyme when Patrik Papley's servants were going to labour. They had their dogs with them, and the dogs hunted her—she in the form of a hare. Very hard pressed, and weary, she had just time to run to her own house, get behind the chest, and repeat—

* On life: alive.

"Hair, hair, God send thé caire,
I am in a hairis likeness now,
But I sall be a woman ewin now;
Hair, hair, God send thé caire!"

Else the dogs would have worried her, and posterity have lost her confessions. Many other doggrels did Isobell teach her judges; but they were all of the same character as those already given: scanty rhymes in the devil's name, when they were not actual paraphrases of the mass book. Some were for healing and some for striking; some in the name of God and all the saints, others in the devil's name, boldly and nakedly used; but both equally damnable in the eyes of the judges, and equally worthy of death. The elf-arrows spoken of before were of great use. The devil gave them to his coven and they shot men and women dead, right and left. Sometimes they missed, as when Isobell shot at the Laird of Park as he was crossing the burn, and missed, for which Bessie Hay gave her a great cuff: also Margaret Brodie, when she shot at Mr Harie Forbes, the minister at Auldearne, he being by the standing stanes; whereupon she asked if she should shoot again, but the devil answered, "Not! for we wold nocht get his lyf at that tym." Finding the elf-arrows useless against Mr Harie Forbes, they tried charms and incantations once when he was sick. They made a bag, into which they put the flesh, entrails, and gall of a toad, a hare's liver, barley grains, nail pairings, and bits of rag, steeping all in water, while Satan stood over them, saying—and they repeating after him—

"He is lying in his bed, and he is seik and sair,
Let him lye in till that bedd monthes two and dayes thrie mair!
He sall lye in till his bed, he salbe seik and sair,
He sall lye in till his bedd, monthes two and dayes thrie mair!"

When they said these words they were all on their knees with their hair about their shoulders and eyes, holding up their hands to the devil, beseeching him to destroy Mr Harry; and then it was decided to go into his chamber and swing the bag over him. Bessie Hay— Able-and-Stout—undertook this office, and she went to his room, being intimate with him, the bag in her hands and her mind set on slaying him by its means; but there were some worthy persons with him at the time, so Bessie did no harm, only swung a few drops on him which did not kill him. They had a hard taskmaster in the devil—

Black Johnnie, as they used to call him among themselves. But he used to overhear them, and would suddenly appear in the midst of them, saying, "I ken weill anewgh what ye wer saying of me," and then would beat and buffet them sore. He was always beating them, specially if they were absent from any of the meetings, or if they forgot anything he had told them to do. Alexander Elder was being continually thrashed. He was very soft and could never defend himself in the least, but would cry and scream when the devil scourged him. The women had more pluck. Margaret Wilson—Pickle-nearest-the-wind—would defend herself finely, throwing up her hands to keep the strokes from her; and Bessie Wilson—Throw-the-corn-yard—"would speak crusty with her tongue and would be belling against him soundly." He used to beat them all up and down with scourges and sharp cords, they like naked ghosts crying, "Pity! pity! mercy! mercy, our Lord!" But he would have neither pity nor mercy, but would grin at them like a dog, and as if he would swallow them up. He would give them most beautiful money, at least to look at; but in four-and-twenty hours it would be all gone, or changed to mere dirt and rubbish. The devil wore sometimes boots and sometimes shoes, but ever his feet were cloven, and ever his colour black. This, with some small variations, was the sum of what Isobell Gowdie confessed in her four depositions taken between the 13th of April and 27th of May in the year of grace 1662.

Janet Braidhead, spouse to John Taylor, followed next. Her first confession, made on the 14th of April, set forth how that she had known nothing of witchcraft until her husband and his mother, Elspeth Nishie, had taught her; her first lesson from them being the making of some "drugs" which were to charm away the fruit and corn, and kill the cattle, of one John Hay in the Mure. After that, she was taken to the kirk at Auldearne, where her husband presented her for the devil's baptism and marking, which were done in the usual manner. She also gave evidence of the clay picture which was to destroy all the male children of the Laird of Park; and she gave a long list of the frequenters of the Sabbaths, including some of the most respectable inhabitants of the place; and in many other things she confirmed Isobell Gowdie's depositions, specially in all regarding the devil and the unequivocal nature of their connection with him, which was put into plain and unmistakable language enough.

We are not told the ultimate fate of Isobell Gowdie and Janet Braidhead, but they had confessed enough to burn half Scotland, and it is not likely that they escaped the doom assigned to their order.

◇

WITCH SPIRITS

Year by year witches became scarcer, none of any special note presenting themselves till we come to the case of Margaret Nin-Gilbert, of Caithness, which happened in the year 1718; the same year as that in which the minister of Redcastle lost his life by witchcraft, and Mr M'Gill's house at Kinross (he was minister there) was so egregiously troubled by a spirit which nipped the sheets and stuck pins into eggs and meat, and clipt away the laps of a gentlewoman's hood and a servant maid's gown tail, and flung stones down the chimney, which "wambled a space" on the floor, and then took a flight out of the window, and threw the minister's bible into the fire, and spoilt the baking, and played all sorts of mad pranks to disquiet the family and defy God. If such things as these could be done in the light of the sun, why should not Margaret Nin-Gilbert have supernatural power? Nin-Gilbert had a friend, one Maragret Olson, a woman of it is said wicked behaviour, whom Mr Frazer put out of her house, taking as his tenant instead one William Montgomerie. Upon this Margaret Olson went to her friend Nin-Gilbert, the notorious witch, and besought her to harm Mr Frazer; but Mr Frazer being a gentleman of rank and fortune was defended from the witches, and Nin-Gilbert confessed she had no power or inclination to hurt him. However, one night as he was crossing a bridge, they attempted him, but succeeded not; and he, on being questioned, said he perfectly remembered "his horse making a great adoe at that place, but that by the Lord's goodness he escaped." Also he had a great sickness at that time these women were taken, but he had common sense enough to refuse to ascribe it to them. Finding that they could not prevail against Mr Frazer, they turned their attention to Montgomerie, "mason, in Burnside of Scrabster," who was also under the ban for having accepted the tenancy of which Margaret Olson had been dispossessed. Suddenly his house became so infested with cats that it was no longer safe for his family to remain there. He himself was away, but his wife sent to him five times, threatening that if he did not return home to protect them, she would flit to Thurso; and his servant left them suddenly, and in mid term, because five of these cats came one night to the fireside where she was alone, and began speaking among themselves with human and intelligible voices. So William Montgomerie, mason at Scrabster, returned home to do battle with the enemy. The cats came in their old way and in their old numbers; and William prepared his best. On Friday night, the 28th of November, one of the cats got into a chest with a hole in it, and when she put her head out of the hole, William made a lunge at her with his sword, which "cutt hir," but for all that he could not hold her. He then opened the chest, and his servant, William Geddes, stuck his dirk into her hind quarters and pinned her to the chest. After which, Montgomerie beat her with his sword and cast her out for dead; but the next morning she was gone; so there was no doubt as to her true character. Four or five nights after this, his servant, being in bed, "cryed out that Some of these catts had come in on him." Montgomerie ran to his aid, wrapt his plaid about the cat and thrust his dirk through her body, then smashed her head with the back of an axe, and cast her out like the first. The next morning she too was gone, and there was proof positive for another case. So as none of these cats belonged to the neighbourhood, and there were eight of them assembled together in one night, "this looking like witchcraft, it being threatened that none should thrive in my said house," William Montgomerie made petition to the Sheriff-Depute of Caithness, to visit "some person of bad fame," who was reported to have fallen sick immediately on this encounter, and search out if she had any wounds on her body or not. "This representation seeming all the time to be very incredulous and fabulous, the sheriff had no manner of regard yrto." But when, on the 12th of February, Margaret Nin-Gilbert was seen by one of her neighbours "to drop at her own door one of her leggs from the midle, and she, being under bad fame for witchcraft, the legg, black and putrified, was brought before the Sheriff-Depute" (not the sheriff himself, the Earl of Caithness, who might have had a little more common sense)—then the said Sheriff-Depute ordered Nin-Gilbert to be seized and examined. Margaret made short work of it. Being interrogated the 8th of

February, 1719, she confessed that she was under compact with the devil, whom she had met in the likeness of a black man as she was travelling some long time byegone in ane evening; confessed also that he sometimes appeared to her as a great black horse, and other times as if riding on a black horse, and sometimes as a black cloud, and sometimes as a black hen. Confessed also that she was at William Montgomerie's house that evening, when he attacked her as a cat, and that he broke her leg with the dirk or axe, which since had fallen off from the rest of her body: also, that Margaret Olson was there with her, who, being stronger than she did cast her on the dirk when her leg was broken. She then delated four other women, one of whom Helen Andrew, had been so crushed and maimed by Montgomerie, "that she dyed that same night of her wounds or few days yrafter:" and another, M'Huistan, "cast herself a few days afterwards from the rocks of Borrowstoun into the sea, since which time she was never seen;" while a third, Jannet Pyper, she identified as having a red petticoat on her. Asked how they managed not be be discovered said, "the devil raised a fog or mist to conceal them." When her confession was ended, her accomplices were apprehended; but she herself died in prison in a fortnight's time. Margaret Olson was then examined. She was "tryed in the shoulders" (for witches' marks), "where there were several small spots, some read, some blewish; after a needle was driven in with great force almost to the eye she felt it not. Mr. Innes, Mr Oswald, minister, and several honest women, and Bailzie Forbes, were witnesses to this. And further, that while the needle was in her shoulder, as aforesaid, she said, 'Am not I ane honest woman now?'" So this instance of human wickedness and folly ended by the usual method of the cord and the stake.

◌

THE LAST OF THE WITCHES

And now we draw near to the close of this fatal superstition. In 1726, Woodrow notes "some pretty odd accounts of witches," had from a couple of Ross-shire men, but fails to give us very accurate details, save only that one of them at her death "confessed that they had, by sorcery, taken away the sight of one of the eyes of an Episcopal minister, who lost the sight of his eye upon a sudden, and could give no reason for it." And early in the year of 1727 the last witch-fire was kindled with which the air of bonnie Scotland was polluted. Two poor Highland women, a mother and daughter, were brought before Captain David Ross of Littledean, deputy-sheriff of Suther-land, charged with witchcraft and consorting with the devil. The mother was accused of having used her daughter as her "horse and hattock," causing her to be shod by the devil, so that she was ever after lame in both hands and feet; and the fact being satisfactorily proved, and Captain David Ross being well assured of the same, the poor old woman was put into a tar-barrel and burned at Dornoch in the bright month of June. "And it is said that after being brought out to execution, the weather proving very severe, she sat composedly warming herself by the fire prepared to consume her, while the other instruments of death were getting ready." The daughter escaped: afterwards she married and had a son who was as lame as herself; and lame in the same manner too; though it does not seem that he was ever shod by the devil and witch-ridden. "And this son," says Sir Walter Scott, in 1830, "was living so lately as to receive the charity of the present Marchioness of Stafford, Countess of Suther-land in her own right."

This, then, is the last execution for witchcraft in Scotland; and in June, 1736, the Acts Anentis Witchcraft were formally repealed. Henceforth, to the dread of the timid, and the anger of the pious, the English Parliament distinctly opposed the express letter of the Law of God, "Thou shalt not suffer a witch to live;" and declared the text upon which so much critical absurdity had been talked, and in support of which so much innocent blood had been shed, vain, super-stitious, impossible, and contrary to that human reason which is the highest law of God hitherto revealed unto men. But if Parliament could stay executions it could not remove beliefs, nor give rationality in place of folly. Not more than sixty years ago an old woman named Elizabeth M'Whirter was "scratched" by one Eaglesham, in the parish of Colmonel, Ayrshire, because his son had fallen sick, and the neighbours said he was betwitched. Poor old Bessie M'Whirter was forced over the hills to the young man's house, a distance of three miles, and there made to kneel by his bedside and repeat the Lord's Prayer. When she had finished, the youth's father took a rusty nail and scratched the poor old creature's brow in the form of a cross; scratched it so effectually that it was many weeks in healing, and the scar remained to the last day of her life. If Elizabeth M'Whirter had lived a generation earlier, she might have run a race with death and a tar barrel, and been defeated at the end, like the poor old wretch at Dornoch.

But still the old faith lingers in those beautiful vales, and hides in the fastnesses of the mountain glens; still brownies haunt the ruined places, and witches send forth blight and bale at their will; still the elfin people ride on the whirlwind and dance in the moonlight; and the hill and the flood and the brae and the streamlet have their attendant spirits which vie with the churchyard ghost in impotent malevolence to men. And the gift of second sight, though dying out because of these degenerate times of utilitarianism and power-loom weaving, is yet to be found where the old blood runs thickest, and the old ideas are least disturbed; and still the whole nation clings with spasmodic force to its gloomy creed of the Predestined and the Elect, and holds by the early faith from whose narrow bounds others have emerged into a brighter and wider path. No more witch-fires are now lighted on the Castle Hill; no more grave and reverend divines give themselves up, like Mr John Aird, to discovering the devil's mark stamped visibly on human flesh; yet the heart of the people has not abandoned its ancient God, and though the altars may be dressed with the flowers of another season, and the name upon the plinth be carved in other characters, yet is the indwelling idol the same. The God which Calvinistic Scotland yet worships is the same God as that to which the witches and wizards of old were sacrificed; he is the God of Superstition, the God of Condemnation, in whose temple Nature has no place, and Humanity no rights.

IRISH WITCH TALES

Lady Wilde

Lady Jane Francisca Speranza Wilde (1826-1896). In Lady Wilde, Ireland has a chronicler of its occult stories as distinguished as Mrs Linton. She, too, was the daughter of a churchman and took to writing to fill in her time in the same way as so many other genteel Victorian ladies. In 1851 she married Sir W. R. Wilde the renowned Irish surgeon and president of the Irish Academy, giving birth to her famous son, Oscar, in 1854. For many years deeply interested in the supernatural in Irish history, Lady Wilde devoted considerable time and effort to producing *Ancient Legends, Mystic Charms and Superstitions of Ireland,* which was published in 1888 and can rightly be regarded as one of the most important books in its field. She also found time to write a great deal of fine poetry under the name of 'Speranza' and conduct the most famous Irish literary salon at her home in Dublin. Though now overshadowed in literature by her son, Lady Wilde has a fluid, entertaining style which is seen to full advantage in these reports on Irish witchcraft and the 'evil eye'.

∞∞∞∞∞∞∞∞∞∞∞∞∞∞∞∞∞∞∞∞∞∞∞∞∞∞

THE LADY WITCH

About a hundred years ago there lived a woman in Joyce's Country, of whom all the neighbours were afraid, for she had always plenty of money, though no one knew how she came by it; and the best of eating and drinking went on at her house, chiefly 'at night—meat and fowls and Spanish wines in plenty for all comers. And when people asked how it all came, she laughed and said, "I have paid for it," but would tell them no more.

So the word went through the country that she had sold herself to the Evil One, and could have everything she wanted by merely wishing and willing, and because of her riches they called her "The Lady Witch."

She never went out but at night, and then always with a bridle and whip in her hand; and the sound of a horse galloping was heard often far on in the night along the roads near her house.

Then a strange story was whispered about, that if a young man drank of her Spanish wines at supper and afterwards fell asleep, she would throw the bridle over him and change him to a horse, and ride him all over the country, and whatever she touched with her whip became hers. Fowls, or butter, or wine, or the new-made cakes—she had but to wish and will and they were carried by spirit hands to her house, and laid in her larder. Then when the ride was done, and she had gathered enough through the country of all she wanted, she took the bridle off the young man, and he came back to his own shape and fell asleep; and when he awoke he had no knowledge of all that had happened, and the Lady Witch bade him come again and drink of her Spanish wines as often as it pleased him.

Now there was a fine brave young fellow in the neighbourhood, and he determined to make out the truth of the story. So he often went back and forwards, and made friends with the Lady Witch, and sat down to talk to her, but always on the watch. And she took a great fancy to him and told him he must come to supper some night, and she would give him the best of everything, and he must taste her Spanish wine.

So she named the night, and he went gladly, for he was filled with curiosity. And when he arrived there was a beautiful supper laid, and plenty of wine to drink; and he ate and drank, but was cautious about the wine, and spilled it on the ground from his glass when her head was turned away. Then he pretended to be very sleepy, and she said—

"My son, you are weary. Lie down there on the bench and sleep, for the night is far spent, and you are far from your home."

So he lay down as if he were quite dead with sleep, and closed his eyes, but watched her all the time.

(*above*) Witches riding to the Sabbat. A superb engraving dated 1844. (*right*) The popular Victorian idea of a witch. An illustration from a collection of witchcraft stories published in 1856

(*above*) The interest in witchcraft during the Victorian era can be judged by the fact that one enterprising firm put out a whole series of specially-posed cards depicting various aspects of the subject. Here is one card showing a 'ducking' scene. (*left*) A harrowing illustration of a suspect under torture. See "The Amber Witch" by Lady Duff-Gordon.

And she came over in a little while and looked at him steadily, but he never stirred, only breathed the more heavily.

Then she went softly and took the bridle from the wall, and stole over to fling it over his head; but he started up, and, seizing the bridle threw it over the woman, who was immediately changed into a spanking grey mare. And he led her out and jumped on her back and rode away as fast as the wind till he came to the forge.

"Ho, smith," he cried, "rise up and shoe my mare, for she is weary after the journey."

And the smith got up and did his work as he was bid, well and strong. Then the young man mounted again, and rode back like the wind to the house of the Witch; and there he took off the bridle, and she immediately regained her own form, and sank down in a deep sleep.

But as the shoes had been put on at the forge without saying the proper form of words, they remained on her hands and feet, and no power on earth could remove them.

So she never rose from her bed again, and died not long after of grief and shame. And not one in the whole country would follow the coffin of the Lady Witch to the grave, and the bridle was burned with fire, and of all her riches nothing was left but a handful of ashes, and this was flung to the four points of earth and the four winds of heaven; so the enchantment was broken and the power of the Evil One ended.

◇

THE DEMON CAT

There was a woman in Connemara, the wife of a fisherman; as he had always good luck, she had plenty of fish at all times stored away in the house ready for market. But, to her great annoyance, she found that a great cat used to come in at night and devour all the best and finest fish. So she kept a big stick by her, and determined to watch.

One day, as she and a woman were spinning together, the house suddenly became quite dark; and the door was burst open as if by the blast of the tempest, when in walked a huge black cat, who went straight up to the fire, then turned round and growled at them.

F

"Why, surely this is the devil," said a young girl, who was by, sorting fish.

"I'll teach you how to call me names," said the cat; and, jumping at her, he scratched her arm till the blood came. "There, now," he said, "you will be more civil another time when a gentleman comes to see you." And with that he walked over to the door and shut it close, to prevent any of them going out, for the poor young girl, while crying loudly from fright and pain, had made a desperate rush to get away.

Just then a man was going by, and hearing the cries, he pushed open the door and tried to get in; but the cat stood on the threshold, and would let no one pass. On this the man attacked him with his stick, and gave him a sound blow; the cat, however, was more than a match in the fight, for it flew at him and tore his face and hands so badly that the man at last took to his heels and ran away as fast as he could.

"Now, it's time for my dinner," said the cat, going up to examine the fish that was laid out on the tables. "I hope the fish is good today. Now, don't disturb me, nor make a fuss; I can help myself." With that he jumped up, and begun to devour all the best fish, while he growled at the woman.

"Away, out of this, you wicked beast," she cried, giving it a blow with the tongs that would have broken its back, only it was a devil; "out of this; no fish shall you have to-day."

But the cat only grinned at her, and went on tearing and spoiling and devouring the fish, evidently not a bit the worse for the blow. On this, both the women attacked it with sticks, and struck hard blows enough to kill it, on which the cat glared at them, and spit fire; then, making a leap, it tore their heads and arms till the blood came, and the frightened women rushed shrieking from the house.

But presently the mistress returned, carrying with her a bottle of holy water; and, looking in, she saw the cat still devouring the fish, and not minding. So she crept over quietly and threw holy water on it without a word. No sooner was this done than a dense black smoke filled the place, through which nothing was seen but the two red eyes of the cat, burning like coals of fire. Then the smoke gradually cleared away, and she saw the body of the creature burning slowly till it became shrivelled and black like a cinder, and finally disappeared.

And from that time the fish remained untouched and safe from harm, for the power of the evil one was broken, and the demon cat was seen no more.

◇

THE EVIL EYE

There is nothing more dreaded by the people, nor considered more deadly in its effects, than the Evil Eye.

There are several modes in which the Evil Eye can act, some much more deadly than others. If certain persons are met the first thing in the morning, you will be unlucky for the whole of that day in all you do. If the evil-eyed comes in to rest, and looks fixedly on anything, on cattle or on a child, there is doom in the glance; a fatality which cannot be evaded except by a powerful counter-charm. But if the evil-eyed mutters a verse over a sleeping child, that child will assuredly die, for the incantation is of the devil, and no charm has power to resist it or turn away the evil. Sometimes the process of bewitching is effected by looking fixedly at the object, through nine fingers; especially is the magic fatal if the victim is seated by the fire in the evening when the moon is full. Therefore, to avoid being suspected of having the Evil Eye, it is necessary at once, when looking at a child, to say "God bless it." And when passing a farmyard where the cows are collected for milking, to say, "The blessing of God be on you and on all your labours." If this form is omitted, the worst results may be apprehended, and the people would be filled with terror and alarm, unless a counter-charm were not instantly employed.

The singular malific influence of a glance has been felt by most persons in life; an influence that seems to paralyze intellect and speech, simply by the mere presence in the room of some one who is mystically antipathetic to our nature. For the soul is like a fine-toned harp that vibrates to the slightest external force or movement, and the presence and glance of some persons can radiate around us a divine joy, while others may kill the soul with a sneer or a frown. We call these subtle influences mysteries, but the early races believed them to be produced by spirits, good or evil, as they acted on the nerves or the intellect.

Some years ago an old woman was living in Kerry, and it was

thought so unlucky to meet her in the morning, that all the girls used to go out after sunset to bring in water for the following day, that so they might avoid her evil glance; for whatever she looked on came to loss and grief.

There was a man, also, equally dreaded on account of the strange, fatal power of his glance; and so many accidents and misfortunes were traced to his presence that finally the neighbours insisted that he should wear a black patch over the Evil Eye, not to be removed unless by request; for learned gentlemen, curious in such things, sometimes came to him to ask for a proof of his power, and he would try it for a wager while drinking with his friends.

One day, near an old-ruin of a castle, he met a boy weeping in great grief for his pet pigeon, which had got up to the very top of the ruin, and could not be coaxed down.

"What will you give me," asked the man, "if I bring it down for you?"

"I have nothing to give," said the boy, "but I will pray to God for you. Only get me back my pigeon, and I shall be happy."

Then the man took off the black patch and looked up steadfastly at the bird; when all of a sudden it fell to the ground and lay motionless as if stunned; but there was no harm done to it, and the boy took it up and went his way, rejoicing.

Some years ago a woman living in Kerry declared that she was "overlooked" by the Evil Eye. She had no pleasure in her life and no comfort, and she wasted away because of the fear that was on her, caused by the following singular circumstance:—

Every time that she happened to leave home alone, and that no one was within call, she was met by a woman totally unknown to her who, fixing her eyes on her in silence, with a terrible expression, cast her to the ground and proceeded to beat and pinch her till she was nearly senseless; after which her tormentor disappeared.

Having experienced this treatment several times, the poor woman finally abstained altogether from leaving the house, unless protected by a servant or companion; and this precaution she observed for several years, during which time she never was molested. So at last she began to believe that the spell was broken, and that her strange enemy had departed for ever.

In consequence she grew less careful about the usual precaution, and one day stepped down alone to a little stream that ran by the house to wash some clothes.

Stooping down over her work, she never thought of any danger, and began to sing as she used to do in the light-hearted days before the spell was on her, when suddenly a dark shadow fell across the water, and looking up, she beheld to her horror the strange woman on the opposite side of the little stream, with her terrible eyes intently fixed on her, as hard and still as if she were of stone.

Springing up with a scream of terror, she flung down her work, and ran towards the house; but soon she heard footsteps behind her, and in an instant she was seized, thrown down to the ground, and her tormentor began to beat her even worse than before, till she lost all consciousness; and in this state she was found by her husband, lying on her face and speechless. She was at once carried to the house, and all the care that affection and rural skill could bestow were lavished on her, but in vain. She, however, regained sufficient consciousness to tell them of the terrible encounter she had gone through, but died before the night had passed away.

It was believed that the power of fascination by the glance, which is not necessarily an evil power like the Evil Eye, was possessed in a remarkable degree by learned and wise people, especially poets, so that they could make themselves loved and followed by any girl they liked, simply by the influence of the glance. About the year 1790, a young man resided in the County of Limerick, who had this power in a singular and unusual degree. He was a clever, witty rhymer in the Irish language; and, probably, had the deep poet eyes that characterize warm and passionate poet-natures—eyes that even without necromancy have been known to exercise a powerful magnetic influence over female minds.

One day, while travelling far from home, he came upon a bright, pleasant-looking farmhouse, and feeling weary, he stopped and requested a drink of milk and leave to rest. The farmer's daughter, a young, handsome girl, not liking to admit a stranger, as all the maids were churning, and she was alone in the house, refused him admittance.

The young poet fixed his eyes earnestly on her face for some time in silence, then slowly turning round left the house, and walked towards a small grove of trees just opposite. There he stood for a few moments resting against a tree, and facing the house as if to take one last vengeful or admiring glance, then went his way without once turning round.

The young girl had been watching him from the windows, and the moment he moved she passed out of the door like one in a dream, and followed him slowly, step by step, down the avenue. The maids grew alarmed, and called to her father, who ran out and shouted loudly for her to stop, but she never turned or seemed to heed. The young man, however, looked round, and seeing the whole family in pursuit, quickened his pace, first glancing fixedly at the girl for a moment. Immediately she sprang towards him, and they were both almost out of sight, when one of the maids espied a piece of paper tied to a branch of the tree where the poet had rested. From curiosity she took it down, and the moment the knot was untied, the farmer's daughter suddenly stopped, became quite still, and when her father came up she allowed him to lead her back to the house without resistance.

When questioned, she said that she felt herself drawn by an invisible force to follow the young stranger wherever he might lead, and that she would have followed him through the world, for her life seemed to be bound up in his; she had no will to resist, and was conscious of nothing else but his presence. Suddenly, however, the spell was broken, and then she heard her father's voice, and knew how strangely she had acted. At the same time the power of the young man over her vanished, and the impulse to follow him was no longer in her heart.

The paper, on being opened, was found to contain five mysterious words written in blood, and in this order—

> Sator.
> Arepo.
> Tenet.
> Opera.
> Rotas.

These letters are so arranged that read in any way, right to left, left to right, up or down, the same words are produced; and when written in blood with a pen made of an eagle's feather, they form a charm which no woman (it is said) can resist; but the incredulous reader can easily test the truth of this assertion for himself.

WITCHCRAFT AND WIZARDRY IN WALES

Miss Mary Lewis

Mary Lewis (1860–1920) set out, like Mrs Linton and Lady Wilde in their countries, to record all the superstitions, strange customs and legends of her native Wales. Her resultant book, *The Queer Side of Things*, has been described as "a veritable treasure trove of material for hunters of strange lore", and it is only surprising that it has been out of print for the past fifty years. Mrs Lewis was born and brought up in rural Wales and had considerable personal knowledge of 'white' witchcraft in particular, as you will read in this extract. Her comment on strange witch cures will certainly be of particular interest to students of the occult as variations of a good many of these are known to have survived in the more remote areas of the British Isles right up to the present day.

Extraordinary though it seems in this practical age, the professional "wise man" and "witch" are, I believe, scarcely yet extinct in the remote country districts of Wales, though, of course, their number, already few, is dwindling yearly. Also it is very difficult to hear of them nowadays, as they rarely display their talents. But there is certainly no doubt that instances could easily be found up to quite a few years ago—perhaps even now—of ailing people consulting the local wise man as a last resort when the ordinary doctor's treatment has failed.

Whatever the quality or attribute peculiar to wise men and witches, it was sometimes said to be confined to certain families. In a hamlet not many miles from my own home there was a "witch" family; that is, there was always some member or another who could claim "witch" powers.

The connection between witches and hares was very widely spread. Addison mentions the belief in one of his Essays, writing of an old crone called Moll White. "If a hare makes an unexpected escape from hounds, the huntsman curses Moll White . . . I have known the master of a pack upon such an occasion send one of his servants to see if Moll White had been out that morning."

Not only was it thought that witches transformed themselves into hares, but Elias Owen, in his "Welsh Folk-lore," tells us that, in his day, aged people in Wales believed that witches, by incantation, could change other people into animals. He quotes instances of a man being turned by witchcraft into a hare, in the neighbourhood of Ystrad Meurig (Cardiganshire). Another case he relates is that of a woman in North Wales, who knew before any one told her that a certain person died at such a time. The clergyman of the parish asked her how she came to know of the death if no one had informed her and she had not been to the house. Her answer was: "I know because I saw a hare come from towards his house and cross over the road before me." Evidently the woman connected the appearance of the hare with the man's death.

Here there seems to have been a trace of the belief, which formerly obtained in some parts of Wales, of the transmigration of souls, the idea being that the departing soul went into the body of some animal.

But it is probable that all through Wales the hare was vaguely regarded as the herald of death. It is said that this animal was much used by the Druids for the purpose of augury, prophecies being made according to its various movements when set running. So it is quite possible that the uncomfortable atmosphere which seems to surround this harmless beast in all Celtic countries is due to its traditional connection with far-away Druidical mysteries.

In olden days Welsh witches used to put spells on the animals of neighbours who annoyed them. If a cow was the victim it would sicken of no apparent disease, cease to give milk and, if the spell were not removed, would die. The effect of "witching" a pig was to cause an odd kind of madness, something like a fit; this, again, ended fatally unless a counter-charm was forthcoming. Quite recently I saw one of these charms quoted in a local paper by a collector of folklore. "An old witch, living not far from Llangadock (in Carmarthenshire) . . . on one occasion when she had witched a pig, was compelled subsequently to 'unwitch' the animal. She came and put her hand on the pig's back, saying, 'Duwa'th gadwo i'th berchenog' (God keep thee to thine owner)"—which seems a mild way of calming a frenzied pig.

A noted witch used to live about a mile and a half from my own home. She was known as "Mary Perllan Peter," from the name of her house "Perllan Peter," deep down in a thickly-wooded ravine, or dingle as we call it in Cardiganshire. This way of designating individuals is common in Wales, where surnames amongst the peasantry are apt to be limited to a few favourites, such as Jones, Davies, Evans, etc. So that a person's Christian name, followed by that of his house, is far more distinctive than using a surname probably common to a third of the people in a parish. Therefore the witch was "Mary of Peter's Orchard" ("perllan" meaning "orchard," though who Peter was, I never found out) and she was undoubtedly a powerful one, as the following stories will show.

One day she asked a neighbour to bring her some corn which she required, and the man only consented unwillingly, as the path down to the cottage was very steep and the corn heavy to carry. On the way he spilt some, and Mary was very angry and muttered threats to her friends when he left. And when he got back to his own home and went to the stable, what was his amazement to see his little mare "sitting like a pig" on her haunches and staring wildly before her. He went to her and pulling at the halter, tried to get on her feet, but in vain; she did not seem able to move. Then the man, very frightened, bethought him of the witch's threats, for he felt sure the mare was spellbound. So he sent off for Mary to come and remove the spell, and when she arrived, she went straight up to the animal; and "*Moron fach*,* what ails thee now?" was all she said, and the mare jumped to her feet as well and lively as ever.

Another time Mary Perllan Peter went to the mill at a neighbouring village to get some corn ground. The miller was very slow over the business, so slow that Mary grew annoyed and cursed the mill.

* Little carrot—term of endearment.

Whereupon it instantly began to turn round the wrong way, and went on like that till the witch was appeased and removed the spell.

These instances were related by a cousin of Mary's, called John Pŵllglas, who apparently quite believed in the uncanny powers possessed by his relative.

In Cardiganshire, as in many other rural districts, it was always firmly believed that when the butter would not "come" on churning-day, the cream or churn had been bewitched. There were many remedies against this trouble—one being a branch of the rowan tree hung over the dairy door; another was a knife put into the churn, for all witches, like fairies, hate iron.

I know a house where, some few years ago, the dairymaid left in a fit of temper. Never had there been any trouble over the churning in that particularly well-regulated dairy, but, strange to say, from the week when "Jane" left the place the butter refused to "come."

Churning, which in spring began early in the morning, went on for hours, everyone in the house taking a turn at the handle, and at length, towards afternoon, the long-delayed butter appeared. But what butter! It was scarcely fit to eat, and this state of things continued for several weeks, no theory of temperature, unsteady churning, or any other reason that scientific butter-makers appreciate, accounting for the extraordinary behaviour of the cream. Of course, all the local people said that Jane departing had bewitched the churn; how that was I do not know, but there is no doubt that after five or six weeks, and quite without apparent cause, the butter suddenly "came" properly again, the "spell" being presumably ended.

When staying at Aberdovey once, I noticed a strangely shaped depression on the hill behind the schools, and inquiring, I was told that it was called the "Witch's Grave," and that a witch was supposed to have been burnt there and her ashes buried on the spot. The old village green used to be on the little plateau where the "grave" is, so that if any burning did take place it is quite likely to have been there.

This is the only tradition I have so far encountered of witches being illtreated in Wales. My own idea is that, unlike many other districts, witches and wise men were never much molested in the Principality, but were rather feared and looked up to. This witch burning at Aberdovey, if the tradition be true, was perhaps due to a backwash of that terrible wave of persecution and burnings that swept over Great Britain and the Continent in the seventeenth and eighteenth centuries.

The practice of "charming" with yarn was, I found, well known in the Aberdovey district, though not much of it is done now. "Witches' butter" is also believed in round there. This is a kind of fungus which shakes and trembles when touched. It is very unlucky to find it, for it means you are bewitched. The remedy is to take up some of the fungus very carefully, and stick it full of pins. These pins will prick the conscience of him or her who has bewitched you, and they will remove the spell.

I heard a quaint little story of an old sea-captain at Aberdovey, whose garden was infested with worms, which he declared was the result of a spell laid on it by a witch woman he had offended.

"Wise men" seem to have flourished from time immemorial in Wales, every village having its "*dyn hysbys*" in old days. It is said that their numbers were kept up by the superstitious practice amongst the very ignorant country-folk of "sacrificing children to the Devil," in order to make "wise men" of them. The Rev. Rees Prichard, of Llaydovery, in a hymn against "conjurors," alludes to this dreadful custom:—

> Tynnu'r plentyn trwy ben crwcca.
> Neu trwy'r fflam ar nos f'lamgaua,
> A'u rhoi ymhinny felyn uchel,
> Yw offrumm plant i Gythraul.

Meaning that "to drag children through a hoop or flame of fire, on All Hallows Eve, and taking them to the mill bin to be shaken, is the way of sacrificing them to the Evil One."

I think the first item of this description—viz., dragging through a hoop—may refer to the old Welsh custom of passing delicate children through a split ash to cure them of rickets and other troubles. I know someone to whom this was done when he was a child, but most certainly in his case the intention was distinctly curative, and had nothing to do with dedication to the Evil One. However, in Vicar Pritchard's time—about three hundred years or so ago—there existed, no doubt, many remnants of beliefs in the country, which have long since died out; just as those which obtain in our day are gradually disappearing, and unless noted by those interested in such things, will be lost to the generations to come.

Of course, the Prince of Welsh wizards was Merlin, of whom many wonderful tales and traditions still linger in the neighbourhood of Carmarthen, in which town the great astrologer and soothsayer is supposed to have been born. A prediction of his in Welsh is preserved, foretelling the attempted landing of the French at Fishguard, in 1797, and its frustration by Lord Cawdor; the lines are very curious, but I will spare readers a further infliction of the vernacular.

It is said that Merlin also prophesied the inundation of Carmarthen, a calamity which fortunately has not yet come to pass.

Leaving the shadowy personality of the great wizard, with the host of lesser lights who followed him, and coming to historical times, we have many records of celebrated "wise men," of whom it may be said that on the whole their influence amongst the people was for good, and that their talents seem to have turned in the direction of benevolence rather than spite. One wizard of North Wales, who died about a century ago, was called "Mochyn y Nant," and was held in great terror by all evil-doers of his district on account of the uncanny knowledge he possessed of their crimes, however secret. De Quincy once visited "Mochyn y Nant," and gives an entertaining description of the experience in his "Confessions."

The following story which I find amongst my notes, well illustrates the kind of affair about which these seers were constantly consulted.

A gentleman in Denbighshire, lost a large silver cup of much value, which had been an heirloom for several generations. After making diligent inquiries respecting the cup without success, he determined to place the affair in the hands of Robin Ddu, the wizard. Robin attended at the hall, and after placing his red cap on his head, he called the inmates of the hall before him, and declared he would find the thief before midnight. All the servants denied the theft. "Then," said Robin, "if you are guiltless, you will have no objection to a magic proof." He then ordered a cockerel to be placed under a pot in the pantry, and told all the servants to go and rub the pot with both their hands. If any of them were guilty, the cockerel would crow whilst the thief was rubbing the vessel. After all had gone through the ceremony, the wizard ordered them to show their hands, when he perceived that the hands of the butler were clean. His conscience had stricken him so that he could not touch the pot. Robin accused him of the theft, which he admitted, and the cup was restored to its owner.

The next stories, told me on excellent authority, relate to the parish of Llanfihangel-Geneurglyn, in Cardiganshire, and the "John Price" referred to was living a very few years ago, and is still alive, for anything I know to the contrary.

There was a man belonging to the village of Llanfihangel who had a sick cow. He could not discover what was the matter with her, and at last, in despair, he went to consult John Price, the wise man, who lived at Llanbadarn-fawr, a few miles away. John immediately declared that the cow was bewitched. "Because," said he, "you will find when you look that every tooth in her head is loose."

"Why, who has done that?" asked the farmer.

"That I cannot tell you," was the reply, "but this I will tell you, that the person who bewitched her has visited your house to-day." He would say no more, and the inquirer hurried off home.

He lost no time in examining the cow's mouth, and, sure enough, every tooth was loose. Then he asked his wife, "Who has been here to-day?"

"No one," she answered, "except indeed So-and-so," naming a poor girl who came sometimes to get work. Then the farmer knew who had ill-wished his cow, which, by the way, recovered.

In the same parish of Llanfihangel there was a child very ill—so ill, in fact, that the doctors gave him up. The father went secretly and consulted John Price, who said that the child was betwiched but would recover; and he did.

I know the clergyman who was the vicar of this parish at the time these two instances occurred, and it was he who made notes of the cases. He is now vicar of a parish in North Pembrokeshire.

Another wise man lived at a farm near Borth (on the coast not far from Aberystwyth) not so long ago, and was often consulted. I heard of the case of a girl who was ailing, and thought by her relations to have had a spell put on her. So they took her to the wizard, who told them that on the way home the first person they met on the road would be the "witch" who had laid the spell on the invalid. They set off home, and before they had gone far, who should they meet but a poor, harmless old man, whom they knew could not have worked the mischief. So they hurried back to the wise man with this information, who coolly replied, "It was not he, but his brother who is dead. And the girl will not be well till the brother's body is decayed—*i.e.*, for about twenty years." History does not relate if the wizard was believed on this occasion, but the person who told me about him said he had many clients, and that one of his accomplishments was the writing of "charms" for people to wear.

At the time I was told of this wizard, my informant asked me if I had ever heard of "Vicar Pritchard of Pŵllheli" (now dead), who in his time was a noted layer of ghosts, and whose fame still survives in Merionethshire, for he was in great demand throughout the country whenever an uneasy spook gave trouble. Armed with candle and book, in the orthodox way, he said to one ghost: "Now, will you promise me to cease troubling this house as long as this candle lasts?" The spirit gladly promised, thinking that was but an hour or two to wait. But the vicar promptly extinguished the flame, put the candle into a lead box, sealed and buried the box beneath a tree, where it lies to this day, and the ghost can do no more harm.

This is a digression; but most readers will excuse the irrelevancy because of its mention of a more or less modern cleric as a professional ghost layer.

The account that follows, of a Pembrokeshire witch, was sent me by an old friend a few years ago, and is best given in his own words, only substituting initials for the personal names.

"I was at Carmarthen last week, and returned in company with Archdeacon H—— and Mr H—— W——. At Whitland a local doctor came into the compartment; I did not know him, but they did, and this is the substance of what he told us. A reputed witch lived near Whitland Abbey. The house she lived in was sold, and bought by a brother-in-law of the teller of the story. A gamekeeper of Mr Z——, the owner of the Abbey, went into the cottage of the witch. She was very angry and gave out that she would be even with all concerned. The following things happened. The keeper's wife (the narrator attended the case) became a mother, and the infant was born with an abnormal number of limbs and died. The doctor's brother-in-law was suddenly seized with a mysterious illness one morning whilst dressing, and was laid up for a long time. The doctor lost a cow, two horses and a sow.

"These happenings made a stir, and even Mr Z—— was troubled.

He was a bit superstitious and was very desirous that the doctor should 'draw the witch's blood' by holding the blade of a penknife between finger and thumb, so that just enough of it should project to draw blood without inflicting a serious wound. The doctor said that would not do, as the woman would run him in for assault!

"When asked to do so, the doctor attended the witch, but for the life of him dared not send in a bill."

If the above facts were correctly reported, they certainly form an extraordinary instance of "ill-wishing"—a power known for many ages to be possessed by a few people of very strong will and a malevolent disposition, and the fear of which is a trait as old as humanity, still lurking, as we have seen, amongst the country-folk in remote districts of this and many other countries.

From the subject of witches one passes naturally to the extraordinary remedies often prescribed by them and the old-fashioned herb doctors up to the beginning of the last century, or perhaps later. There are still people to be found who visit and consult herbalists, sometimes finding them hidden away in dark and dusty little shops in the quiet back streets of towns, or living, often solitary, in isolated cottages near wood or moor in remote country districts. And there is no doubt that some of the mixtures prescribed by these modern "herb doctors" possess virtue and are probably nowadays derived from more or less wholesome and certainly harmless plants and normal food materials. It is hardly likely, for instance, that a twentieth century herbalist would sell dried earth worms to a patient as a remedy for fits, or advise oil of earth worms as beneficial for the nerves, and to "ease pain of the joints." Even if this kind of dose were prescribed, nobody now would swallow anything so nauseous.

But little more than a hundred years ago, not only did "wise men" and herbalists use such unpleasant things in their prescriptions, but there is every reason to believe that ingredients which seem to us quite horrible were taken docilely and with perfect faith in their efficacy by people of intelligence, and not only by the ignorant and less fastidious classes.

A quaint old book was lent to me once; it was called "A General Dispensatory," by R. Brookes, M.D., and the date of publication was 1753. There was a long list, arranged alphabetically, of all the *materia medica* used in the eighteenth century, and very odd some of those "materials" were. Much store was set on preparations made from various stones; of these, the chief were Eagle-stone, Jew's stone, Bezoar and Blood stone. Bezoar was taken from a certain species of "Mountain-goat, called by some, Capricarva. . . . It is a most timourous animal, and delights in the mountains, seldom descending into the plains. . . . The stones are cried up as an antidote against all manner of poisons, plagues, contagious diseases, malignant fevers, the small-pox and measles. . . ."

This stone was ground and given in powder. Others were applied outwardly by rubbing the part affected. I know of the existence of a stone in Cardiganshire, about the size of a large marble, which was formerly used for the cure of goitre; it was lent to sufferers from that complaint and rubbed on the neck. Its present owner, an old lady, knows of undoubted cures wrought by it in former years. There seems to be an idea that this stone has some connection with a snake, though apparently the exact relation has been forgotten. But it is very probable that in old times it was called a snake stone, and believed to have been taken out of the head of a snake; for it was thought in Wales that such stones were sometimes found in the heads of toads and adders, and were endowed with wonderful powers of healing and magic.

Blood stone, of course, has been used from times unknown to stop bleeding, and among other cures for the same thing was the bone or "stone" taken from the head of the manatee or sea-cow. Hare's fur as an application to the wound was also advised. A hare's foot, carried in the pocket prevented heartburn. Another "pocket" remedy was a piece of potato for rheumatism, which I have known practised very lately. Crabs' eyes—probably dried and powdered—seem to have been a popular medicine; a pike's jaw was supposed to have much the same virtue as crabs' eyes, but was more "efficacious in the pleurisy and peripneumony." Amber, burnt and reduced to powder was thrown on a chafing-dish, and the smoke inhaled to stop bleeding of the nose. In Wales this beautiful sea-product was worn as a powerful charm against witches, the Evil Eye,* and blindness.

---

* In South Pembrokeshire hot-cross buns left over from Good Friday were carefully preserved throughout the year. They were considered efficacious as a remedy for disease if eaten—and also highly useful to scare away witches and avert the Evil Eye.

G

Snail broth was a great country remedy for consumption in old days. Culpepper, in his "Herbal," gives a recipe for it. "Snails with shells on their backs, being first washed from the dirt, then the shells broken, and then boiled in spring water, but not scummed at all, for the scum will sink of itself, and the water drank for ordinary drink, is a most admirable remedy for consumption." "Snail water" is also prescribed for the same complaint; this was a really terrible mixture, as besides "Of Garden Snails two pounds," there was included the juice of ground ivy, colt's foot, scabious lungwort, purslain, ambrosia, Paul's betony, hog's blood and white wine, dried tobacco leaves, liquorice elecampane, orris, cotton seeds, annis seeds, saffron, the flowers of red roses and of violets and borage; all to be steeped three days and then distilled. One wonders if the unfortunate patient who imbibed this decoction had any idea of what he was swallowing. A fox's lung dried and made into a "lohoch" (a substance to be licked up, rather thicker than a syrup) and sucked off the end of a liquorice stick was also "a present remedy in pthisicks."

Flummery, or wheat boiled to a jelly, was another country cure for consumption, especially in Wales, where the old people also extolled the virtues of nettle tea as "very good for the chest," and for other ills besides.

A decoction of nettle seeds was supposed to cure hydrophobia, but many other remedies were advised for this dread disease. One which I found in a very old manuscript collection of recipes, headed "For the Bite of a Mad Dog," was simple in the extreme. "Pare an onion, mix it with honey and salt and lay it on the wound." A piece of onion rubbed on a bee or wasp sting is certainly an excellent impromptu relief, but one would scarcely imagine it could do much to counteract the deadly poison of hydrophobia. The root of liverwort—*lichen caninus*—was thought to be an infallible cure or preventive in the case of a mad dog's bite. One was bidden to mix the ground liverwort with black pepper, and the patient "is to lose nine or ten ounces of blood, and then a dram and a half of the powder is to be taken fasting every morning, for four mornings successively, in half a pint of warm cow's milk; after this he must go into a cold bath, cold spring, or river for thirty days together early in the morning, and before breakfast, and to be dipped all over; but he is not to remain in it with his head above water, not longer than half a minute, if the water be very cold."

Another curious specific for hydrophobia is mentioned by Iolo Morganŵg in his Diary, dated 1802. When on a walk to Llanfernach, in North Pembrokeshire, he met a man "who carries a stone about the country, which he calles Llysfaen. Scrapes it into powder with a knife, and sells it at about five shillings an ounce as an infallible remedy for the canine madness. He says this stone is only to be found on mountains after a thunder-storm, and that every eye cannot see it. I assured him it was only a piece of Glamorganshire alabaster; but I was surprised to hear many positively assert that they had actually seen the hydrophobia cured in dogs and man from this powder, given in milk and used as the only liquid taken for nine days and the only food also."

A far more drastic method of treating hydrophobia patients than the above is quoted by Mrs Trevelyan,* as being formerly very popular all along the coast of Wales. The person bitten was taken out to sea in a boat. "Before starting, he was securely bound by the hands and feet, and when out at a distance from the shore, two men plunged him in the water three times. Each time the man or woman as the case might be, was asked if he or she had had enough. But just as he opened his mouth to reply he was dipped again. This dipping was repeated nine times, with a pause between each three dips, to enable the patient to have an opportunity for breathing. The shock or temporary fright caused by repeated dips into the sea, and the quantity of water swallowed, worked the cure."

The use of the number nine in so many of these old cures, is remarkable, and shows that originally there was a mystic meaning behind these rude treatments in which the "curative" power lay, and which possibly did really continue to heal those who used them with faith, long after the knowledge of their mystical significance was lost.

Very extraordinary were some of the remedies administered for "the falling sickness," as epilepsy used to be called. I have already mentioned the use of earth worms dried and powdered; but decoctions of the wood and leaves of the mistletoe were also taken, and an elk hoof, either worn in a ring, or scraped and taken internally, was much recommended. "But," says an authority, "it must be the hoof of the right foot behind." Most firmly believed in as a potent cure was a powder made from the human skull, which dreadful ingredient

* "Folk-lore of Wales."

figures in a recipe I have for "convulsion fits." "Take native cinnabar, the roots of male Piony and Human Skull prepared, of each an ounce, castor and salt of amber of each a dram, mix them and divide into forty-eight equal parts. This is Dr Pughe's Receipt."

Especially valuable were the skulls of those who had died a violent death, and the heads of criminals were eagerly bought for that reason. Hedgehog's liver, dried, powdered and drunk in wine was another specific for epilepsy.

Vipers were much esteemed as medicine in various parts of the country, and prepared in different ways were swallowed with the greatest faith. The old "Dispensatory" before quoted, said: 'Viper's flesh is looked upon as a great restorative, to be very balsamic, an enemy to all malignity and excellent to purify the blood, hence it is given to prolong life and to resist poisons."

I have read an old recipe for "viper broth," which included chicken as well as snake, so let us hope the prevailing flavour was of fowl and not of serpent.

There is some plausibility about the idea that various herbs possessed efficacy in clearing the sight; the common "eyebright" was much used for this purpose. But we can hardly believe that the eating of young swallows, which was also advised, can have benefited the eyes much, unless a great deal of faith was taken with the fledglings.

In some districts a dried toad worn in the armpit was thought to ward off fever. The poor creatures were put alive into an earthen pot, and gradually dried in a moderate oven till they were fit to reduce to powder. Bees were treated in the same way; and an old prescription says, "Burnt to ashes and a lye made with the ashes, trimly decks a bald head being washed with it."

A strange remedy for jaundice was a live spider rolled in butter to form a pill and then swallowed. Quite lately I saw a case reported in a paper of a child found wearing a spider enclosed in a nut round its neck to cure whooping-cough; but that, of course, was worn as a "charm"; a form of remedy which seems likely to be popular as long as the world goes round.

Diet drinks were formerly much used in amateur doctoring in rural districts, and recipes for their manufacture are sure to be found in any of those quaint "house books" treasured in old country houses. In one of these which I have handled, there is a recipe for a "Dyet drink," composed of no fewer than nineteen ingredients, mostly herbs, such as dwarf elder, salendin, broom robin, brook lime, wormwood, eyebright, etc., etc., all making "two payls and a half of Drink." Pity the poor victim who had to begin the day by swallowing a mugful of such nauseous mixtures.

In Cardiganshire to-day, a decoction of the wild ragwort is believed to be excellent for rheumatism; also another of garlic for "the indigestion." I have known blackberry leaves applied to heal sores in the same county; this is a very old remedy, and its survival is interesting. So is the fact that in the parish of Talybont, in North Cardiganshire, there is a family owning a recipe for the cure of erysipelas, which has quite a local fame, but of which no one knows the secret but themselves.

This element of secrecy is nearly always a feature of these rural "cures"; doubtless a vestige of the ancient belief that medical treatment to be successful must be wrapped in mystery.

PART TWO

Fiction

"As might be expected the witch has appealed to the picturesque imagination of the romancist in many times and countries."

Lady Duff-Gordon

THE MAGIC RING

Mrs H. L.

Mrs H. L. A cursory glance at magazines and journals from the beginning of the Victorian era soon reveals that very few stories were signed by their authors; anonymity, in fact, cloaked much of the writing population and this has not aided the researcher on the track of literary gentle-women. However, the occasional story has emerged which we have established beyond doubt was written by a woman and "The Magic Ring" (1839) is in this category. 'Mrs H. L.' was apparently the wife of a provincial doctor—possibly from Essex—who was deeply interested in witch lore and legends. Her tale, which sees the light of print here for the first time in well over 100 years, is almost poetic in its simplicity yet vividly evocative of the dark rites of witchcraft.

<hr>

At the midnight hour they met, the moon was in the wane, they dared not gaze upon her whilst they framed the magic spell. From the mossy bank the glow-worm's glimmering light played on the stream below. They stood beneath the alders dank, and spake the words of fear. He placed the mystic circlet on her hand, and watched the appointed time. From a maniac's grave, they had stolen the earth, they scattered the dust on the stream, they gazed on the northern star. That star withdrew her sparkling rays, and veiled her in a cloud in darkness, and with dread they uttered the awful spell.—The spirits of evil rejoiced, the wind moaned sadly around, the glow-worms quenched their fires, and they who had tempted their fate, who had scattered the maniac's dust, read their doom in the sighs of the wind, and wished the dread accents untold.

The forester departed, he roamed in other climes, the past appeared a dream, he thought not of his plighted vows, nor remembered the force of the spell. She dwelt in the forest glades, beside that limpid stream, far from the haunts of men in deepest solitude. Now days and months had fled, but the forester returned not; the fifth day of the week, when clouds enveloped the norther star, the wind was abroad in the oaks, and the mist and rain were eddying in the valley, the maiden bent her steps to that half-dreaded spot, beside the alders dank. She gazed upon the bright blue gem, the token of the spell; its colour was unchanged, for the wearer still was true. She longed to prove her lover's faith, and watched the heavens with dread; she uttered the words that wake the dead, and looked on the magic ring; the blue stone turned to deadly white, and she knew her lover false. The spirits that heard the charm rejoiced in the echoes around, the midnight fogs fell damp and thick, but the chill was in her soul; consumption hovered in the mist and crept into her breast.

Her eye was bright, her cheek was fair, but the spell had numbered her days.—She dropt like the flower of the field, and passed from the face of the earth.—She sleeps beside the maniac's grave, beneath the northern star.—The forester returned.—The abode of her he once loved was desolate—the thoughts of former days resumed their power, the secret spell still worked upon his mind; it haunted him in sleep, it haunted him by day, it was around, unseen, but every where—it stamped his features with a dire deceit, the eye that met avoided him, the hearts of all turned from him, he sought affection but he found it not, he lived unloved, unwept he died; no holy prayers e'er blessed his grave, or bid his troubled spirit rest—his ashes moulder in the wind, the pilgrim shuns the spot, for there the spirits of evil perform their unearthly rites, and frame the spells of death.

THE AMBER WITCH

Lady Duff-Gordon

Lady Lucie Duff-Gordon (1821-1869). This fascinating story brings together probably the greatest female translator of the Victorian era and one of the best nineteenth Century European witchcraft novels. Lady Duff-Gordon was the daughter of the distinguished English philosopher, John Austin, and Sarah Taylor, a noted writer and translator. She was involved in the literary circles of London from a very early age and counted John Stuart Mill among her childhood companions. After her marriage to Sir Alexander Duff-Gordon in 1840, she quickly became a brilliant literary hostess and began her life-long study of German writing; this leading to her meeting and friendship with Heine. One of her great literary achievements is undoubtedly her translation of "The Amber Witch"—"the most interesting trial for witchcraft ever known" according to its title page—written by the German Lutheran clergyman, Wilhelm Meinhold. At the time of its initial publication in 1843, "The Amber Witch" was widely believed to be an actual record of a witchcraft trial at the time of the Thirty Years War (particularly as it contained what purported to be actual photographs of the witch). However, while it is loosely based on a real case it is primarily fiction—and very good, evocative fiction at that. When we take up the tale here, the storyteller, a German Pastor named Abraham Schweidler, is describing the trial of his daughter, Rea, who he believes is being falsely accused of practising witchcraft by an old crone named Lizzie Kolken.

When we were summoned before the court again, the whole place was full of people, and some shuddered when they saw us, but others wept; my child Rea again denied she was a witch. But when our old servant Ilse was called, who sat on a bench behind, so that we had not seen her, the strength wherewith the Lord had gifted her was again at an end, and she repeated the words of our Saviour, "He that eateth bread with Me hath lift up his heel against Me:" and she held fast by my chair. Old Ilse, too, could not walk straight for very grief, nor could she speak for tears, but she twisted and wound herself about before the court, like a woman in travail. But when *Dom. Consul* threatened that the constable should presently help her to her words, she testified that my child had very often got up in the night, and called aloud upon the foul fiend.

Q. Whether she had ever heard Satan answer her?—*R*. She never had heard him at all.

Q. Whether she had perceived that *Rea* had a familiar spirit, and in what shape? She should think upon her oath, and speak the truth. —*R*. She had never seen one.

Q. Whether she had ever heard her fly up the chimney?—*R*. Nay, she had always gone softly out at the door.

Q. Whether she never at mornings had missed her broom or pitch-fork?—*R*. Once the broom was gone, but she had found it again behind the stove, and may be left it there herself by mistake.

Q. Whether she had never heard *Rea* cast a spell, or wish harm to this or that person?—*R*. No, never; she had always wished her neighbours nothing but good, and even in the time of bitter famine had taken the bread out of her own mouth to give it to others.

Q. Whether she did not know the salve which had been found in *Rea*'s coffer?—*R*. Oh, yes! her young mistress had brought it back from Wolgast for her skin, and had once given her some when she had chapped hands, and it had done her a vast deal of good.

Q. Whether she had anything further to say?—*R*. No. nothing but good.

Hereupon my man Claus Neels was called up. He also came forward in tears, but answered every question with a "nay," and at last testified that he had never seen nor heard anything bad of my child, and knew naught of her doings by night, seeing that he slept in the stable with the horses; and that he firmly believed that evil folks—

and here he looked at old Lizzie—had brought this misfortune upon her, and that she was quite innocent.

When it came to the turn of this old limb of Satan, who was to be the chief witness, my child again declared that she would not accept old Lizzie's testimony against her, and called upon the court for justice, for that she had hated her from her youth up, and had been longer by habit and repute a witch than she herself.

But the old hag cried out, "God forgive thee they sins; the whole village knows that I am a devout woman, and one serving the Lord in all things;" whereupon she called up old Zuter Witthahn and my churchwarden Claus Bulk, who bore witness hereto. But old Paasch stood and shook his head; nevertheless when my child said, "Paasch, wherefore dost thou shake thy head?" he started, and answered, "Oh, nothing!"

Howbeit, *Dom. Consul* likewise perceived this, and asked him, whether he had any charge to bring against old Lizzie; if so, he should give glory to God, and state the same; *item*, it was competent to every one so to do; indeed, the court required of him to speak out all he knew.

But from fear of the old dragon, all were still as mice, so that you might have heard the flies buzz about the inkstand. I then stood up, wretched as I was, and stretched out my arms over my amazed and faint-hearted people, and spake: "Can ye thus crucify me together with my poor child? have I deserved this at your hands? Speak, then; alas, will none speak?" I heard, indeed, how several wept aloud, but not one spake; and hereupon my poor child was forced to submit.

And the malice of the old hag was such that she not only accused my child of the most horrible witchcraft, but also reckoned to a day when she had given herself up to Satan to rob her of her maiden honour; and she said that Satan had, without doubt, then defiled her. Hereupon my child said naught, save that she cast down her eyes and blushed deep for shame at such filthiness; and to the other blasphemous slander which the old hag uttered with many tears, namely, that my daughter had given up her (Lizzie's) husband, body and soul, to Satan, she answered as she had done before. But when the old hag came to her re-baptism in the sea, and gave out that while seeking for strawberries in the coppice she had recognised my child's voice, and stolen towards her, and perceived these devil's doings, my child fell in smiling, and answered, "Oh, thou evil woman! how couldst thou hear my voice speaking down by the sea, being thyself in the forest upon the mountain? surely thou liest, seeing that the murmur of the waves would make that impossible." This angered the old dragon, and seeking to get out of the blunder she fell still deeper into it, for she said, "I saw thee move thy lips, and from that I knew that thou didst call upon thy paramour the devil!" for my child straightway replies, "Oh, thou ungodly woman! thou saidst thou wert in the forest when thou didst hear my voice; how then up in the forest couldst thou see whether I, who was below by the water, moved my lips or not?"

Such contradictions amazed even *Dom. Consul*, and he began to threaten the old hag with the rack if she told such lies; whereupon she answered and said, "List, then, whether I lie! When she went naked into the water she had no mark on her body, but when she came out again I saw that she had between her breasts a mark the size of a silver penny, whence I perceived that the devil had given it her, although I had not seen him about her, nor, indeed, had I seen any one, either spirit or child of man, for she seemed to be quite alone."

Hereupon the sheriff jumped up from his seat, and cried, "Search must straightway be made for this mark;" whereupon *Dom. Consul* answered, "Yea, but not by us, but by two women of good repute," for he would not hearken to what my child said, that it was a mole, and that she had it from her youth up. Wherefore the constable's wife was sent for, and *Dom. Consul* muttered somewhat into her ear, and as prayers and tears were of no avail, my child was forced to go with her. Howbeit, she obtained this favour, that old Lizzie Kolken was not to follow her, as she would have done, but our old maid Ilse. I, too, went in my sorrow, seeing that I knew not what the women might do to her. She wept bitterly as they undressed her, and held her hands over her eyes for very shame.

Well-a-day, her body was just as white as my departed wife's; although in her childhood, as I remember, she was very yellow, and I saw with amazement the mole between her breasts, whereof I had never heard aught before. But she suddenly screamed violently and started back, seeing that the constable's wife, when nobody watched her, had run a needle into the mole, so deep that the red blood ran down over her breasts. I was sorely angered thereat, but the woman said that she had done it by order of the judge,* which, indeed, was true; for when we came back into court, and the sheriff asked how it was, she testified that there was a mark of the size of a silver penny, of a yellowish colour, but that it had feeling, seeing that *Rea* had screamed aloud, when she had, unperceived, driven a needle therein. Meanwhile, however, *Dom. Camerarius* suddenly rose, and stepping up to my child, drew her eyelids asunder and cried out, beginning to tremble, "Behold the sign which never fails:" whereupon the whole court started to their feet, and looked at the little spot under her right eyelid, which in truth had been left there by a sty, but this none would believe. *Dom. Consul* now said, "See, Satan hath marked thee on body and soul! and thou dost still continue to lie unto the Holy Ghost; but it shall not avail thee, and thy punishment will only be the heavier. Oh, thou shameless woman! thou hast refused to accept the testimony of old Lizzie; wilt thou also refuse that of these people, who have all heard thee on the mountain call upon the devil thy paramour, and seen him appear in the likeness of a hairy giant, and kiss and caress thee?"

Hereupon old Paasch, goodwife Witthahn, and Zuter, came forward and bare witness, that they had seen this happen about midnight, and that on this declaration they would live and die; that old Lizzie had awakened them one Saturday night about eleven o'clock, had given them a can of beer, and persuaded them to follow the parson's daughter privately, and to see what she did upon the mountain. At first they refused; but in order to get at the truth about the witch-craft in the village, they had at last, after a devout prayer, consented, and had followed her in God's name.

They had soon through the bushes seen the witch in the moon-shine; she seemed to dig, and spake in some strange tongue the while, whereupon the grim arch-fiend suddenly appeared, and fell upon her neck. Hereupon they ran away in consternation, but, by the help of the Almighty God, on whom from the very first they had set their faith, they were preserved from the power of the evil one. For, not-withstanding he had turned round on hearing a rustling in the bushes, he had had no power to harm them.

* It was believed that these marks were the infallible sign of a witch when they were insensible, and that they were given by the devil; and every one suspected of witchcraft was invariably searched for them.

Finally, it was even charged to my child as a crime, that she had fainted on the road from Coserow to Pudgla, and none would believe that this had been caused by vexation at old Lizzie's singing, and not from a bad conscience, as stated by the judge.

When all the witnesses had been examined, *Dom. Consul* asked her whether she had brewed the storm, what was the meaning of the frog that dropped into her lap, *item*, the hedgehog which lay directly in his path? To all of which she answered, that she had caused the one as little as she knew of the other. Whereupon *Dom. Consul* shook his head and demanded that she be put to the torture to determine what the truth might be. The court forthwith agreed that this should be done on a day hence and one and all withdrew; my dear child being taken to prison where she should await her examination.

On Thursday, 25th *Augusti*, at noon the worshipful court drove into the prison yard as I sat in the cell with my child, as I was wont. The tall constable peeped in at the door grinning, and cried, "Oh, ho! they are come, they are come; now the tickling will begin:" whereat my poor child shuddered, but less at the news than at sight of the fellow himself. Scarce was he gone than he came back again to take off her chains and to fetch her away. So I followed her into the judgment-chamber, where *Dom. Consul* read out the sentence of the honourable high court as follows:—That she should once more be questioned in kindness touching the articles contained in the indictment; and if she then continued stubborn she should be subjected to the *peine forte et dure*, for that the *defensio* she had set up did not suffice, and that there were *indicia legitima, prægnantia et sufficientia ad torturam ipsam;* to wit—

1. *Mala fama.*
2. *Maleficium, publicè commissum.*
3. *Apparitio dæmonis in monte.*

Whereupon the most honourable central court cited about 20 *auctores*, whereof, howbeit, we remember but little. When *Dom. Consul* had read out this to my child, he once more lift up his voice and admonished her with many words to confess of her own free will, for that the truth must now come to light.

Hereupon she steadfastly replied, that she had indeed hoped for a better sentence; but that, as it was the will of God to try her yet more

hardly, she resigned herself altogether into His gracious hands, and
could not confess aught save what she had said before, namely, that
she was innocent, and that evil men had brought this misery upon
her. Hereupon *Dom. Consul* motioned the constable, who straight-
away opened the door of the next room, and admitted *Pastor Benzensis* in his surplice, who had been sent for by the court to admonish her
still better out of the Word of God. He heaved a deep sigh, and said,
"Mary, Mary, is it thus I must meet thee again?" Whereupon she
began to weep bitterly, and to protest her innocence afresh. But he
heeded not her distress; and as soon as he had heard her pray, "Our
Father," "The eyes of all wait upon Thee," and "God the Father
dwell with us," he lift up his voice and declared to her the hatred of
the living God to all witches and warlocks, seeing that not only is the
punishment of fire awarded to them in the Old Testament, but that
the Holy Ghost expressly saith in the New Testament (Gal. v.),
"That they which do such things shall not inherit the kingdom of
God;" but "shall have their part in the lake which burneth with fire
and brimstone; which is the second death" (Apocal. xxi.). Wherefore
she must not be stubborn nor murmur against the court when she
was tormented, seeing that it was all done out of Christian love, and
to save her poor soul. That, for the sake of God and her salvation,
she should no longer delay repentance, and thereby cause her body
to be tormented and give over her wretched soul to Satan, who
certainly would not fulfil those promises in hell which he had made
her here upon earth; seeing that "he was a murderer from the beginning—a liar and the father of it" (John viii.). "Oh!" cried he, "Mary,
my child, who so oft hast sat upon my knees, and for whom I now
cry every morning and every night unto my God, if thou wilt have
no pity upon thee and me, have pity at least upon thy worthy father,
whom I cannot look upon without tears, seeing that his hairs have
turned snow white within a few days, and save thy soul, my child,
and confess! Behold, thy Heavenly Father grieveth over thee no less
than thy fleshly father, and the holy angels veil their faces for sorrow
that thou, who wert once their darling sister, art now become the
sister and bride of the devil. Return, therefore, and repent! This day
thy Saviour calleth thee, poor stray lamb, back into His flock, 'And
ought not this woman, being a daughter of Abraham, whom Satan
hath bound . . . be loosed from this bond?' Such are His merciful
H

words (Luke xiii.); *item*, 'Return, thou backsliding Israel, saith the Lord, and I will not cause Mine anger to fall upon you, for I am merciful' (Jer. iii). Return then, thou backsliding soul, unto the Lord thy God! He who heard the prayer of the idolatrous Manasseh when 'he besought the Lord his God and humbled himself' (2 Chron. xxxiii); who, through Paul, accepted the repentance of the sorcerers at Ephesus (Acts xix.), the same merciful God now crieth unto thee as unto the angel of the church of Ephesus, 'Remember, therefore, from whence thou art fallen and repent' (Apocal. ii.), O Mary, Mary, remember, my child, from whence thou art fallen, and repent!"

Hereupon he held his peace, and it was some time before she could say a word for tears and sobs; but at last she answered, "If lies are no less hateful to God than witchcraft, I may not lie, but must rather declare, to the glory of God, as I have ever declared, that I am innocent."

Hereupon *Dom. Consul* was exceeding wroth, and frowned, and asked the tall constable if all was ready, *item*, whether the women were at hand to undress *Rea ;* whereupon he answered with a grin, as he was wont, "Ho, ho, I have never been wanting in my duty, nor will I be wanting to-day; I will tickle her in such wise that she shall soon confess."

When he had said this, *Dom. Consul* turned to my daughter and said, "Thou art a foolish thing, and knowest not the torment which awaits thee, and therefore is it that thou still art stubborn. Now then, follow me to the torture-chamber, where the executioner shall show thee the *instrumenta*, and thou mayest yet think better of it, when thou hast seen what the question is like."

Hereupon he went into another room, and the constable followed him with my child. And when I would have gone after them, *Pastor Benzensis* held me back, with many tears, and conjured me not to do so, but to tarry where I was. But I hearkened not unto him, and tore myself from him, and swore that so long as a single vein should beat in my wretched body, I would never forsake my child. I therefore went into the next room, and from thence down into a vault, where was the torture-chamber, wherein were no windows, so that those without might not hear the cries of the tormented. Two torches were already burning there when I went in, and although *Dom. Consul* would at first have sent me away, after a while he had pity upon me, so that he suffered me to stay.

And now that hell-hound the constable stepped forward, and first showed my poor child the ladder, saying with savage glee, "See here! first of all, thou wilt be laid on that, and thy hands and feet will be tied. Next the thumb-screw here will be put upon thee, which straightway will make the blood to spirt out at the tips of thy fingers; thou mayest see that they are still red with the blood of old Gussy Biehlke, who was burnt last year, and who, like thee, would not confess at first. If thou still wilt not confess, I shall next put these Spanish boots on thee, and should they be too large, I shall just drive in a wedge, so that the calf, which is now at the back of thy leg, will be driven to the front, and the blood will shoot out of thy feet, as when thou squeezest blackberries in a bag.

"Again, if thou wilt not yet confess—holla!" shouted he, and kicked open a door behind him, so that the whole vault shook, and my poor child fell upon her knees for fright. Before long two women brought in a bubbling cauldron, full of boiling pitch and brimstone. This cauldron the hell-hound ordered them to set down on the ground, and drew forth, from under the red cloak he wore, a goose's wing, whereupon he plucked five or six quills, which he dipped into the boiling brimstone. After he had held them awhile in the cauldron he threw them upon the earth, where they twisted about and spirited the brimstone on all sides. And then he called to my poor child again, "See! these quills I shall throw upon thy while loins, and the burning brimstone will presently eat into thy flesh down to the very bones, so that thou wilt thereby have a foretaste of the joys which await thee in hell."

When he had spoken thus far, amid sneers and laughter, I was so overcome with rage that I sprang forth out of the corner where I stood leaning my trembling joints against an old barrel, and cried, "Oh, thou hellish dog! sayest thou this of thyself, or have others bidden thee?" Whereupon, however, the fellow gave me such a blow upon the breast that I fell backwards against the wall, and *Dom. Consul* called out in great wrath, "You old fool, if you needs must stay here, at any rate leave the constable in peace, for if not I will have you thrust out of the chamber forthwith. The constable has said no more than is his duty; and it will thus happen to thy child if she confess not, and if it appear that the foul fiend hath given her some charm against the torture."* Hereupon this hell-hound went on to speak to my poor child, without heeding me, save that he laughed in my face: "Look here! when thou hast thus been well shorn, ho, ho, ho! I shall pull thee up by means of these two rings in the floor and the roof, stretch thy arms above thy head, and bind them fast to the ceiling; whereupon I shall take these two torches, and hold them under thy shoulders, till thy skin will presently become like the rind of a smoked ham. Then thy hellish paramour will help thee no longer, and thou wilt confess the truth. And now thou hast seen and heard all that I shall do to thee, in the name of God, and by order of the magistrates."

And now *Dom. Consul* once more came forward and admonished her to confess the truth. But she abode by what she had said from the first; whereupon he delivered her over to the two women who had brought in the cauldron, to strip her naked as she was born, and to clothe her in the black torture-shift; after which they were once more to lead her barefooted up the steps before the worshipful court. But one of these women was the sheriff's housekeeper (the other was the impudent constable's wife), and my daughter said that she would not suffer herself to be touched save by honest women, and assuredly not by the housekeeper, and begged *Dom. Consul* to send for her maid, who was sitting in her prison reading the Bible, if he knew of no other decent woman at hand. Hereupon the housekeeper began to pour forth a wondrous deal of railing and ill words, but *Dom. Consul* rebuked her, and answered my daughter that he would let her have her wish in this matter too, and bade the impudent constable's wife call the maid hither from out of the prison. After he had said this, he took me by the arm, and prayed me so long to go up with him, for that no harm would happen to my daughter as yet, that I did as he would have me.

Before long she herself came up, led between the two women, barefooted, and in the black torture-shift, but so pale that I myself should scarce have known her. The hateful constable, who followed close behind, seized her by the hand, and led her before the worshipful court.

* It was believed that when witches endured the torture with unusual patience, or even slept during the operation, which, strange to say, frequently occurred, the devil had gifted them with insensibility to pain by means of an amulet which they concealed in some secret part of their persons.—Zedler's Universal Lexicon, vol. xliv., art. "Torture."

Hereupon the admonitions began all over again, and *Dom. Consul* bade her look upon the brown spots that were upon the black shift, for that they were the blood of old wife Biehlke, and to consider that within a few minutes it would in like manner be stained with her own blood. Hereupon she answered, "I have considered that right well, but I hope that my faithful Saviour, who hath laid this torment upon me, being innocent, will likewise help me to bear it, as He helped the holy martyrs of old; for if these, through Gods' help, overcame by faith the torments inflicted on them by blind heathens, I also can overcome the torture inflicted on me by blind heathens, who, indeed, call themselves Christians, but who are more cruel than those of yore; for the old heathens only caused the holy virgins to be torn of savage beasts, but ye which have received the new commandment, 'That ye love one another; as your Saviour hath loved you, that ye also love one another. By this shall all men know that ye are His disciples' (St. John xiii.); yourselves will act the part of savage beasts, and tear with your hands the body of an innocent maiden, your sister, who has never done aught to harm you. Do then as ye list, but have a care how ye will answer it to the highest Judge of all. Again, I say, the lamb feareth naught, for it is in the hand of the Good Shepherd."

When my matchless child had thus spoken, *Dom. Consul* rose, pulled off the black skull-cap which he ever wore, because the top of his head was already bald, bowed to the court, and said, "We hereby make known to the worshipful court, that the question ordinary and extraordinary of the stubborn and blaspheming witch, Mary Schweidler, is about to begin, in the name of the Father, and of the Son, and of the Holy Ghost. Amen."

Hereupon all the court rose save the sheriff, who had got up before, and was walking uneasily up and down in the room. But of all that now follows, and of what I myself did, I remember not one word, but will relate it all as I have received it from my daughter and other *testes*, and they have told me as follows:—

That when *Dom. Consul* after these words had taken up the hourglass which stood upon the table, and walked on before, I would go with him, whereupon *Pastor Benzensis* first prayed me with many words and tears to desist from my purpose, and when that was of no avail my child herself stroked my cheeks, saying, "Father, have you ever read that the Blessed Virgin stood by when her guileless Son was scourged? Depart, therefore, from me. You shall stand by the pile whereon I am burned, that I promise you; for in like manner did the Blessed Virgin stand at the foot of the cross. But now, go; go, I pray you, for you will not be able to hear it, neither shall I!"

And when this also failed, *Dom. Consul* bade the constable seize me, and by main force lock me into another room; whereupon, however, I tore myself away, and fell at his feet, conjuring him by the wounds of Christ not to tear me from my child; that I would never forget his kindness and mercy, but pray for him day and night; nay, that at the day of judgment I would be his intercessor with God and the holy angels if that he would but let me go with my child; that I would be quite quiet, and not speak one single word, but that I must go with my child.

This so moved the worthy man that he burst into tears, and so trembled with pity for me that the hour-glass fell from his hands and rolled right before the feet of the sheriff, as though God Himself would signify to him that his glass was soon to run out; and, indeed, he understood it right well, for he grew white as any chalk when he picked it up, and gave it back to *Dom. Consul*. The latter at last gave way, saying that this day would make him ten years older; but he bade the impudent constable, who also went with us, lead me away if I made any *rumor* during the torture. And hereupon the whole court went below, save the sheriff, who said his head ached, and that he believed his old *malum*, the gout, was coming upon him again, wherefore he went into another chamber, *item, Pastor Benzensis* likewise departed.

Down in the vault the constables first brought in tables and chairs, whereon the court sat, and *Dom. Consul* also pushed a chair toward me, but I sat not thereon, but threw myself upon my knees in a corner. When this was done they began again with their vile admonitions, and as my child, like her guileless Saviour before His unrighteous judges, answered not a word, *Dom. Consul* rose up and bade the tall constable lay her on the torture-bench.

She shook like an aspen leaf when he bound her hands and feet; and when he was about to bind over her sweet eyes a nasty old filthy clout wherein my maid had seen him carry fish but the day before, and which was still all over shining scales, I perceived it, and pulled off my silken neckerchief, begging him to use that instead, which he did. Hereupon the thrumb-screw was put on her, and she was once more asked whether she would confess freely, but she only shook her poor blinded head, and sighed with her dying Saviour, "Eli, Eli, lama sabachthani," and then in Greek, "Θεε μου, Θεε μου, ινα τι με εγκατελιπες."* Whereat *Dom. Consul* started back, and made the sign of the cross (for inasmuch as he knew no Greek, he believed, as he afterwards said himself, that she was calling upon the devil to help her), and then called to the constable with a loud voice, "Screw!"

But when I heard this I gave such a cry that the whole vault shook; and when my poor child, who was dying of terror and despair, had heard my voice, she first struggled with her bound hands and feet like a lamb that lies dying in the slaughter-house, and then cried out, "Loose me, and I will confess whatsoe'er you will." Hereat *Dom. Consul* so greatly rejoiced, that while the constable unbound her, he fell on his knees, and thanked God for having spared him this anguish. But no sooner was my poor desperate child unbound, and had laid aside her crown of thorns (I mean my silken neckerchief), than she jumped off the ladder, and flung herself upon me, who lay for dead in the corner in a deep swound.

This greatly angered the worshipful court, and when the constable had borne me away, *Rea* was admonished to make her confession according to promise. But seeing she was too weak to stand upon her feet, *Dom. Consul* gave her a chair to sit upon, although *Dom. Camerarius* grumbled thereat, and these were the chief questions which were put to her by order of the most honourable high central court, as *Dom. Consul* said, and which were registered *ad protocollum.*

Q. Whether she could bewitch?—*R.* Yes, she could bewitch.

Q. Who taught her to do so?—*R.* Satan himself.

Q. How many devils had she?—*R.* One devil was enough for her.

Q. What was this devil called?—*Illa* (considering). His name was *Disidæmonia.*

Hereat *Dom. Consul* shuddered and said that that must be a very terrible devil indeed, for that he had never heard such a name before, and that she must spell it, so that *Scriba* might make no error; which she did, and he then went on as follows:—

Q. In what shape had he appeared to her?—*R.* In the shape of the sheriff, and sometimes as a goat with terrible horns.

* "My God, My God, why hast thou forsaken Me?"—Matt. xxvii. 46.

_Q_. Whether Satan had re-baptized her, and where ?—_R_. In the sea.

_Q_. What name had he given her?—_R_. ——.

_Q_. Whether any of the neighbours had been by when she was re-baptized, and which of them ?—_R_. Hereupon my matchless child cast up her eyes towards heaven, as though doubting whether she should fyle old Lizzie or not, but at last she said, No!

_Q_. She must have had sponsors; who were they ? and what gift had they given her as christening money ?—_R_. There were none there save spirits; wherefore old Lizzie could see no one when she came and looked on at her re-baptism.

_Q_. Whether she had ever lived with the devil ?—_R_. She never had lived anywhere save in her father's house.

_Q_. She did not choose to understand. He meant whether she had ever played the wanton with Satan, and known him carnally ? Hereupon she blushed, and was so ashamed that she covered her face with her hands, and presently began to weep and to sob: and as, after many questions, she gave no answer, she was again admonished to speak the truth, or that the executioner should lift her up on the ladder again. At last she said "No!" which howbeit the worshipful court would not believe, and bade the executioner seize her again, whereupon she answered "Yes!"

_Q_. Whether she had found the devil hot or cold ?—_R_. She did not remember which.

_Q_. Whether she had ever conceived by Satan, and given birth to a changeling, and of what shape ?—_R_. No, never.

_Q_. Whether the foul fiend had given her any sign or mark about her body, and in what part thereof?—_R_. That the mark had already been seen by the worshipful court.

She was next charged with all the witchcraft done in the village, and owned to it all, save that she still said that she knew naught of the death of old Seden, _item_, or of little Paasch's sickness, nor, lastly, would she confess that she had, by the help of the foul fiend, raked up my crop or conjured the caterpillars into my orchard. And albeit they again threatened her with the question, and even ordered the executioner to lay her on the bench and put on the thumb-screw to frighten her; she remained firm, and said, "Why should you torture me, seeing that I have confessed far heavier crimes than these, which it will not save my life to deny?"

Hereupon the worshipful court at last were satisfied, and suffered her to be lifted off the torture-bench, especially as she confessed the *articulus principalis;* to wit, that Satan had really appeared to her on the mountain in the shape of a hairy giant. Of the storm and the frog, *item,* of the hedgehog, nothing was said, inasmuch as the worshipful court had by this time seen the folly of supposing that she could have brewed a storm while she quietly sat in the coach. Lastly, she prayed that it might be granted to her to suffer death clothed in the garments which she had worn when she went to greet the King of Sweden; *item,* that they would suffer her wretched father to be driven with her to the stake, and to stand by while she was burned, seeing that she had promised him this in the presence of the worshipful court.

Hereupon she was once more given into the charge of the tall constable, who was ordered to put her into a stronger and severer prison. But he had not led her out of the chamber before the sheriff's bastard, whom he had had by the house-keeper, came into the vault with a drum, and kept drumming and crying out, "Come to the roast goose! come to the roast goose!" whereat *Dom. Consul* was exceeding wroth, and ran after him, but he could not catch him, seeing that the young varlet knew all the ins and outs of the vault. It was at this point that the Good Lord caused me to swoon and my senses were taken from this terrible place where there seemed no relief for me or my poor misjudged child.

[*Editor's Note : Thanks mainly to the efforts of her father (our storyteller) Rea is eventually cleared of the charges of witchcraft, but not until after a whole series of further dramatic episodes which bring her perilously close to the stake. The reader wishing to pursue the story is advised that copies of the work, usually in two volumes, can be obtained from most of the major libraries.*]

THE WITCH SPECTRE

Anonymous

Anonymous. As was noted in the first item in the fictional section of this book, numerous Victorian periodicals did not carry the name of the author on many of their contributions. Probably the most distinguished of the journals to fall into this category, and at the same time cater for those who liked their stories spiced with the supernatural, was *The Dublin Review*. (It is perhaps not surprising that this monthly magazine should have shown such a penchant for the macabre when one considers that its editor for a great many years was the distinguished ghost story writer, Joseph Sheridan Le Fanu.) From the many volumes of this publication through which I have happily researched, I would like to present the following item which the editor noted was from "A society lady in County Cork" and based on a true occurrence. (1845).

∽∽∽∽∽∽∽∽∽∽∽∽∽∽∽∽∽∽∽∽∽∽∽∽∽∽∽∽∽∽∽∽

IT was about eighty years ago, in the month of May that a Roman Catholic clergyman, near Rathdowney, in the Queen's County, was awakened at midnight to attend a dying man in a distant part of the parish. The priest obeyed without a murmur, and having performed his duty to the expiring sinner, saw him depart this world before he left the cabin. As it was yet dark, the man who had called on the priest offered to accompany him home, but he refused, and set forward on his journey alone. The grey dawn began to appear over the hills. The good priest was highly enraptured with the beauty of the scene, and rode on, now gazing intently at every surrounding object, and again cutting with his whip at the bats and big beautiful night-flies which flitted ever and anon from hedge to hedge across his lonely way. Thus engaged, he journeyed on slowly, until the nearer approach of sunrise began to render objects completely discernible, when he dismounted from his horse, and slipping his arm out of the rein, and drawing forth his "Breviary" from his pocket, he commenced reading his "morning office" as he walked leisurely along.

He had not proceeded very far, when he observed his horse, a very spirited animal, endeavouring to stop on the road, and gazing intently into a field on one side of the way where there were three or four cows grazing. However, he did not pay any particular attention to this circumstance, but went on a little farther, when the horse suddenly plunged with great violence, and endeavoured to break away by force. The priest with great difficulty succeeded in restraining him, and, looking at him more closely, observed him shaking from head to foot, and sweating profusely. He now stood calmly, and refused to move from where he was, nor could threats or entreaty induce him to proceed. The father was greatly astonished, but recollecting to have often heard of horses labouring under affright being induced to go by blindfolding them, he took out his handkerchief and tied it across his eyes. He then mounted, and striking him gently, he went forward without reluctance, but still sweating and trembling violently. They had not gone far, when they arrived opposite a narrow path or bridle-way, flanked at either side by a tall, thick hedge, which led from the high road to the field where the cows were grazing. The priest happened by chance to look into the lane, and saw a spectacle which made the blood curdle in his veins. It was the legs of a man from the hips downwards, without head or body, trotting up the avenue at a smart pace. The good father was very much alarmed, but, being a man of strong nerve, he resolved, come what might, to stand, and be further acquainted with this singular spectre. He accordingly stood, and so did the headless apparition, as if afraid to approach him. The priest, observing this, pulled back a little from the entrance of the avenue, and the phantom again resumed its progress. It soon arrived on the road, and the priest now had sufficient opportunity to view it minutely. It wore yellow buckskin breeches, tightly fastened at the knees with green ribbon, it had neither shoes nor stockings on, and its legs were covered with long, red hairs, and all full of wet, blood, and clay, apparently contracted in its progress through the thorny hedges. The priest, although very much alarmed, felt eager to examine the phantom, and for this purpose summoned all his philosophy to enable him to speak to it. The ghost was now a little ahead, pursuing its march at its usual brisk trot, and the priest urged on his horse speedily until he came up with it, and thus addressed it—

"Hilloa, friend! who art thou, or whither art thou going so early?"

The hideous spectre made no reply, but uttered a fierce and superhuman growl, or "Umph."

"A fine morning for ghosts to wander abroad," again said the priest.

Another "Umph" was the reply.

"Why don't you speak?"

"Umph."

"You don't seem disposed to be very loquacious this morning."

"Umph," again.

The good man began to feel irritated at the obstinate silence of his unearthly visitor, and said, with some warmth—

"In the name of all that's sacred, I command you to answer me, Who art thou, or where art thou travelling?"

Another "Umph," more loud and more angry than before, was the only reply.

"Perhaps," said the father, "a taste of whipcord might render you a little more communicative;" and so saying, he struck the apparition a heavy blow with his whip on the breech.

The phantom uttered a wild and unearthly yell, and fell forward on the road, and what was the priest's astonishment when he perceived the whole place running over with milk. He was struck dumb with amazement; the prostrate phantom still continued to eject vast quantities of milk from every part; the priests' head swam, his eyes got dizzy; a stupor came all over him for some minutes, and on his recovering, the frightful spectre had vanished, and in its stead he found stretched on the road, and half drowned in milk, the form of Sarah Kennedy, an old woman of the neighbourhood, who had been long notorious in that district for her witchcraft and superstitious practices, and it was now discovered that she had, by infernal aid, assumed that monstrous shape, and was employed that morning in sucking the cows of the village. Had a volcano burst forth at his feet, he could not be more astonished; he gazed awhile in silent amazement—the old woman groaning, and writhing convulsively.

"Sarah," said he, at length, "I have long admonished you to repent of your evil ways, but you were deaf to my entreaties; and now, wretched woman, you are surprised in the midst of your crimes."

"Oh father, father," shouted the unfortunate woman, "can you do nothing to save me? I am lost; hell is open for me and legions of devils surround me this moment, waiting to carry my soul to perdition."

The priest had not power to reply; the old wretch's pains increased; her body swelled to an immense size; her eyes flashed as if on fire, her face was black as night, her entire form writhed in a thousand different contortions; her outcries were appalling, her face sunk, her eyes closed, and in a few minutes she expired in the most exquisite tortures.

The priest departed homewards, and called at the next cabin to give notice of the strange circumstances. The remains of Sarah Kennedy were removed to her cabin, situate at the edge of a small wood at a little distance. She had long been a resident in that neighbourhood, but still she was a stranger, and came there no one knew from whence. She had no relation in that country but one daughter, now advanced in years, who resided with her. She kept one cow, but sold more butter, it was said, than any farmer in the parish, and it was generally suspected that she acquired it by devilish agency, as she never made a secret of being intimately acquainted with sorcery and fairyism. She professed the Roman Catholic religion, but never compiled with the practices enjoined by that church, and her remains were denied Christian sepulture, and were buried in a sand-pit near her own cabin.

On the evening of her burial, the villagers assembled and burned her cabin to the earth. Her daughter made her escape, and never after returned.

POSSESSED BY DEMONS

Catherine Crowe

Catherine Crowe (1800-1870) is another Victorian writer whose name is still familiar in occult literature through one book, *The Night Side of Nature*, which was published in 1848. Miss Crowe spent much of her life in Scotland and according to her biographers suffered from a morbid disposition and frequently went through long periods of despondency—one of these leading to a brief but violent bout of insanity. Much of her best work is in the area of tragedy and there can be little doubt that she gave herself wholeheartedly to the task of collecting weird and supernatural stories for *The Night Side of Nature*. From this work I have selected her thoughtful and well-researched piece on the dark subject of demonic possession; it is included here rather than in the factual section as it provides an ideal introduction to several of the tales which follow.

Of all the areas of witchcraft and the supernatural to which I have directed my attention, that of 'demonic possession' exerts probably the greatest fascination. Many German physicians maintain, that to this day instances of genuine possession occur, and there are several works published in their language on the subject; and for this malady they consider magnetism the only remedy, all others being worse than useless. Indeed, they look upon possession itself as a demono-magnetic state, in which the patient is in rapport with mischievous or evil spirits. They assert, that although instances are comparatively rare, both sexes and all ages are equally subject to this misfortune; and that it is quite an error to suppose, either, that it has ceased since the Resurrection of Christ, or that the expression used in the Scriptures "possessed by a devil," meant merely insanity or convulsions. This disease, which is not contagious, was well known to the Greeks; and in later times Hofman has recorded several well established instances. Amongst the distinguishing symptoms, they reckon the patient's speaking in a voice that is not his own, frightful convulsions and motions of the body, which arise suddenly, without any previous indisposition—blasphemous and obscene talk, a knowledge of what is secret, and of the future—a vomiting of extraordinary things, such as hair, stones, pins, needles, &c., &c. I need scarcely observe that this opinion is not universal in Germany; still it obtains amongst many who have had considerable opportunities for observation.

Dr Bardili had a case in the year 1830, which he considered decidedly to be one of possession. The patient was a peasant woman, aged thirty-four, who never had any sickness whatever; and the whole of whose bodily functions continued perfectly regular whilst she exhibited the following strange phenomena. I must observe that she was happily married, had three children, was not a fanatic, and bore an excellent character for regularity and industry, when, without any warning or perceptible cause, she was seized with the most extraordinary convulsions, whilst a strange voice proceeded from her. which assumed to be that of an unblessed spirit, who had formerly inhabited a human form. Whilst these fits were on her, she entirely lost her own individuality, and became this person; on returning to herself, her understanding and character were as entire as before. The blasphemy and cursing, and barking and screeching, were dreadful. She was wounded and injured severely by the violent falls and blows she gave herself; and when she had an intermission, she could do nothing but weep over what they told her had passed, and the state in which she saw herself. She was moreover reduced to a skeleton; for when she wanted to eat, the spoon was turned round in her hand, and she often fasted for days together. This affliction lasted for three years; all remedies failed, and the only alleviation she obtained was by the continued and earnest prayers of those about her and her own; for although this demon did not like prayers, and violently opposed her kneeling down, even forcing her to outrageous fits of laughter, still they had a power over him. It is remarkable that pregnancy, confinement, and the nursing her child, made not the least difference in this woman's condition. All went on regularly, but the demon kept his post. At length, being magnetised, the patient fell into a partially somnambulic state in which another voice was heard to proceed from her, being that of her protecting spirit, which encouraged her to patience and hope, and promised that the evil guest would be obliged to vacate his quarters. She often now fell into a magnetic state without the aid of a magnetiser. At the end of three years she was entirely relieved, and as well as ever.

In the case of Rosina Wildin, aged ten years, which occurred at Pleidelsheim, in 1834, the demon used to announce himself by crying out, "Here I am again!" Whereupon the weak exhausted child, who had been lying like one dead, would rage and storm in a voice like a man's, perform the most extraordinary movements and feats of violence and strength, till he would cry out, "Now I must be off again!" This spirit spoke generally in the plural number, for he said, she had another beside himself, a dumb devil, who plagued her most. "He it is that twirls her round and round, distorts her features, turns her eyes, locks her teeth, &c. What he bids me, I must do!" This child was at length cured by magnetism.

Barbara Rieger, of Steinbach, aged ten, in 1834, was possessed by two spirits, who spoke in two distinctly different male voices and dialects; one said he had formerly been a mason, the other gave himself out for a deceased provisor; the latter of whom was much the worst of the two. When they spoke, the child closed her eyes, and when she opened them again, she knew nothing of what they had said. The mason confessed to have been a great sinner, but the provisor was proud and hardened, and would confess nothing. They often commanded food, and made her eat it, which, when she recovered her individuality, she felt nothing of, but was very hungry. The mason was very fond of brandy, and drank a great deal; and if not brought when he ordered it, his raging and storming was dreadful. In her own individuality, the child had the greatest aversion to this liquor. They treated her for worms and other disorders, without the least effect; till at length, by magnetism, the mason was cast out. The provisor was more tenacious, but, finally, they got rid of him, too, and the girl remained quite well.

In 1835, a respectable citizen, whose full name is not given, was brought to Dr Kerner. He was aged thirty-seven, and till the last seven years had been unexceptionable in conduct and character. An unaccountable change had, however, come over him in his thirtieth year, which made his family very unhappy; and at length, one day, a strange voice suddenly spoke out of him, saying, that he was the late magistrate, S., and that he had been in him for six years. When this spirit was driven out, by magnetism, the man fell to the earth, and was almost torn to pieces by the violence of the struggle; he then lay for a space as if dead, and arose quite well and free.

In another case, a young woman at Gruppenbach was quite in her senses, and heard the voice of her demon (who was also a deceased person) speak out of her, without having any power to suppress it.

In short, instances of this description seem by no means rare; and if such a phenomenon as possession ever did exist, I do not see what right we have to assert that it exists no longer, since, in fact, we know nothing about it; only, that being determined to admit nothing so contrary to the ideas of the present day, we set out by deciding that the thing is impossible.

Since these cases occur in other countries, no doubt they must do so in this; and, indeed, I have met with one instance much more remarkable in its details than any of those above-mentioned, which occurred at Bishopwearmouth, near Sunderland, in the year 1840; and as the particulars in this case have been published and attested by two physicians and two surgeons, not to mention the evidence of numerous other persons, I think we are bound to accept the facts, whatever interpretation we may choose to put upon them.

The patient, named Mary Jobson, was between twelve and thirteen years of age; her parents, respectable people in humble life, and herself an attendant on a Sunday school. She became ill in November, 1839, and was soon afterwards seized with terrific fits, which continued, at intervals, for eleven weeks. It was during this period that the family first observed a strange knocking, which they could not account for. It was sometimes in one place, and sometimes in another; and even about the bed, when the girl lay in a quiet sleep, with her hands folded outside the clothes. They next heard a strange voice, which told them circumstances they did not know, but which they afterwards found to be correct. Then there was a noise like the clash-

I

ing of arms, and such a rumbling that the tenant below thought the house was coming down; footsteps where nobody was to be seen, water falling on the floor, no one knew whence, locked doors opened, and above all, sounds of ineffably sweet music. The doctors and the father were suspicious, and every precaution was taken, but no solution of the mystery could be found. This spirit, however, was a good one, and it preached to them, and gave them a great deal of good advice. Many persons went to witness this strange phenomenon, and some were desired to go by the voice, when in their own homes. Thus Elizabeth Gauntlett, whilst attending to some domestic affairs at home, was startled by hearing a voice say, "Be thou faithful, and thou shalt see the works of thy God, and shalt hear with thine ears!" She cried out, "My God! what can this be!" and presently she saw a large white cloud near her. On the same evening, the voice said to her, "Mary Jobson, one of your scholars, is sick; go and see her; and it will be good for you." This person did not know where the child lived; but having inquired the address, she went: and at the door she heard the same voice bid her go up. On entering the room, she heard another voice, soft and beautiful, which bade her be faithful, and said, "I am the Virgin Mary." This voice promised her a sign at home; and accordingly that night, whilst reading the Bible, she heard it say, "Jemima, be not afraid; it is I: if you keep my commandments, it shall be well with you." When she repeated her visit, the same things occurred, and she heard the most exquisite music.

The same sort of phenomena were witnessed by everybody who went—the immoral were rebuked, the good encouraged. Some were bidden instantly depart, and were forced to go. The voices of several deceased persons of the family were also heard, and made revelations.

Once the voice said, "Look up, and you shall see the sun and moon on the ceiling!" and immediately there appeared a beautiful representation of these planets in lively colours, viz., green, yellow, and orange. Moreover, these figures were permanent; but the father, who was a long time sceptical, insisted on whitewashing them over; however, they still remained visible.

Amongst other things, the voice said that though the child appeared to suffer, that she did not; that she did not know where her body was, and that her own spirit had left it and another had entered; and that her body was made a speaking-trumpet. The voice told the family and visitors many things of their distant friends, which proved true.

The girl twice saw a divine form standing by her bedside who spoke to her, and Joseph Ragg, one of the persons who had been invited by the voice to go, saw a beautiful and heavenly figure come to his bedside about eleven o'clock at night, on the 17th January. It was in male attire, surrounded by a radiance; it came a second time on the same night. On each occasion it opened his curtains and looked at him benignantly, remaining about a quarter of an hour. When it went away, the curtains fell back in their former position. One day, whilst in the sick child's room, Margaret Watson saw a lamb, which passed through the door and entered a place where the father, John Jobson, was; but he did not see it.

One of the most remarkable features in this case is the beautiful music which was heard by all parties, as well as the family, including the unbelieving father, and, indeed, it seems to have been, in a great degree, this that converted him at last. This music was heard repeatedly during a space of sixteen weeks; sometimes it was like an organ, but more beautiful; at others, there was singing of holy songs, *in parts*, and the words distinctly heard. The sudden appearance of water in the room, too, was most unaccountable; for they felt it, and it was really water. When the voice desired that water should be sprinkled, it immediately appeared as if sprinkled. At another time a sign being promised to the sceptical father, water would suddenly appear on the floor; this happened "not once, but twenty times."

During the whole course of this affair the voices told them that there was a miracle to be wrought on this child; and accordingly, on the 22nd of June, when she was as ill as ever, and they were only praying for her death, at five o'clock the voice ordered that her clothes should be laid out, and that everybody should leave the room, except the infant, which was two years and a half old. They obeyed; and having been outside the door a quarter of an hour, the voice cried, "Come in!" and when they entered they saw the girl completely dressed and quite well, sitting in a chair with the infant on her knee, and she had not an hour's illness from that time till the report was published, which was on the 30th of January, 1841.

Now, it is very easy to laugh at all this, and assert that these things never happened, because they are absurd and impossible; but whilst honest, well-meaning, and intelligent people, who were on the spot, assert that they did, I confess I find myself constrained to believe them, however much I find in the case which is discrepant with my notions. It was not an affair of a day or an hour: there was ample time for observation, for the phenomena continued from the 9th of February to the 22nd of June; and the determined unbelief of the father, with regard to the possibility of spiritual appearances, insomuch that he ultimately expressed great regret for the harshness he had used— is a tolerable security against imposition. Moreover, they pertinaciously refused to receive any money or assistance whatever, and were more likely to suffer in public opinion than otherwise by the avowal of these circumstances.

Dr Reid Clanny, who publishes the report, with the attestations of the witnesses, is a physician of many years' experience, and is also, I believe, the original inventor of the safety lamp; and he declares his entire conviction of the facts, assuring his readers that "many persons holding high rank in the Established Church, ministers of other denominations, as well as many lay-members of society, highly respected for learning and piety, are equally satisfied." When he first saw the child lying on her back, apparently insensible, with her eyes suffused with florid blood, he felt assured that she had a disease of the brain; and he was not in the least disposed to believe in the mysterious part of the affair, till subsequent investigation compelled him to do so; and that his belief is of a very decided character we may feel assured, when he is content to submit to all the obloquy he must incur by avowing it.*

He adds, that since the girl has been quite well, both her family and that of Joseph Ragg have frequently heard the same heavenly music as they did during her illness; and a Mr Torbock, a surgeon, who expresses himself satisfied of the truth of the above particulars, also mentions another case, in which he as well as a dying person he was attending, heard divine music just before the dissolution.

Of this last phenomenon, namely, sounds as of heavenly music being heard when a death was occurring, I have met with numerous instances.

From investigation of the above case, Dr Clanny has arrived at

---

* Dr Clanny informs me that Mary Jobson is now a very well educated and extremely respectable young woman.

the conviction that the spiritual world do occasionally identify themselves with our affairs, and Dr Drury asserts, that besides this
instance he has met with another circumstance which has left him
firmly convinced that we live in a world of spirits, and that he has
been in the presence of an unearthly being, who had "passed that
bourne from which, it is said, no traveller returns."

MY BROTHER'S GHOST STORY

Amelia Edwards

Amelia Blandford Edwards (1831-1892) is perhaps the most famous contributor to this anthology. Her novels such as *My Brother's Wife* (1855) and *Lord Brackenbury* (1880) are still in circulation, and occasionally one of her short stories will find its way into a new anthology. Born in London, she was deeply interested in Egypt and was founder of the Egyptian Exploration Fund. She was also fascinated by ghost lore and wrote a number of stories based on alleged sightings. Her light, well-paced tales were popular in an age when so much prose was leaden and pedantic, and indeed this is probably the main reason for her work surviving in print to the present day. From one of the collections of her work I have selected the following memorable ghost tale with its hints of possession and diabolism (1860).

∽∽∽∽∽∽∽∽∽∽∽∽∽∽∽∽∽∽∽∽∽∽∽∽∽∽∽∽∽∽∽∽∽∽∽∽∽

Mine is my brother's Ghost Story. It happened to my brother about thirty years ago, while he was wandering, sketch-book in hand, among the High Alps, picking up subjects for an illustrated work on Switzerland. Having entered the Oberland by the Brunig Pass, and filled his portfolio with what he used to call "bits" from the neighbourhood of Meyringen, he went over the Great Scheideck to Grindlewald, where he arrived one dusky September evening, about three-quarters of an hour after sunset. There had been a fair that day, and the place was crowded. In the best inn there was not an inch of space to spare—there were only two inns at Grindlewald, thirty years ago—so my brother went to one at the end of the covered bridge next to the church, and there, with some difficulty, obtained the promise of a pile of rugs and a mattress, in a room which was already occupied by three other travellers.

The Adler was a primitive hostelry, half farm, half inn, with great rambling galleries outside, and a hugh general room, like a barn. At the upper end of this room stood long stoves, like metal counters, laden with steaming-pans, and glowing underneath like furnaces. At the lower end, smoking, supping, and chatting, were congregated some thirty or forty guests, chiefly mountaineers, char drivers and guides. Among these my brother took his seat, and was served, like the rest, with a bowl of soup, a platter of beef, a flagon of country wine, and a loaf made of Indian corn. Presently, a huge St. Bernard dog came and laid his nose upon my brother's arm. In the meantime he fell into conversation with two Italian youths, bronzed and dark-eyed, near whom he happened to be seated. They were Florentines. Their names, they told him, were Stefano and Battisto. They had been travelling for some months on commission, selling cameos, mosaics, sulphur casts, and the like pretty Italian trifles, and were now on their way to Interlaken and Geneva. Weary of the cold North, they longed, like children, for the moment which should take them back to their own blue hills and grey-green olives; to their workshops on the Ponte Vecchio, and their home down by the Arno.

It was quite a relief to my brother, on going up to bed, to find that these youths were to be two of his fellow-lodgers. The third was already there, and sound asleep, with his face to the wall. They scarcely looked at this third. They were all tired, and all anxious to rise at daybreak, having agreed to walk together over the Wengern Alp as far as Lauterbrunnen. So, my brother and the two youths exchanged a brief good night, and, before many minutes, were all as far away in the land of dreams as their unknown companion.

My brother slept profoundly—so profoundly that, being roused in the morning by a clamour of merry voices, he sat up dreamily in his rugs, and wondered where he was.

"Good day, signor," cried Battisto. "Here is a fellow-traveller going the same way as ourselves."

"Christien Baumann, native of Kandersteg, musical-box maker by trade, stands five feet eleven in his shoes, and is at monsieur's service to command," said the sleeper of the night before.

He was as fine a young fellow as one would wish to see. Light, and strong, and well proportioned, with curling brown hair, and bright honest eyes that seemed to dance at every word he uttered.

"Good morning," said my brother. "You were asleep last night when we came up."

"Asleep! I should think so, after being all day in the fair, and walking from Meyringen the evening before. What a capital fair it was!"

"Capital, indeed," said Battisto. "We sold cameos and mosaics yesterday, for nearly fifty francs."

"Oh, you sell cameos and mosaics, you two! Show me your cameos and I will show you my musical boxes. I have such pretty ones, with coloured views of Geneva and Chillon on the lids, playing two, four, six, and even eight tunes. Bah! I will give you a concert!"

And with this he unstrapped his pack, displayed his little boxes on the table, and wound them up, one after the other, to the delight of the Italians.

"I helped to make them myself, every one," said he, proudly. "Is it not pretty music? I sometimes set one of them when I go to bed at night, and fall asleep listening to it. I am sure, then, to have pleasant dreams! But let us see your cameos. Perhaps I may buy one for Marie, if they are not too dear. Marie is my sweetheart, and we are to be married next week."

"Next week!" exclaimed Stefano. "That is very soon, Battisto has a sweetheart also, up at Impruneta; but they will have to wait a long time before they can buy the ring."

Battisto blushed like a girl.

"Hush, brother!" said he. "Show the cameos to Christien, and give your tongue a holiday!"

But Christien was not so to be put off.

"What is her name?" said he. "Tush! Battisto you must tell me her name! Is she pretty? Is she dark, or fair? Do you often see her when you are at home? Is she very fond of you? Is she as fond of you as Marie is of me?"

"Nay, how should I know that?" asked the soberer Battisto. "She loves me, and I love her—that is all."

"And her name?"

"Margherita."

"A charming name! And she is herself as pretty as her name, I'll engage. Did you say she was fair?"

"I said nothing about it one way or the other," said Battisto, unlocking a green box clamped with iron, and taking out tray after tray of his pretty wares. "There! Those pictures all inlaid in little bits are Roman mosaics—these flowers on a black ground are Florentine. The ground is of hard dark stone, and the flowers are made of thin slices of jasper, onyx, cornelian, and so forth. Those forget-me-nots, for instance, are bits of turquoise, and that poppy is cut from a piece of coral."

"I like the Roman ones best," said Christien. "What place is that with all the arches?"

"This is the Coliseum, and the one next to it is St Peter's. But we Florentines care little for the Roman work. It is not half so fine or so valuable as ours. The Romans make their mosaics of composition."

"Composition or no, I like the little landscapes best," said Christien. "There is a lovely one, with a pointed building, and a tree and, mountains at the back. How I should like that one for Marie!"

"You may have it for eight francs," replied Battisto; "we sold two of them yesterday for ten each. It represents the tomb of Caius Cestius, near Rome."

"A tomb!" echoed Christien, considerably dismayed. "Diable! That would be a dismal present to one's bride."

"She would never guess that it was a tomb, if you did not tell her," suggested Stefano.

Christien shook his head.

"That would be next door to deceiving her," said he.

"Nay," interposed my brother, "the owner of that tomb has been dead these eighteen or nineteen hundred years. One almost forgets that he was ever buried in it."

"Eighteen or nineteen hundred years? Then he was a heathen?"

"Undoubtedly, if by that you mean that he lived before Christ."

Christien's face lighted up immediately.

"Oh, that settles the question," said he, pulling out his little canvas purse, and paying his money down at once. "A heathen's tomb is as good as no tomb at all. I'll have it made into a brooch for her, at

Interlaken. Tell me, Battisto, what shall you take home to Italy for your Margherita?"

Battisto laughed, and chinked his eight francs, "That depends on trade," said he; "if we make good profits between this and Christmas, I may take her a Swiss muslin from Berne; but we have already been away seven months, and we have hardly made a hundred francs over and above our expenses."

And with this, the talk turned upon general matters, the Florentines locked away their treasures, Christien restrapped his pack, and my brother and all went down together, and breakfasted in the open air outside the inn.

It was a magnificent morning; cloudless and sunny, with a cool breeze that rustled in the vine upon the porch, and flecked the table with shifting shadows of green leaves. All around and about them stood the great mountains, with their blue-white glaciers bristling down to the verge of the pastures, and the pine-woods creeping darkly up their sides. To the left, the Wetterhorn; to the right, the Eigher; straight before them, dazzling and imperishable, like an obelisk of frosted silver, the Schreckhorn, or Peak of Terror. Breakfast over, they bade farewell to their hostess, and, mountain-staff in hand took the path to the Wengern Alp. Half in light, half in shadow, lay the quiet valley, dotted over with farms, and traversed by a torrent that rushed, milk-white, from its prison in the glacier. The three lads walked briskly in advance, their voices chiming together every now and then in chorus of laughter. Somehow my brother felt sad. He lingered behind, and, plucking a little red flower from the bank, watched it hurry away with the torrent, like a life on the stream of time. Why was his heart so heavy, and why were their hearts so light?

As the day went on, my brother's melancholy, and the mirth of the young men, seemed to increase. Full of youth and hope, they talked of the joyous future, and built up pleasant castles in the air. Battisto, grown more communicative, admitted that to marry Margherita, and become a master mosaicist, would fulfil the dearest dream of his life. Stefano, not being in love, preferred to travel. Christien, who seemed to be the most prosperous, declared that it was his darling ambition to rent a farm in his native Kander Valley, and lead the patriarchal life of his fathers. As for the musical-box trade, he said, one should live in Geneva to make it answer; and, for his part, he loved the pine-forests and the snow-peaks, better than all the towns in Europe. Marie, too, had been born among the mountains, and it would break her heart, if she thought she were to live in Geneva all her life, and never see the Kander Thal again. Chatting thus, the morning wore on to noon, and the party rested awhile in the shade of a clump of gigantic firs festooned with trailing banners of grey-green moss.

Here they ate their lunch, to the silvery music of one of Christien's little boxes, and by-and-by heard the sullen echo of an avalanche far away on the shoulder of the Jungfrau.

Then they went on again in the burning afternoon, to heights where the Alp-rose fails from the sterile steep, and the brown lichen grows more and more scantily among the stones. Here, only the bleached and barren skeletons of a forest of dead pines varied the desolate monotony; and high on the summit of the pass, stood a little solitary inn, between them and the sky.

At this inn they rested again, and drank to the health of Christien and his bride, in a jug of country wine. He was in uncontrollable spirits, and shook hands with them all, over and over again.

"By nightfall to-morrow," said he, "I shall hold her once more in my arms! It is now nearly two years since I came home to see her, at the end of my apprenticeship. Now I am foreman, with a salary of thirty francs a week, and well able to marry."

"Thirty francs a week!" echoed Battisto. "Corpo di Bacco! that is a little fortune."

Christien's face beamed.

"Yes." said he, "we shall be very happy; and, by-and-by—who knows?—we may end our days in the Kander Thal, and bring up our children to succeed us. Ah! If Marie knew that I should be there to-morrow night, how delighted she would be!"

"How so, Christien?" said my brother. "Does she not expect you?"

"Not a bit of it. She has no idea that I can be there till the day after to-morrow—nor could I, if I took the road all round by Unterseen and Frütigen. I mean to sleep to-night at Lauterbrunnen, and to-morrow morning shall strike across the Tschlingel glacier to Kander-steg. If I rise a little before daybreak, I shall be at home by sunset."

At this moment the path took a sudden turn, and began to descend in sight of an immense perspective of very distant valleys. Christien flung his cap into the air, and uttered a great shout.

"Look!" said he, stretching out his arms as if to embrace all the dear familiar scene: "O! Look! There are the hills and woods of Interlaken, and here, below the precipices on which we stand, lies Lauterbrunnen! God be praised, who has made our native land so beautiful!"

The Italians smiled at each other, thinking their own Arno valley far more fair; but my brother's heart warmed to the boy, and echoed his thanksgiving in that spirit which accepts all beauty as a birthright and an inheritance. And now their course lay across an immense plateau, all rich with corn-fields and meadows, and studded with substantial homesteads built of old brown wood, with huge sheltering eaves, and strings of Indian corn hanging like golden ingots along the carven balconies. Blue whortleberries grew beside the footway, and now and then came upon a wild gentian, or a star-shaped immortelle. Then the path became a mere zigzag on the face of the precipice, and in less than half an hour they reached the lowest level of the valley. The glowing afternoon had not yet faded from the uppermost pines, when they were all dining together in the parlour of a little inn looking to the Jungfrau. In the evening my brother wrote letters, while the three lads strolled about the village. At nine o'clock they bade each other good night, and went to their several rooms.

Weary as he was, my brother found it impossible to sleep. The same unaccountable melancholy still possessed him, and when at last he dropped into an uneasy slumber, it was but to start over and over again from frightful dreams, faint with a nameless terror. Towards morning, he fell into a profound sleep, and never woke until the day was fast advancing towards noon. He then found, to his regret, that Christien had long since gone. He had risen before daybreak, breakfasted by candlelight, and started off in the grey dawn— "as merry," said the host, "as a fiddler at a fair."

Stefano and Battisto were still waiting to see my brother, being charged by Christien with a friendly farewell message to him, and an invitation to the wedding. They, too, were asked, and meant to go; so, my brother agreed to meet them at Interlaken on the following

Tuesday, whence they might walk to Kandersteg by easy stages, reaching their destination on the Thursday morning, in time to go to church with the bridal party. My Brother then bought some of the little Florentine cameos, wished the two boys every good fortune, and watched them down the road till he could see them no longer.

Left now to himself, he wandered out with his sketch-book, and spent the day in the upper valley; at sunset, he dined alone in his chamber, by the light of a single lamp. This meal despatched, he drew nearer to the fire, took out a pocket edition of Goethe's Essays on Art, and promised himself some hours of pleasant reading. (Ah, how well I know that very book, in its faded cover, and how often I have heard him describe that lonely evening!) The night had by this time set in cold and wet. The damp logs spluttered on the hearth, and a wailing wind swept down the valley, bearing the rain in sudden gusts against the panes. My brother soon found that to read was impossible. His attention wandered incessantly. He read the same sentence over and over again, unconscious of its meaning, and fell into long trains of thought leading far into the dim past.

Thus the hours went by, and at eleven o'clock he heard the doors closing below, and the household retiring to rest. He determined to yield no longer to this dreaming apathy. He threw on fresh logs, trimmed the lamp, and took several turns about the room. Then he opened the casement, and suffered the rain to beat against his face, and the wind to ruffle his hair, as it ruffled the acacia leaves in the garden below. Some minutes passed thus, and when, at length, he closed the window and came back into the room, his face and hair and all the front of his shirt were thoroughly saturated. To unstrap his knapsack and take out a dry shirt was, of course, his first impulse —to drop the garment, listen eagerly, and start to his feet, breathless and bewildered, was the next.

For, borne fitfully upon the outer breeze, now sweeping past the window, now dying in the distance, he heard a well-remembered strain of melody, subtle and silvery as the "sweet airs" of Prospero's isle, and proceeding unmistakably from the musical-box which had, the day before, accompanied the lunch under the fir-trees of the Wengern Alp!

Had Christien come back, and was it thus that he announced his return? If so, where was he? Under the window? Outside in the corridor? Sheltering in the porch, and waiting for admittance? My brother threw open the casement again, and called him by his name.

"Christien! Is that you?"

All without was intensely silent. He could hear the last gust of wind and rain moaning farther and farther away upon its wild course down the valley, and the pine-trees shivering, like living things.

"Christien!" he said again, and his own voice seemed to echo strangely on his ear. "Speak! Is it you?"

Still no one answered. He leaned out into the dark night; but could see nothing—not even the outline of the porch below. He began to think that his imagination had deceived him, when suddenly the strain burst forth again;—this time, apparently in his own chamber.

As he turned, expecting to find Christien at his elbow, the sounds broke off abruptly, and a sensation of intensest cold seized him in every limb—not the mere chill of nervous terror, not the mere physical result of exposure to wind and rain, but a deadly freezing of every vein, a paralysis of every nerve, an appalling consciousness that in a few moments more the lungs must cease to play, and the heart to beat! Powerless to speak or stir, he closed his eyes, and believed that he was dying.

This strange faintness lasted but a few seconds. Gradually the vital warmth returned, and, with it, strength to close the window, and stagger to a chair. As he did so, he found the breast of his shirt all stiff and frozen, and the rain clinging in solid icicles upon his hair.

He looked at his watch. It had stopped at twenty minutes before twelve. He took his thermometer from the chimney-piece, and found the mercury at sixty-eight. Heavenly powers! How were these things possible in a temperature of sixty-eight degrees, and with a large fire blazing on the hearth?

He poured out half a tumbler of cognac, and drank it at a draught. Going to bed was out of the question. He felt that he dared not sleep—that he scarcely dared to think. All he could do, was, to change his linen, pile on more logs, wrap himself in his blankets, and sit all night in an easy-chair before the fire.

My brother had not long sat thus, however, before the warmth, and probably the nervous reaction, drew him off to sleep. In the morning he found himself lying on the bed, without being able to remember in the least how or when he reached it.

It was again a glorious day. The rain and wind were gone, and the Silverhorn at the end of the valley lifted its head into an unclouded sky. Looking out upon the sunshine, he almost doubted the events of the night, and, but for the evidence of his watch, which still pointed to twenty minutes before twelve, would have been disposed to treat the whole matter as a dream. As it was, he attributed more than half his terrors to the prompting of an overactive and over-wearied brain. For all this, he still felt depressed and uneasy, and so very unwilling to pass another night at Lauterbrunnen, that he made up his mind to proceed that morning to Interlaken. While he was yet loitering over his breakfast, and considering whether he should walk the seven miles of road, or hire a vehicle, a char came rapidly up to the inn door and a young man jumped out.

"Why, Battisto!" exclaimed my brother, in astonishment, as he came into the room; "what brings *you* here to-day? Where is Stefano?"

"I have left him at Interlaken, signor," replied the Italian.

Something there was in his voice, something in his face, both strange and startling.

"What is the matter?" asked my brother, breathlessly. "He is not ill? No accident has happened?"

Battisto shook his head, glanced furtively up and down the passage, and closed the door.

"Stefano is well, signor; but—but a circumstance has occurred— a circumstance so strange!—Signor, do you believe in spirits?"

"In spirits, Battisto?"

"Ay, signor; for if ever the spirit of any man, dead or living, appealed to human ears, the spirit of Christien came to me last night at twenty minutes before twelve o'clock."

"At twenty minutes before twelve o'clock!" repeated my brother.

"I was in bed, signor, and Stefano was sleeping in the same room. I had gone up quite warm, and had fallen asleep, full of pleasant thoughts. By-and-by, although I had plenty of bed-clothes, and a rug over me as well, I woke, frozen with cold and scarcely able to breathe. I tried to call to Stefano; but I had no power to utter the slightest sound. I thought my last moment was come. All at once, I heard a sound under the window—a sound which I knew to be Christien's musical-box; and it played as it played when we lunched under the fir-trees, except that it was more wild and strange and melancholy and most solemn to hear—awful to hear! Then, signor, it grew fainter and fainter—and then it seemed to float past upon the wind, and die away. When it ceased, my frozen blood grew warm again, and I cried out to Stefano. When I told him what had happened, he declared I had been only dreaming. I made him strike a light, that I might look at my watch. It pointed to twenty minutes before twelve, and had stopped there; and—stranger still—Stefano's watch had done the very same. Now tell me, signor, do you believe that there is any meaning in this, or do you think, as Stefano persists in thinking, that it was all a dream?"

"What is your own conclusion, Battisto?"

"My conclusion, signor, is that some harm has happened to poor Christien on the glacier, and that his spirit came to me last night."

"Battisto, he shall have help if living, or rescue for his poor corpse if dead; for I, too, believe that all is not well."

And with this, my brother told him briefly what had occurred to himself in the night; despatched messengers for the three best guides in Lauterbrunnen; and prepared ropes, ice-hatchets, alpenstocks, and all such matters necessary for a glacier expedition. Hasten as he would, however, it was nearly mid-day before the party started.

Arriving in about half an hour at a place called Stechelberg, they left the char, in which they had travelled so far, at a châlet, and ascended a steep path in full view of the Breithorn glacier, which rose up to the left, like a battlemented wall of solid ice. The way now lay for some time among pastures and pine-forests. Then they came to a little colony of châlets, called Steinberg, where they filled their water-bottles, got their ropes in readiness, and prepared for the Tschlingel glacier. A few minutes more, and they were on the ice.

At this point, the guides called a halt, and consulted together. One was for striking across the lower glacier towards the left, and reaching the upper glacier by the rocks which bound it on the south. The other two preferred the north, or right side; and this my brother finally took. The sun was now pouring down with almost tropical intensity, and the surface of the ice, which was broken into long treacherous fissures, smooth as glass and blue as the summer sky, was both difficult and dangerous. Silently and cautiously, they went, tied together at intervals of about three yards each: with two guides in front, and the third bringing up the rear. Turning presently to the right, they found themselves at the foot of a steep rock, some forty feet in height, up which they must climb to reach the upper glacier. The only way in which Battisto or my brother could hope to do this, was by the help of a rope steadied from below and above. Two of the guides accordingly clambered up the face of the crag by notches in the surface, and one ramained below. The rope was then let down, and my brother prepared to go first. As he planted his foot in the first notch, a smothered cry from Battisto arrested him.

"Santa Maria! Signor! Look yonder!"

My brother looked, and there (he ever afterwards declared), as surely as there is a heaven above us all, he saw Christien Baumann standing in the full sunlight, not a hundred yards distant! Almost in the same moment that my brother recognised him, he was gone. He neither faded, nor sank down, nor moved away; but was simply gone, as if he had never been. Pale as death, Battisto fell upon his knees, and covered his face with his hands. My brother, awe-stricken and speechless, leaned against the rock, and felt that the object of his journey was but too fatally accomplished. As for the guides, they could not conceive what had happened.

"Did you see nothing?" asked my brother and Battisto, both together.

But the men had seen nothing, and the one who had remained below, said, "What should I see but the ice and the sun?"

To this my brother made no other reply than by announcing his intention to have a certain crevasse, from which he had not once removed his eyes since he saw the figure standing on the brink, thoroughly explored before he went a step farther; whereupon the two men came down from the top of the crag, resumed the ropes, and followed my brother, incredulously. At the narrow end of the fissure, he paused, and drove his alpenstock firmly into the ice. It was an unusually long crevasse—at first a mere crack, but widening gradually as it went, and reaching down to unknown depths of dark deep blue, fringed with long pendent icicles, like diamond stalactites. Before they had followed the course of this crevasse for more than ten minutes, the youngest of the guides uttered a hasty exclamation.

"I see something!" cried he. "Something dark, wedged in the teeth of the crevasse, a great way down!"

K

They all saw it: a mere indistinguishable mass, almost closed over by the ice-walls at their feet. My brother offered a hundred francs to the man who would go down and bring it up. They all hesitated.

"We don't know what it is," said one.

"Perhaps it is only a dead chamois," suggested another.

Their apathy enraged him.

"It is no chamois," he said, angrily. "It is the body of Christien Baumann, native of Kandersteg. And, by Heaven, if you are all too cowardly to make the attempt, I will go down myself!"

The youngest guide threw off his hat and coat, tied a rope about his waist, and took a hatchet in his hand.

"I will go, monsieur," said he; and without another word, suffered himself to be lowered in. My brother turned away. A sickening anxiety came upon him, and presently he heard the dull echo of the hatchet far down in the ice. Then there was a call for another rope, and then—the men all drew aside in silence, and my brother saw the youngest guide standing once more beside the chasm, flushed and trembling, with the body of Christien lying at his feet.

Poor Christien! They made a rough bier with their ropes and alpenstocks, and carried him, with great difficulty, back to Steinberg. There, they got additional help as far as Stechelberg, where they laid him in the char, and so brought him on to Lauterbrunnen. The next day, my brother made it his sad business to precede the body to Kandersteg, and prepare his friends for its arrival. To this day, though all these things happened thirty years ago, he cannot bear to recall Marie's despair, or all the mourning that he innocently brought upon that peaceful valley. Poor Marie has been dead this many a year; and when my brother last passed through the Kander Thal on his way to the Ghemmi, he saw her grave, beside the grave of Christien Baumann, in the village burial-ground.

This is my brother's Ghost Story.

THE ENCHANTED WOMAN

Anna Kingsford

Anna Bonus Kingsford (1846-1888) was widely known and respected in Victorian scientific circles in the latter part of the nineteenth century and was for a time the distinguished President of The Hermetic Society. Educated at the Paris Faculty of Medicine, Miss Kingsford was a woman deeply devoted to learning and able to bring an enquiring and careful mind to her studies. It was this facility that enabled her to gain serious attention for her life-long study of dreams—a study undertaken primarily because she was herself particularly prone to them. She recorded a number of her own dreams, "written down as soon as possible after awaking from the slumber during which they presented themselves", and from the body of these I have selected the following item (dated 1877) which is heavily tinged with the occult. In her preface Miss Kingsford thought it best to note that "never have I taken opium, hashish or any other dream-producing agent—a cup of tea or coffee being the extent of my indulgences in this direction".

<hr/>

The first consciousness which broke my sleep last night was one of floating, of being carried swiftly by some invisible force through a vast space; then, of being gently lowered; then of light, until, gradually, I found myself on my feet in a broad noon day brightness, and before me an open country. Hills, hills, as far as the eye could reach, —hills with snow on their tops, and mists around their gorges. This was the first thing I saw distinctly. Then, casting my eyes towards the ground, I perceived that all about me lay huge masses of grey material which, at first, I took for blocks of stone, having the form of lions; but as I looked at them more intently, my sight grew clearer, and I saw, to my horror, that they were really alive. A panic seized me, and I tried to run away; but on turning, I became suddenly aware that the whole country was filled with these awful shapes; and the faces of those nearest to me were most dreadful for their eyes, and something in the expression, though not in the form, of their faces, were human. I was absolutely alone in a terrible world peopled with lions, too, of a monstrous kind. Recovering myself with an effort, I resumed my flight, but, as I passed through the midst of this concourse of monsters, it suddenly struck me that they were perfectly unconscious of my presence. I even laid my hands, in passing, on the heads and manes of several, but they gave no sign of seeing me or of knowing that I touched them. At last I gained the threshold of a great pavilion, not, apparently, built by hands, but formed by Nature. The walls were solid, yet they were composed of huge trees standing close together, like columns; and the roof of the pavilion was formed by their massive foliage, through which not a ray of outer light penetrated. Such light as there was seemed nebulous, and appeared to rise out of the ground. In the centre of this pavilion I stood alone, happy to have got clear away from those terrible beasts and the gaze of their steadfast eyes.

As I stood there, I became conscious of the fact that the nebulous light of the place was concentrating itself into a focus on the columned wall opposite to me. It grew there, became intenser, and then spread, revealing, as it spread, a series of moving pictures that appeared to be scenes actually enacted before me. For the figures in the pictures were living, and they moved before my eyes, though I heard neither word nor sound. And this is what I saw. First there came a writing on the wall of the pavilion:—"This is the History of our World." These words, as I looked at them, appeared to sink into the wall as they had risen out of it, and to yield place to the pictures which then began to come out in succession, dimly at first, then strong and clear as actual scenes.

First I beheld a beautiful woman, with the sweetest face and most perfect form conceivable. She was dwelling in a cave among the hills with her husband, and he, too, was beautiful, more like an angel than a man. They seemed perfectly happy together; and their dwelling was like Paradise. On every side was beauty, sunlight, and repose. This picture sank into the wall as the writing had done. And then came out another; the same man and woman driving together in a sleigh drawn by reindeer over fields of ice; with all about them glaciers and snow, and great mountains veiled in wreaths of slowly moving mist. The sleigh went at a rapid pace, and its occupants talked gaily to each other, so far as I could judge by their smiles and the movement of their lips. But, what caused me much surprise was that they carried between them, and actually in their hands, a glowing flame, the fervour of which I felt reflected from the picture upon my own cheeks. The ice around shone with its brightness. The mists upon the snow mountains caught its gleam. Yet, strong as were its light and heat, neither the man nor the woman seemed to be burned or dazzled by it. This picture, too, the beauty and brillancy of which greatly impressed me, sank and disappeared as the former.

Next, I saw a terrible looking man clad in an enchanter's robe, standing alone upon an ice-crag. In the air above him, poised like a dragon-fly, was an evil spirit, having a head and face like that of a human being. The rest of it resembled the tail of a comet, and seemed made of a green fire, which flickered in and out as though swayed by a wind. And as I looked, suddenly, through an opening among the hills, I saw the sleigh pass, carrying the beautiful woman and her husband; and in the same instant the enchanter also saw it, and his face contracted, and the evil spirit lowered itself and came between me and him. Then this picture sank and vanished.

I next beheld the same cave in the mountains which I had before seen, and the beautiful couple together in it. Then a shadow darkened the door of the cave; and the enchanter was there, asking admittance; cheerfully they bade him enter, and, as he came forward with his snake-like eyes fixed on the fair woman, I understood that he wished to have her for his own and was even then devising how to bear her away. And the spirit in the air beside him seemed busy suggesting schemes to this end. Then this picture melted and became confused, giving place for but a brief moment to another, in which I saw the enchanter carrying the woman away in his arms, she struggling and lamenting, her long bright hair streaming behind her. This scene passed from the wall as though a wind had swept over it, and there rose up in its place a picture, which impressed me with a more vivid sense of reality than all the rest.

It represented a market place, in the midst of which was a pile of faggots and a stake, such as were used formerly for the burning of heretics and witches. The market place, round which were rows of seats as though for a concourse of spectators, yet appeared quite deserted. I saw only three living beings present,—the beautiful woman, the enchanter, and the evil spirit. Nevertheless, I thought that the seats were really occupied by invisible tenants, for every now and then there seemed to be a stir in the atmosphere as of a great multitude; and I had, moreover, a strange sense of facing many witnesses. The enchanter led the woman to the stake, fastened her there with iron chains, lit the faggots about her feet and withdrew to a short distance, where he stood with his arms folded, looking on as the flames rose about her. I understood that she had refused his love, and that in his fury he had denounced her as a sorceress. Then in the fire, above the pile, I saw the evil spirit poising itself like a fly, and rising and sinking and fluttering in the thick smoke. While I wondered what this meant, the flames which had concealed the beautiful woman, parted in their midst, and disclosed a sight so horrible and unexpected as to thrill me from head to foot, and curdle my blood. Chained to the stake there stood, not the fair woman I had seen there a moment before, but a hideous monster,—a woman still, but a woman with three heads, and three bodies linked in one. Each of her long arms ended, not in a hand, but in a claw like that of a bird of rapine. Her hair resembled the locks of the classic Medusa, and her faces were inexpressibly loathsome. She seemed, with all her dreadful heads and limbs, to writhe in the flames and yet not to be consumed by them. She gathered them in to herself; her claws caught them and drew them down; her triple body appeared to suck the fire into itself, as though a blast drove it. The sight appalled me. I covered my face and dared look no more.

When at length I again turned my eyes upon the wall, the picture that had so terrified me was gone, and instead of it, I saw the enchanter flying through the world, pursued by the evil spirit and that dreadful woman. Through all the world they seemed to go. The scenes changed with marvellous rapidity. Now the picture glowed with the wealth and gorgeousness of the torrid zone; now the ice-fields of the North rose into view; anon a pine-forest; then a wild sea-shore; but always the same three-flying figures; always the horrible three-formed harpy pursuing the enchanter, and besides her the evil spirit with the dragon-fly wings.

At last this succession of images ceased, and I beheld a desolate region, in the midst of which sat the woman with the enchanter beside her, his head reposing in her lap. Either the sight of her must have become familiar to him and, so, less horrible, or she had subjugated him by some spell. At all events, they were mated at last, and their offspring lay around them on the stony ground, or moved to and fro. These were lions,—monsters with human faces, such as I had seen in the beginning of my dream. Their jaws dripped blood; they paced backwards and forwards, lashing their tails. Then too, this picture faded and sank into the wall as the others had done. And through its melting outlines came out again the words I had first seen:—"This is the History of our World," only they seemed to me in some way changed, but how, I cannot tell. The horror of the whole thing was too strong upon me to let me dare look longer at the wall. And I awoke, repeating to myself the question, "How could one woman become three?"

BOUND BY A SPELL

The Hon. Mrs Greene

The Honourable Mrs Louisa Greene (1833-1886), was the daughter of the third Baron Plunket and like a great many other Victorian authoresses, produced a large number of novels and stories during her lifetime, few of which have survived the period and most of which are completely unknown today. It has been my pleasure here, and in a previous anthology, to remedy this state of affairs by reprinting some of the best of their work. In the case of Mrs Greene it gives me especial pleasure because she was an adventurous writer who always sought to introduce new and unusual elements to her stories. *Bound By A Spell* (1885)— or "The Hunted Witch of the Forest" as the novel is subtitled— is a good example of her skill with its plot and counterplot. Beginning simply as the story of the persecution of a much-feared witch, it subsequently introduces episodes about the art of levitation, a pact with the devil and a particularly good section about a werewolf. As the art of lycanthropy has not yet been mentioned in these pages—and as it is an important element of witchcraft—it is from this part of the book which I take the following piece of splendid macabre storytelling.

∞∞∞∞∞∞∞∞∞∞∞∞∞∞∞∞∞∞∞∞∞∞∞∞∞∞∞∞∞∞

In the eyes of the villagers of Protogno, Christine Delemont was nothing more or less than a witch, a God-forsaken woman, whose life was appointed to be a bane and a terror to all who came in contact with her or within the range of her ill-omened presence. If one yielded credence to all these stories, one would have to believe tales so dark and strange of the doings at her deserted cottage, that one could not but shudder at the very name of so inhuman a woman; and many people were even found to swear that they had been eye-witnesses of Christine's mysterious and cruel doings: how they had seen her child, little Paul, beaten and dashed upon the floor of the cottage and dragged by the hair of his head about the garden. How, also, flames were seen at night-time issuing from the doors and windows of the house, and direful howlings and groanings were heard both by day and night in the woods around. And strange and appalling as were these stories, few voices were raised to deny them, or other tales as extraordinary, which were freely adduced to darken the history of Christine.

But even these wild reports might have found in time few believers, and have perished for want of evidence, had it not been for other and fresh circumstances which fanned into a fiery blaze the smouldering doubts and suspicions of the village folk.

It was late on an autumn afternoon, when the reapers, who had been toiling all day under a blazing sun, were returning from their work into the little town of Protogno. Many had taken off their broad shady hats, so that the little breeze which had sprung up with the decline of the sun might blow through their hair and cool their over-heated heads. As if by one accord they filed down the main street of the town, neither halting at house or shop until they reached the market-place, in front of which stood the Fountain of St Agnes, and whose bright and cool waters had an attraction for their parched lips which only those who, like themselves, had toiled all day long under a meridian sun, could understand. Besides, this fountain was, as it were, the village club. As the hour of six tolled from the high bell-tower of the church which crowned the summit of an over-shadowing hill, not only the workmen from the fields, but artisans, shopkeepers, and, above all, the village gossips assembled round the Fountain of St Agnes, which, with its shady row of trees, and comfortable benches set here and there in every nook and corner, made a most inviting resting-place; and here the village politics, the daily doings, the births, deaths, and marriages of the little town were chronicled with more or less solemnity as the importance of the cases required.

This evening the fountain, with its picturesque and quaint

carvings, looked particularly tempting, for the sun, which was setting in a crimson flood of light behind the hill, had caught the market-place with its last and most lovely rays, and the fountain, the trees, and the waters tossing high up into the rose-coloured air, looked more like some painted scene in a theatre than the quiet and every-day resort of the poor and the weary. The benches were speedily filled with those who had already quenched their thirst, their bright sickles lying at their feet on the ground, or hanging from the branches of the trees above their heads. Many were still gathered around the base of the fountain, satisfying their thirst, while a few, who could not find a place by the fountain itself, handed their tin pannikins over the heads of their neighbours into some friendly hands, which returned them again filled with the fresh water their parched throats so much coveted to taste.

But all at once, while the jest and the laugh went round, and Frau Gartmann, the queen-gossip of the town, was quizzing in a covert whisper a handsome couple who stood near the fountain, chatting playfully with each other, there was a sudden hoarse cry of horror and surprise raised amongst the crowd, and, as if to add to the theatrical appearance of the scene, a man suddenly appeared in their midst, whose blood-stained garments, blenched face, and panic-stricken eyes carried a sudden terror into the hearts of all who looked upon him.

It was no other than Silvestro Milano, a reaper like themselves, who had been out all day cutting corn in a distant field near Madeline l'Estrange's Wood. He was a brave and honest-hearted fellow, courageous as a lion, and tender-hearted as a woman, and now he stood among them with his blouse stained with gore, and hanging in ribbons from his bleeding arms; his sickle also had been dipped in blood up to its wooden handle, and he staggered, as he approached the fountain, like a drunken man. He gazed around him at first in a vacant way, and then, pointing towards the fountain, he stretched out his torn and bleeding arm. The neighbours understood his unspoken request, and instantly a score of pannikins running over with clear water were pressed upon his acceptance.

He drank deeply, and then, tottering towards a seat, sank upon it, and remained for some time in a semi-unconscious state, unable to answer the questions of those who pressed around him, and yet looking at them with an anxiety in his eyes which told of a troubled spirit within.

At last he spoke, and so great was the silence that ensued that a grasshopper on a neighbouring tree could be distinctly heard rasping out its evening call.

"I have met the accursed wolf that killed Alexandre Delemont in the forest, and I have slain it. It is now lying cold and dead in the flower-garden where I plunged this sickle into its heart."

At these words a murmur, which had been gradually rising out of the previous hush, now burst into a loud shout or yell of triumph and applause.

"Bravo, bravo, Silvestro! tell us, good friend, how did it all happen?" cried the foremost of the group, as they pressed forwards to catch his gasping efforts at speech.

"Aye, aye; give me time, give me time; for the horror of the thing is still upon me, and I fancy even now I hear the cry of the miserable child."

"What child?"

"Peace, peace! leave me a moment to recall my thoughts. Aye, it was thus that it happened. I had finished my reaping for the day, and I was weary; my back ached and my head was giddy from the long stooping under the most burning sun that ever crossed the sky; so, withdrawing under the shadow of a tree close by the Count's cottage, I sat down to rest, and presently I fell asleep. I do not know how long I slept, but I awoke feeling something soft touching the back of my hand, and then my cheek. I opened my eyes quietly, thinking perhaps a lizard or field mouse had run up my coat-sleeve, when, standing by me, I saw a little child, all dressed in white. I tell ye," cried Silvestro, raising himself up in his excitement, and almost rising to his feet as he spoke, "I tell ye, good folk, I thought it was a vision sent from Heaven. The babe was fair as wax, and beautiful as the child which the Madonna carries in her arms. Its hair, which was of the purest flaxen, hung long over its shoulders, and its eyes gazed into mine as if it sought to gain my love.

"For a moment, awaking as it were from a dream, I thought in my confusion it was our blessed Lord Himself standing once more as a child on the earth beside me—that He had a message, perhaps, to give me; but presently, seeing the boy smile and stretch out his hands to me, I shook off the foolish impression, and I cried out encouragingly, 'Eh, little one, to whom dost thou belong?'

"It smiled again, and with a clear sweet voice it answered me strangely enough, 'A Dieu.' "

Again a low sympathetic murmur rose around Silvestro, but it came chiefly from the women, and there was the sound of a dry sob not far off, followed by the words, "Go on, go on—what next?" and Silvestro, looking up, saw, through a haze of weakness, the lovely face of Marie Fedele gazing earnestly at him.

"Aye, what next?" he repeated, as if questioning himself, for a faintness was stealing over him and his mind was growing clouded and uncertain; "I cannot just now remember what came next, only I know the child, hearing a sound in the garden, turned anxiously and hurried from me, but it cannot have been many minutes, when crossing the field on my way home I heard a piercing cry. May I never hear such a cry on this earth again!" said Silvestro, as he passed his hand languidly across his forehead. "I stopped, and turning towards the cottage, I listened. There was silence for a space, and I was thinking of continuing my way home, when I heard the same cry once more, only this time even more bitter in its anguish, and repeated again and yet again.

"I did not hesitate now, but ran as fast as my feet could carry me towards the spot from which the sound came; and as I drew near to the garden hedge, just where a narrow path leads down across the bridge into the forest, I saw a wolf, dark, large, and terrible to look at, hurrying down this very path with something white in its mouth, which all at once I perceived to be nothing else than the child which had stood before me but a few minutes previously, smiling in the security of its innocent trust and love.

"Yes! but the sight was so pitiful, my very limbs seemed to grow weak with horror, and though I strove to run, my legs doubled under me like hempstalks. I know not how I ran, nor how often I stumbled in this nightmare chase, until I came on a lock of fair flaxen hair torn from the little one's glossy head and caught on a bramble at my side, and then, as it were, the strength and courage of something more powerful than myself seemed to enter into me. I stumbled no longer, but cutting through the thicket I doubled on the beast, and came, for a moment, face to face with its burning eyes and its bristling mane, while the child still drooped from the creature's mouth, and its white arm trailed along the ground."

"Ah, say no more; is it not dead?" sobbed Marie Fedele, as she laid her head on her husband's shoulder and hid her face from view.

"Have patience for a moment. When I am questioned I lose the thread of my thoughts." Once again Silvestro passed his hand across his eyes as if to hide out some vision of horror, and then he proceeded slowly.

"It turned, the great coward, as I drew my sickle from my belt, and fearing to meet me, it leaped over a low bush, and made back with haste across the wooden bridge towards the house. I saw then what I had to deal with—no common brute such as God Himself places in the forest, but one of those tailless monsters whose existence until now I had never believed in: a wicked were-wolf, with slinking steps, whose every movement filled me with disgust. Full of some strange and ever-increasing strength, I followed after it, gaining each moment on its track, though it hurried forward with ever longer and more sinuous steps. At last, driven as it were almost to bay, it took the direct path towards the cottage, and, slinking through the narrow garden gate, passed in. At once I saw my advantage; I closed the gate with a sudden click that sent the hasp straight into the lock, and then, unless it dashed in at the open housedoor, it had no hole or possible outlet for escape. Round and round the garden I hunted it, my sharp sickle ever in my outstretched arm, until at last, with a kind of crying snarl, it dropped the child from its blood-stained jaws, and, turning with a sudden fury towards me, it sprang forward to meet me. It was its last hope, its last chance for life, and verily I gave myself up for lost; but seeing the child lie in a white heap on the gravel path, the same infant which had stood before me so lately in its purity and love, I thought of Him who carries the little lambs in His bosom, and though the beast leaped on me, and as it were wrestled with me, and though I felt its jaws snap on my shoulder and its claws tear the flesh from my arm, still the good God guided the weapon in my hand so that I struck it right home to its craven heart, and with a kind of human cry it fell backwards upon the flower-beds behind us, and then rolled over on its side, dead; aye, dead." Silvestro paused: "Aye, dead and stiff, as I shall be myself by-and-by."

It was not a murmur, but a loud yell of stunning overpowering applause which followed on the recital of Silvestro's victory; but he motioned to them to be quiet, and taking up his story from where he had left off, he continued—

"When I saw that the beast was dead, and would no more rise to attack us, I leaped over its carcase, and stepping across a bed of roses and lavender, I came to the spot where the child still lay, to all appearances dead. I stooped to raise it in my arms, but as I did so I heard behind me a loud, sharp cry of pain or anger or surprise, and looking up, I saw Christine Delemont rushing out of the cottage towards the child; she pushed me aside with a frantic gesture, and when I would have stretched out my arm to stay her, she rushed past me and herself lifted up the little one, whose head hung quite loosely to one side, and whose white frock was all stained with blood.

"I know not whether it was a wild despair or a fierce anger or a mad fit which had come over the woman, but Christine screamed and beat herself on her breast and tore her hair from her head, and at length she rushed into the house with the boy in her arms, and the door slammed behind her in my face, in my very face! and though I sought to follow after her, she either did not or would not hear me. I waited in the garden and paced up and down the paths till I grew weak from loss of blood. It was all in vain. At last I turned back and tapped at a window, the curtain of which was drawn. I felt too weak to return without a glass of wine or something wherewith to strengthen myself ere I ventured on the long walk home, but I could obtain no answer; only just as I moved aside, I heard a voice inside the room raised as it were in bitter anguish, and crying aloud, 'Speak, speak, in the name of God, speak, child, speak!" And then, like as it were a sigh or a sound of some far-off voice, I heard the words 'A Dieu,' and I knew it was the babe I had seen in the wood, and I offered up thanks that it still lived."

"Now, Heaven be praised!" cried Marie Fedele; "for if ever there was an angel on earth, it is that child."

"Aye," cried Frau Gartmann, "and if ever there was a foul witch, it is Christine Delemont. From the day she entered that cottage until now, death and destruction have followed in her path."

"Yes," cried a third, "she is a witch, and worse than a witch. It is well known that she keeps that miserable child as a decoy to entice those she hates into her power, and afterwards to wreak her vengeance on them. Ah, the wretch! She ought to be shot through the heart herself; the were-wolf will not cease to haunt the town till her own heart's blood has been spilled."

"How so, Janette?" cried several voices in the crowd; "Did not Silvestro slay it with his sickle?"

"Aye, aye, he slew the shadow, but the real wolf is bound up in the heart of that wicked woman, and, believe me, she will never cease to revenge herself on all who come within her reach until the sickle is plunged into her own bosom. Let those who do not know what a were-wolf is, ask me," cried Janette Chaudron; "I can tell them all about it."

"Then how came it to pass that Christine called on God in her anguish? Didst not thou say so, good Silvestro?" said Marie Fedele, her voice tremulous with anger; but if any explanation was given to her question it was lost in the murmur of the crowd, for Silvestro Milano, while speaking, had suddenly fainted away upon the bench, and as his tall son Pierre and others lifted him up tenderly in their arms, it was noticed how, all the time he had been relating his adventure, a pool of blood had been gathering on the ground at his feet.

[*Editor's Note. As the story of* Bound By A Spell *continues, it becomes obvious that the unfortunate Christine Delemont is not a willing practitioner of witchcraft but possessed by an evil spirit which had bound her to the were-wolf. The intervention of a friendly traveller eventually enables her to not only rid herself of the spirit but also end the dreadful suspicions of the villagers of Protogno.*]

THE WITCH OF THE MARSH

Mrs Ethel Marriott-Watson

Mrs Ethel Marriott-Watson (1858-1903) was born and lived for most of her life in a remote area of Cornwall and much of the atmosphere of the following story is obviously derived from that part of the country. She contributed a great deal of poetry to women's weekly newspapers and magazines, but her fictional tales are few and far between. To anyone who was familiar with her gentle and lilting verse, "The Witch of the Marsh" (1893) may well have come as something of a surprise, containing as it does several quite unnerving incidents. And, limited as it may be in some ways, it still has a nice ring of horror about it which many writers since have struggled to achieve.

It was nigh upon dusk when I drew close to the Great Marsh, and already the white vapours were about, riding across the sunken levels like ghosts in a churchyard. Though I had set forth in a mood of wild delight, I had sobered in the lonely ride across the moor and was now uneasily alert. As my horse jerked down the grassy slopes that fell away to the jaws of the swamp I could see thin streams of mist rise slowly, hover like wraiths above the long rushes, and then, turning gradually more material, go blowing heavily away across the flat. The appearance of the place at this desolate hour, so remote from human society and so darkly significant of evil presences, struck me with a certain wonder that she should have chosen this spot for our meeting. She was a familiar of the moors, where I had invariably encountered her; but it was like her caprice to test my devotion by some such dreary assignation.

The prospect depressed me beyond reason, but the fact of her neighbourhood drew me on, and my spirits mounted at the thought that at last she was to put me in possession of herself. Tethering my horse upon the verge of the swamp, I soon discovered the path that crossed it, and entering struck out boldly for the heart. The track could have been little used, for the reeds, which stood high above the level of my eyes upon either side, straggled everywhere across in low arches, through which I dodged, and broke my way with some inconvenience and much impatience. A full half hour I was solitary in that wilderness, and when at last a sound other than my own footsteps broke the silence the dusk had fallen.

I was moving very slowly at the time, with a mind half disposed to turn from the expedition, which it seemed to me now must surely be a jest she had played upon me. While some such reluctance held me, I was suddenly arrested by a hoarse croaking which broke out upon my left, sounding somewhere from the reeds in the black mire. A little farther it came again from close at hand, and when I had passed on a few more steps in wonder and perplexity, I heard it for the third time. I stopped and listened, but the marsh was as a grave, and so taking the noise for the signal of some raucous frog, I resumed my way. But in a little the croaking was repeated, and coming quickly to a stand I pushed the reeds aside and peered into the darkness.

I could see nothing, but at the immediate moment of my pause I thought I detected the sound of somebody trailing me through the rushes. My distaste for the adventure grew with this suspicion, and had it not been for my infatuation I would have assuredly turned back and ridden home. The sound pursued me at intervals along the track, until at last, irritated beyond endurance by the sense of this persistent and invisible company, I broke into a sort of run. This, it seemed, the creature (whatever it was) could not achieve, for I heard no more of it, and continued my way in peace. My path at length ran out from among the reeds upon the smooth flat of which she had spoken, and here my heart quickened, and the gloom of the place lifted.

The flat lay in the very centre of the marsh, and here and there in it a gaunt brush or withered tree rose like a spectre against the white

L

mists. At the farther end I fancied some kind of building loomed up; but the fog which had been gathering ever since my entrance upon the passage sailed down upon me at that moment and the prospect went out with suddenness. As I stood waiting for the clouds to pass, a voice cried to me out of its centre, and I saw her next second with bands of mist swirling about her body, come rushing to me from the darkness. She put her long arms about me, and, drawing her close, I looked into her deep eyes. Far down in them, it seemed to me, I could discern a mystic laughter dancing in the wells of light.

"At last," she said, "at last, my beloved!" I caressed her.

"Why," said I, tingling at the nerves, "why have you put this journey between us? And what mad freak is your presence in this swamp?"

She uttered her silver laugh, and nestled to me again.

"I am the creature of this place," she answered. "This is my home. I have sworn you should behold me in my native sin ere you ravished me away."

"Come, then," said I, "I have seen; let there be an end of this. I know you, what you are. This marsh chokes up my heart. God forbid you should spend more of your days here. Come."

"You are in haste," she cried. "There is yet much to learn. Look, my friend," she said, "you who know me, what I am. This is my prison, and I have inherited its properties. Have you no fear?"

For answer I pulled her to me, and her warm lips drove out the horrid humours of the night; but the swift passage of a flickering mockery over her eyes struck me as a flash of lightning, and I grew chill again.

"I have the marsh in my blood," she whispered; "the marsh and the fog of it. Think ere you vow to me, for I am the cloud in a starry night."

A lithe and lovely creature, palpably of warm flesh, she lifted her magic face to mine and besought me plaintively with these words. The dews of the nightfall hung on her lashes, and seemed to plead with me for her forlorn and solitary plight.

"Behold!" I cried, "witch or devil of the marsh, you shall come with me! I have known you on the moors, a roving apparition of beauty; nothing more I know, nothing more I ask. I care not what this dismal haunt means, nor again these strange and mystic eyes.

You have powers and senses above me; your sphere and habits are as mysterious and incomprehensible as your beauty. But that." I said, "is mine, and the world that is mine shall be yours also."

She moved her head nearer to me with an antic gesture, and her gleaming eyes glanced up at me with a sudden flash, the similitude (great heavens!) of a hooded snake. Starting, I fell away, but at that moment she turned her face and set it fast towards the fog that came rolling in thick volumes over the flat. Noiselessly the great cloud crept down upon us, and all dazed and troubled I watched her watching it in silence. It was as if she awaited some omen, and I too trembled in the fear of its coming.

Then suddenly out of the night issued the hoarse and hideous croaking I had head upon my journey here. I reached out my arm to take her hand, but in an instant the mists broke over us, and I was groping in the vacancy. Something like panic took hold of me, and, beating through the blind obscurity, I rushed over the flat, calling upon her. In a little the swirl went by, and I perceived her upon the margin of the swamp, her arm raised as in imperious command, I ran to her, but stopped, amazed and shaken by a fearful sight. Low by the dripping reeds crouched a small squat thing, in the likeness of a monstrous frog, coughing and choking in its throat. As I stared, the creature rose upon its legs and disclosed a human resemblance. Its face was white and thin, with long black hair; its body gnarled and twisted as with the ague of a thousand years. In a flash of horror I realised this monster had once been a man!

Shaking, the creature whined in a breathless voice, pointing a skeleton finger at the woman by my side.

"Your eyes were my guide," it quavered. "Do you think that after all these years I have no knowledge of your eyes? Lo, is there aught of evil in you I am not instructed in? This is the Hell you designed for me, and now you would leave me to a greater one still."

The wretch paused, and panting leaned upon a bush, while she stood silent, mocking him with her eyes, and soothing my terror with her soft touch.

"Hear!" he cried, turning to me, "hear the tale of this woman that you may know her as she is. She is the witch of the marshes. Woman or Devil I know not, but only that the accursed marsh has crept into her soul and she herself has become its Evil Spirit; she herself, that lives and grows young and beautiful by it, has its full power to blight and chill and slay. I, who was once as you are, have this knowledge. What bones lie deep in this swamp who can say but she? She has drained of health, she has drained of mind and of soul; what is between her and her desire that she should not drain also of life? She has made me a devil in her Hell, and now she would leave me to my solitary pain, and go search for another victim. But she shall not!" he screamed through his chattering teeth; "she shall not! My Hell is also hers! She shall not!"

Her smiling untroubled eyes left his face and turned to me: she put out her arms, swaying towards me, and so fervid and so great a light glowed in her face that, as one distraught of superhuman means, I took her into my embrace. And then the madness seized me.

"Woman or witch," I said, "I will go with you! Of what account this pitiful past? Blight me even as that wretch, so long as you are with me!"

She laughed, and, disengaging herself, leaned, half-clinging to me, towards the coughing creature by the mire.

"Come," I cried, catching her by the waist. "Come!" She laughed again a silver-ringing laugh. She moved with me slowly across the flat to where the track started for the portals of the marsh. She laughed and clung to me.

But at the edge of the track I was startled by a shrill, hoarse screaming; and behold, from my very feet, that loathsome creature rose up and wound his long black arms about her, shrieking and crying in his pain. Stooping I pushed him from her skirts, and with one sweep of my arm drew her across the pathway; as her face passed mine her eyes were wide and smiling.

Then of a sudden the still mist enveloped us once more; but ere it descended I had a glimpse of that contorted figure trembling on the margin, the white face drawn and full of desolate pain. At the sight an icy shiver ran through me. And then through the yellow gloom the shadow of her darted past me to the further side. I heard the hoarse cough, the dim noise of a struggle, a swishing sound, a thin cry, and then the sucking of the slime over something in the rushes. I leapt forward: and once again the fog thinned, and I beheld her, woman or devil, standing upon the verge, and peering with smiling eyes into the foul and sickly bog.

With a sharp cry wrung from my nerveless soul, I turned and fled down the narrow way from that accursed spot; and as I ran the thickening fog closed round me, and I heard far off, yet never lessening, the silver sound of her mocking laughter.

YE LYTTLE SALEM MAIDE

Pauline Mackie

Pauline Bradford Mackie (1859–1919) a noted writer of historical
stories appears in this anthology because her contribution
deals with the most famous of all witchcraft 'outbreaks'—that at
Salem in 1692. There can be few readers who are not familiar
with this dark chapter in American history when a group of men
and women were tried and sentenced on the flimsiest of evidence,
accused of practising witchcraft and devilry. Several major
historical figures emerged from the trials, probably the most
infamous being Cotton Mather, a Boston minister, who ruthlessly
led many of the persecutions and whose name spread terror
throughout the country. In her novel, *Ye Lyttle Salem Maide*
(1901), copies of which are now very rare, Miss Mackie cleverly
combined fact with fiction telling the story of a small girl innocently caught up in the witch hysteria and encountering several
of the real-life characters. In this extract the child, Deliverance,
is already being held in prison for questioning on a charge brought
by a bigoted town official, Sir Jonathan Jamieson. And any hope
of her acquittal seems in imminent danger by the arrival in the
town of Mr Cotton Mather.

∽∽∽∽∽∽∽∽∽∽∽∽∽∽∽∽∽∽∽∽∽∽∽∽∽∽∽∽∽∽∽∽∽

Now, upon the day of our story, ye godly minister Mr Cotton
Mather was in Salem in attendance upon the trial of an old woman,
whose spectre had appeared to several people and terrified them with
horrible threats. Furthermore, the Beadle had testified to having

seen her "Dead Shape" lurking in the very pulpit of the church. It was with unusual relish Cotton Mather had heard her condemnation to death, considering her crime, in particular, deliberate treason to the Lord.

As he stepped from the hot and dusty court into the fresh air, salt with the sea and bright with the sunshine, a great rush of gladness filled his heart, and he mentally framed a prayer that with God's assistance he might rid this fair, new land of witches, and behold the church of his fathers firmly established. Leaving his horse for the present where it was tied to the hitching-post, outside the meeting-house, he walked slowly down the village street to the inn, there to have luncheon before setting out for Boston Town.

The fruit trees growing adown the street were green, and cast little clumps of shadow on the cobblestone pavement. And he thought of their fruitage—being minded to happy thoughts at remembrance of duty done—in the golden autumn, when the stern Puritans held a feast day in thanksgiving to the Lord.

All the impassioned tenderness of the poet awoke in him at the sight of these symbolical little trees.

"And there are the fair fruit trees," he murmured, "and also the trees of emptiness."

Now he bowed to a group of the gossips knitting on a door-stoop in the sun, and now he stooped to set upon its feet a little child that had fallen. At the stocks he dispelled sternly a group of boys who were tickling the feet of the writhing prisoners.

Thus, in one of the rarely serene moments of his troubled life, he made his leisurely way.

But only his exalted mood, wrapping him as an invisible, impenetrable garment, enabled him to pass thus serenely.

To every one else a weight of terror hung like a pall. The awful superstition seemed in the very air they breathed. How unnatural the blue sky! What a relief to their strained nerves would have been another mighty storm! Then might they have shrieked the terror which possessed them, but now the villagers spoke in whispers, so terrible the silence of the bright noonday. And many, although aware of the fact that the evil spirits were mostly abroad at night, yet longed for the darkness to come and cover them. No man dared glance at his neighbour. From one cottage came the cry of a babe yet in swaddling clothes, deserted by its panic-stricken mother, who believed it possessed by an evil spirit.

Yet, mechanically the villagers pursued their daily duties.

At the tavern Cotton Mather found Judge Samuel Sewall and the schoolmaster—who acted as clerk in court—conversing over their mugs of sack. Pleased to fall in with such company, he drew his stool up to their table.

"Alas, my dear friend," said the good judge, "this witchery business weighs heavy on my soul! I cannot forseee an end to it, and know not who will next be cried out upon. 'Tis a sorry jest, I wot, but meseemeth, in time, the hangman will be the only man left in this afflicted township. E'en my stomach turns 'gainst my best loved dishes."

On the younger man's serene, almost exalted face came a humanizing gleam of gentle ridicule. "Then indeed has the Lord used this witchery business to one godly purpose, at least, if you do turn from things of the flesh, Samuel." A rare sweetness, born of the serenity of his mind and his friendship, was in his glance.

"Nay, nay," spoke the good judge, gruffly, " 'tis an ill conscience and an haughty stomach go together. No liking have I for the man who turns from his food. Alas, that such a man should be I and I should be such a man!" he groaned. "The face of that child we condemned troubles me o' nights."

A menacing frown transformed Cotton Mather's face, and he was changed from the genial friend into the Protestant priest, imperious in his decisions. He struck his hand heavily on the table. "Shall we, then, be wrought upon by a round cheek and tender years, and shrink from doing the Lord's bidding? Most evil is the way of such a maid, and more to be dreaded than all the old hags of Christendom."

"Ay," joined in the schoolmaster, "most evil is the way of such a maid! Strange rumours are afloat regarding her. 'Tis said, that for the peace of the community she cannot be hanged too soon. 'Tis whispered that the glamour of her way has e'en cast a spell on the old jailer. Moreover, the woman of Ipswich, who was hanged a fortnight ago, did pray that the witch-maid be saved. Now 'tis an uncanny thing, as all the world knows, that one witch should desire good to another witch."

Cotton Mather turned a terrible glance upon the great judge. "O fool!" he cried, "do you not perceive the work of the Devil in all this? The woman of Ipswich would have had the witch-maid saved that her own black spirit might pass into this fair child's form, and thus, with double force, working in one body, the two would wreak evil on the world."

"Nay, nay," protested the judge, "my flesh is weaker than my willing spirit, and, I fear me, wrought upon by a fair seeming and the vanity of outward show. But we must back to court, my good friend," he added, addressing the schoolmaster.

So the two arose and donned their steeple-hats and took their walking-sticks, and arm-in-arm they went slowly down the middle of the street.

Cotton Mather, as he lunched, became absorbed in troubled thought. The conviction grew that it was his duty to investigate to the full and personally these rumours of the witch-maid. Also, he would seek to lead her to confession to the salvation of her own soul, and, further, that he might learn something regarding the evil ways of witches, and by some good wit turn their own methods against them to the establishment of the Lord.

Full of eager resolve, he did not finish his luncheon, but left the tavern and proceeded to the jail.

There he had the old jailer open the door of the cell very softly, that he might, by some good chance, surprise the prisoner in evil doing.

Quietly the old jailer swung open the door.

Cotton Mather saw a little maiden seated on a straw pallet, knitting. Some wisps of the straw clung to her fair hair, some to her linsey-woolsey petticoat. Where the iron ring had slipped on her white ankel was a red mark.

All the colour went from Deliverance's face as she looked up and perceived her visitor. Before his stern gaze she trembled, and her head drooped, and she ceased her knitting. The ball of yarn rolled out from her lap over to the young minister's feet.

She waited for him to speak. The moments passed and still he did not speak, and the torture of his silence grew so great that at last she lifted her head and met his glance, and out of her pain she was enabled to speak. "What would ye have with me, good sir?"

"I have come to pray with you, and to exhort you to confession," he answered.

"Nay, good sir," protested Deliverance, "I be no witch."

The old jailer entered with a stool for Mr Mather, and having set it down, went out and left the two together.

Ere either could speak, there was a rapping at the door.

In answer to the young minister's summons to enter, Sir Jonathan Jamieson came in.

Deliverance glanced dully at him, all uncaring; for she felt he had harmed her all he could, and now might nevermore injure her.

The young minister, having much respect for Sir Jonathan, rose and begged that he be seated. But Sir Jonathan, minded to be equally polite, refused to deprive Mr Mather of the stool. So they might have argued and bowed for long, had not the jailer appeared with another stool.

"I did but see you enter now, as I chanced to come out of the tavern near by," remarked Sir Jonathan, seating himself comfortably, leaning back against the wall, "and, being minded to write a book upon the evil ways of witchery, I followed you in, knowing you came to exhort the prisoner to repentance. So I beg that you will grant me the privilege to listen in case she should confess, that I may thereby obtain some valuable notes." As he spoke he shot a quick glance at Deliverance.

She could not divine that menacing look. Was he fearful lest she should confess, or did he indeed seek to have her do so?

Cotton Mather turned, his face filled with passionate and honest fervour, toward the speaker.

"Most gladly," he answered with hearty sympathy; "it is a noble and useful calling. I oft find more company with the dead in their books than in the society of the living, and it has ever been one of my chief thanksgivings that the Lord blessed me with a ready pen. But more of this later. Let us now kneel in prayer."

They both knelt.

But Deliverance remained seated.

"Wicked and obstinate o' heart I be," she said, "but Sir Jonathan holds me from prayer. I cannot kneel in company with him."

She no longer felt any fear to speak her mind.

At her words Cotton Mather glanced at Sir Jonathan and saw the man's face go red. His suspicions were aroused thereat, and he forgot all his respect for Sir Jonathan's great position and mickle gold, and spoke sternly, as became a minister, recognizing in his profession neither high nor low.

"Do you indeed exercise a mischievous spell to hold this witch-maid from prayer when she would seem softened toward godliness?"

"Nay," retorted Sir Jonathan, " 'tis the malice of her evil, invisible spectre whispering at her ear to cast a reflection on me."

"I prithee go, however, and stand in the corridor outside, and we will see if the witch-maid, relieved of your presence, will pray," advised Cotton Mather.

Sir Jonathan was secretly angered at this command, yet he rose with what fair show of grace he could muster, and went out into the corridor. But an indefinable fear had sprung to life in his heart. For lo, but a look, a word, an accusation, and one was put upon as a witch.

Deliverance, although she feared the young minister, yet knew him to be not only a great but a good man, and desirous for her soul's good. Thus willingly she knelt opposite him.

Long and fervently he prayed. Meanwhile, Sir Jonathan sauntered up and down the corridor, swinging his blackthorn stick lightly, humming his Old World tune.

Every time he passed the open door, he cast a terrible glance at Deliverance over the minister's kneeling figure, so that she shuddered, feeling she was indeed besieged by the powers of darkness on one hand, and an angel of light on the other.

Cotton Mather could not see those terrible glances, but even as he prayed, he was conscious of Sir Jonathan's unconcerned humming and light step. This implied some disrespect, so that it was with displeasure he called upon him to return.

"I cannot understand, Sir Jonathan," he remarked, rising and resuming his seat, "how it is that you who are so godly a man, should exercise a spell to hold this witch-maid from prayer."

Sir Jonathan shrugged his shoulders. "She has a spectre which would do me evil. 'Tis a plot of the Devil's to put reproach on me, in that I have refused to do his bidding." An expression of low cunning came into his glance. "Have not you had similar experience, Mr Mather? Methinks I have heard that the tormentors of an afflicted young woman did cause your very image to appear before her."

"Yea," rejoined Mr Mather with some heat, "the fiends did make themselves masters of her tongue, so in her fits she did complain I put upon her preternatural torments. Yet her only outcries when she recovered her senses were for my poor prayers. At last my exhortations did prevail, and she, as well as my good name, was delivered from the malice of Satan."

Sir Jonathan stooped to flick some dust off his buckled shoe with his kerchief. "One knows not on whom the accusation of witchery may fasten. Even the most godly be not spared some slander." Now when he stooped, Deliverance thought she had seen a smile flicker over his face, but when he lifted his head, his expression was deeply grave. He met the young minister's suspicious and uncomfortable glance serenely. "What most convinces me," he continued easily, "of the prisoner's guilt, e'en more than the affliction she put upon me, is the old yeoman's testimony that he saw her conversing in the woods with Satan. Could we but get to the root of that matter, perchance the whole secret may be revealed. But I would humbly suggest she tell it in my ear, alone, lest the tale prove of too terrible and scandalous a nature to reach thy pious ear. Then I would repeat it to you with becoming delicacy."

"Nay," answered Cotton Mather, "a delicate stomach deters me not from investing aught that may result to the better establishment of the Lord in this district."

Deliverance began to feel that some story would be torn from her against her will. Alas, what means of self-defence remained to her! Her fingers closed convulsively upon the unfinished stocking in her lap. The feminine instinct to seek relief from painful thought by some simple occupation of sewing or knitting, awakened in her. She resolved to continue her knitting, counting each stitch to herself, never permitting her attention to swerve from the task, no matter what words were addressed to her.

So in her great simplicity, and innocent of all worldly conventionalities, she sought security in her knitting.

This action was so unprecedented, it suggested such quiet domesticity and the means by which good women righteously busied themselves, that both priest and layman were disconcerted, and knew not what to do.

Suddenly Sir Jonathan laughed harshly. "The witch has a spice of her Master's obstinacy," he cried. "Methinks 'twere right good wisdom, since your prayers and exhortations avail not with her, to try less gentle means and use threats," his crafty mind catching at the fact that whatever strange, but, he feared to him, familiar tale, the little maid might tell, it could be misconstrued as the malice of one who had given herself over to Satan.

"Perchance 'twould be as well," assented Cotton Mather, greatly perplexed.

Sir Jonathan shook his forefinger at Deliverance. "Listen, mistress," said he, and sought to fix her with his menacing eye.

Deliverance, counting her stitches, heeded him not.

How pale her little face! How quick the glancing needles flashed! And ever back of her counting ran an undercurrent of thought, the words of her dream,—A little life sweetly lived.

"This would I threaten you," spoke Sir Jonathan. "You have heard how old Giles Corey is to be put to death?"

The knitting-needles trembled in the small hands. Now she dropped a stitch, and now another stitch.

"And because he will say neither that he is guilty, nor yet that he is not guilty, it is rumoured that he is to be pressed to death beneath stones," continued Sir Jonathan.

A sigh of horror followed his words. The involuntary sound came from Cotton Mather, whose imaginative, highly-strung organism responded to the least touch. His eyes were fixed upon the little maid. He saw the small hands shaking so that they could not guide the needles. How small those hands, how stamped with the innocent seeming of childhood! Oh, that the Devil should take upon himself such a disguise!

"And so, if you do not confess," spoke Sir Jonathan's cold, menacing voice, "you shall not be accorded even the mercy of being hanged, but tied hands and feet, and laid upon the ground. And the villagers shall come and heap stones on you, and I, whom you have afflicted, shall count them as they fall. I shall watch the first stone strike you—"

A loud cry from the tortured child interrupted him. She sprang to her feet with arms outstretched. "And when that first stone strikes me," she cried, "God will take me to Himself! Ye can count the stones the others throw upon me, but I shall never ken how fast they fall!"

Cotton Mather was moved to compassion. "Let us use all zeal to do away with these evil sorcerers and their fascinations, good Sir Jonathan, but yet let us deal in mercy as far as compatible with justice, lest to do any living thing torture be a reflection on our manhood." With gentleness he then addressed himself to Deliverance, who had sunk upon her pallet and covered her face with her hands. "Explain to us why the woman of Ipswich, that was hanged, did seek that you be saved."

Deliverance made no reply. Nor could he prevail upon her in any way; so, after a weary while spent in prayers and exhortations, he and Sir Jonathan rose and went away. At the threshold Cotton Mather glanced back over his shoulder at the weeping little maid.

"This affair savours ill," he remarked, laying his hand heavily on his companion's shoulder as the two went down the corridor; "my heart turned within me, and strange feelings waked at her cry."

It was late in the afternoon. It would not be possible for the young minister to reach Boston Town until after midnight, so he decided to postpone his journey until the next day. Moreover, he rather seized at an excuse to remain for the morrow's court, having great relish in these witch-trials.

But that night Cotton Mather did not sleep easy in his bed for his mind was much troubled with the maid and whether or not she was guilty of the charges laid. . . .

[*Editor's Note: After a further series of cross-examinations the 'Witch Maid' is found innocent of the charges brought against her—and the man she has most to thank for her rescue from hanging is the unlikely Mr Mather! It certainly took an author of courage to use such a fictional device at a time when most readers still saw all the characters involved in the notorious trials— particularly the prosecutors—in very definite shades of white and black!*]

A WITCH BURNING

Mrs Baillie Reynolds

Mrs Baillie Reynolds (1842–1912) can also be numbered among the many Victorian writers who, like Miss Mackie, were fascinated by the infamous witch trials and used them as a basis for their fiction. She was a popular contributor to journals like *The Windsor Magazine* and *The Strand Magazine* and it is from the fading pages of the latter that I extracted this evocative and dramatic story of terror (1901). Mrs Reynolds also wrote a number of full-length novels containing elements of the supernatural and was an enthusiastic member of several organisations devoted to research into psychic phenomena. A selection of her best short stories were published just after the First World War under the title *The Terrible Baron.*

∽∽∽∽∽∽∽∽∽∽∽∽∽∽∽∽∽∽∽∽∽∽∽∽∽∽∽∽∽∽∽∽∽∽∽∽

The dusk was falling upon the hard, frozen ground, covered with light, powdery snow. Gilbert Caton sat by the window of his lowly lodging, looking forth into the wide market-square of the populous New England village of Mizpah.

There before his eyes were the figures of men, warmly wrapped about from the piercing cold, busily engaged in piling faggots for the witch who was to be burned upon the morrow.

As he looked forth the young man was raging in his heart. He could not stop this thing that was to be. Or he could stop it only as in bygone days the monk Telemachus stopped the Public Games at Rome—by being himself a martyr.

He was an Englishman, and for two years had been an exile from his country, ministering to the handful of his own faith who dwell here among the Nonconformists. He had no position, no influence. He could but sit by and see what horror men could work in the name of righteousness. He and his flock were taboo to the other inhabitants, and, though there was no open persecution now, there was a persistent hostility which gave Churchmen a poor chance in the law courts and no chance at all in the way of public posts.

And now a hideous tendency, dormant of late in the people, had awoke again in new strength. They had taken to witch-burning. Only six months before an old woman, widow of a sailor—who held the secret of a herbal preparation, brought by her husband from far countries—had been dragged to the water, flung in, and cruelly tormented before being done to death. With that the hunting instinct of the mob had been roused. Having once tasted the savage joy of pursuit, capture, and destruction, they thirsted for it again. And ere many months had passed there came tales of two witches most undoubtedly possessed of occult powers, who lived in the depths of Haranec Wood, wherein, as everybody knew, there lurked cougars, so that no woman unprotected by Satanic powers could dwell there in safety.

Day after day there sifted in tales of the skill of these women—of the marvels wrought by the mere muttering of a spell, in which the waving of hands played great and wondrous part. Two men dispatched to take the offenders came back daunted and trembling, afraid to lay a hand on either of them. And thereupon the blood lust swept raging through the town, the people turned out, and the women were hunted down with dogs and dragged to the town jail.

At first there was a division of opinion respecting their equal guilt. One of them, who was evidently the leader, had been burnt a week ago. And now news had come down that the second captive, who had been reported penitent, had been tampering with her jailers— had been bribing them to connive at her escape. So she, too, was to burn upon the morrow.

And Caton sat there, wondering what judgment God would send upon a town which, within a year, had murdered three defenceless women. He had some vague ideas floating through his head, of trying to assemble half-a-dozen men to form a rescue. But he doubted if even that were possible. And as he mused, there was sharp knocking against his door from the street without. He rose, and opened; there stood the burly form and harsh-lined face of Brading, the village constable. He held a lantern in his hand, for dusk was falling and the night would be very dark.

"His worship, in his mercy, has sent for you," he said, in his husky tones. "Let no man say we give not even the most degraded their fair chance. The baggage down yonder, that is to burn to-morrow, says she belongs to the English faith. So come you down and say a prayer for her, and try to turn her thoughts from Satan to the Lord, for she will not listen to the godly exhorting of Master Lupton."

Gilbert rose and stared wide-eyed, at the messenger. What? Go and speak to this poor despairing creature of the mercy of God when she was to have no mercy from man! He quailed in his heart at the task. The constable burst into a hateful, husky titter.

"He's afraid—afraid the witch'll put a spell on him," he chuckled. "Lord love you, man. Master Lupton, he's been in her cell nigh two hours—and that against her will—and she's not been able to hurt him, through his faith in the Lord. But you that put your trust in forms and ceremonies, ye fear, and who can wonder at it?"

A sudden impulse swept over Gilbert, calming him utterly.

Without having spoken one word he turned to a desk which stood by his table, took his books of devotions, and stowed them in the pocket of his cassock, which, like the clergy of his day, he wore habitually. Then he took from a peg his long cloak with thick capes and his wide-brimmed hat, and intimated that he was ready to follow Brading.

It was almost night as they came out into the street and made their way—past the wide space where the pile of faggots rose a ghastly blot against the surrounding whiteness—up to the narrow throat of the street, where the houses began to cluster close, and so to the low, narrow stone archway which was the entrance to the town jail.

Brading let himself in with his own key and they stood in the small waiting-room, where two or three men were lounging by the glowing heat of a great fire. The men greeted Gilbert with half-surely respect. His powerful physique and great strength procured for him a consideration which his blameless life and sincere simplicity might not have commanded. One of them told Brading that he had been

M

summoned to go to the house of the mayor with regard to the proceedings of to-morrow. Brading was by no means unwilling, knowing that hot supper would be forthcoming at the mayor's house; so he forthwith departed, taking his lantern with him and making a kind of apology that Gilbert must needs walk home in the dark.

Gilbert hardly heard. He was watching the selection of a key by a man who had risen to attend him, and who now led the way down a corkscrew stair which seemed to descend to the bowels of the earth.

The condemned cell!

All was dark and silent within. Caton took the torch from the man who held it, flashed the light round, saw an iron ring in the wall and fixed the light there.

"Knock loud when you want to come out," said the turnkey, and retired, slamming the iron door with a bang.

Gilbert fixed his eyes upon the heap of rags huddled in a corner.

"Good evening," he said, in his clear, high-bred voice. "God be with you."

There was a rustle in the straw. The heap of rags moved, turned towards him, and displayed, to his horror, the face of a young girl, hardly more than a child. She seemed all eyes—the stare of them burned his very soul. Her face was chalk-white, her streaming dark hair hung about it on either side, showing it up like a silver moon upon the dark sky. Her young, fresh mouth was piteously curved. She had that terrible dumbness of appeal which one sees in the eyes of ill-treated animals. The sight of her froze the man's blood in his veins. "My daughter!" he said, in a voice which was almost a sob of compassion.

There came a quiver to her mouth—to her whole face. On her two hands she crawled nearer to him, a fearful questioning in her wild look. Was this really a human being speaking kind words to her? Not cursing her?

The young man threw off his cloak and hat and knelt down beside her in the straw. She laid her small hand, freezing cold, upon his outstretched palm.

"You are warm," she said, in a murmuring voice. "And you have brought a light! I have been in the dark—alone—so cold."

In a transport of pity he lifted her up and drew her into his arms, holding her head in the hollow of his elbow.

"What do they mean?" he said, unsteadily. "What do they mean by calling you a witch?"

She faintly shook her head. "I don't—know," she faltered, in laboured gasps. He looked about the horrible dungeon and saw on a shelf a water-pitcher and mug. In his pocket was, as it chanced, a flask of wine and some biscuit which he had taken with him to bestow upon a poor parishioner earlier in the day, and found him away. He mixed wine and water and gave her to eat and drink; in his anxiety for her bodily needs forgetting all else, as one does in such a case.

The taste of the delicate biscuit drew her to eat; the wine made the blood flow again in her veins. As she ate and drank he held her warmly wrapped in his cloak, and felt the icy rigidity of her limbs relax.

And yet—was it kindness or cruelty, he asked himself. Had it been better to leave her in her stupor of cold and hunger? Might she have cheated the flames after all? Had he not brought her back to the full sense of her misery?

"Tell me," he said at last, as she sat silent, her head fallen sideways against his shoulder, "what have you done? What have you said that they have condemned you for a witch?"

She sighed wearily. "Nothing that I know of. They said grannie was a witch; and I lived with her."

"Was it true? Did your grandmother practise magic arts?"

"She could put them to sleep by waving her hands about. She could cure pain by stroking the place. Is that wicked?"

"Alas, I know not. Who taught her these things?"

"She learned them long ago of a nurse she had, who was a gipsy. They were very rich, my grandparents, and they had a large estate. The Indians attacked them and killed my father and mother and—and almost everybody. Only grannie and I were left, and she was always queer after that. She would not live in the town, she was full of strange fancies. But she was good to me. We were very happy till Joseph, our servant, died."

"How long ago was that?"

"I do not know; I forget. We buried him, and then grannie would not stay in that house. She said she would go to my uncle, who had a fine home in England and a park with swans and a lake, and many servants. So we started off to walk to the coast, but she was old and ill. We found a little house in the wood, and rested there; and the people found us out, and they were good to us till they came hunting us. Oh!" Suddenly she sat erect, threw up her hands, and screamed. "They will burn me! They will burn me!" she cried, madly. . . . She flung her arms about his knees. "Are you kind? Are you human?" she cried. "Can't you save me from them? Can't you?"

The sweat stood on the young man's forehead. It had come suddenly—so suddenly. Not a moments' interval between the everyday quiet of his usual existence and this sudden plunge into a life and death struggle.

"Have you ever been baptized?" he asked her, hurriedly.

"Oh, yes; and confirmed, too, by a Bishop," she said, faintly.

She was a sheep of his fold, and he must save her or die with her.

Her name, she told him, was Luna Clare. The clear shining of the moon! He thought her well named.

Rapidly his mind reviewed the position. The wild idea of passing her out in his habiliments crossed his mind. But the thing was impossible. She was much less than half his bulk. And even could he hope that, the jailers being drunk, such a plot could be carried out—once beyond the prison alone what would become of her? She must die of exposure, be eaten by wild beasts, or re-taken.

She sat, watching with craving eyes the thoughts, the doubts, the trouble in his face. Her soft hand touched his "Kill me," she breathed. "Kill me here, with your own hand. I do not fear death— I have nothing to live for—I fear only torture—only to die shrieking with devilish men gloating on my agony. Kill me now—it is the only way."

For a moment he thought it was. Her head fell limply against his rough cassock. He held her in his arms, his clear, grey eyes gazing out over her head, contemplating the situation.

And then, suddenly, as he reflected upon the emaciation of the slight thing he held, an idea broke upon his mind that sent the blood with a rush to his face—that made his head reel a moment, then flooded him with a calmness and strength which surprised himself.

"Luna," he said, in a new voice, "will you swear to do whatever I bid you?"

She moved, so that her small, white face, with its piteous, pointed chin, was upturned to his. She just breathed "Yes," and hung upon his words.

"Luna, you must trust me to the uttermost. In the eyes of God I am your brother—you are safe with me."

He rose to his feet. "Let me try how heavy you are," he muttered; and lifted her slip of a body with an ease that astonished him.

"It can be done," he said, through his teeth. "God helping, it shall be done."

From upstairs he caught a loud, vacant laugh, a snatch of drunken song. In Brading's absence the jailers were making merry. There was a slender chance for the success of his plan. His hesitation was over; he turned upon her, short and sharp. "I am going to put you on my back," he said, "and to carry you out of the prison under my cassock." In spite of his resolution, his face flamed as he said it.

Luna looked neither afraid nor shocked. Her eye lit up. "Oh, I will be very still," she said, with quick breathlessness.

He was already divesting himself of his long garment, and stood before her, well-knit and sturdy, in his grey flannel shirt and knee-breeches.

"Take off your frock," he bade her. "We must arrange it, with a stuffing of straw, in the corner to look like you."

She caught his idea, stripped it off her, and there she was, bare-armed and fragile, in her poor petticoat—a creature of cloud and air.

The hearts of the two young creatures throbbed with violence. They felt themselves alone against the world. Gilbert stooped and lifted the girl upon his back, so that her arms were locked about his shoulders. Her feet hung clear of the ground. With the broad sash of his cassock he bound her firmly to him to decrease the weight upon her arms. With his knife he had previously slit his cassock all up the back, from below the waist to the neckband. Now he buttoned it round them both and flung over all his big cloak, which concealed the rent behind. The weight was greater than he had anticipated, but not greater than he could bear.

All was ready. The frock, stuffed with straw, looked like a girl crouching in the corner. The imprisoned Luna hung perfectly quiet, her arms hardly perceptible under the thick cloak, whose hood concealed her head behind. He felt the warmth of her cheek against his shoulder.

Then, standing on the threshold of his venture, he spoke a brief but strenuous prayer, and heard a soft voice sigh "Amen," as he knocked and shouted for the turnkey to release him. The men above were so heavy with drink and the heat of their great fire that he had to knock and shout for some time before the man came.

"Can you bear it?" he asked, hastily, at the last moment. She merely answered, "Yes."

But the strength of ten men seemed to uphold him, as the door slowly opened.

"God be good to us! God be good to us!" he muttered, lifting his hands in horror at the failure of his mission.

"What, no success? Well, 'twasn't likely you should succeed where brother Lupton failed," sniggered the turnkey.

"Perhaps solitude—and darkness—may prevail," said Gilbert, harshly, taking the torch and stamping it out with his feet. "Leave her to think over my words."

It was more difficult than he had foreseen to ascend the narrow corkscrew stair. As he went slowly up, bumping his burden against the wall, he felt an insane desire to laugh, mingling with his fear. The sweat stood on his forehead, and his heart thumped like a machine as they emerged into the outer room, where the blaze of the fire lit up the place and threw the distorted outline of Master Caton's figure upon the wall.

The dungeon below was locked for the night—between them and their slender hope of escape stood now but one door.

Fortunately, Gilbert had a small silver coin in his pocket. At the door he bestowed it on the turnkey, whose fellow was stretched upon the bench in a drunken slumber.

"A cold night, friend," he said. "Here is somewhat to keep you warm."

The turnkey muttered something inaudible. He was very tipsy indeed. He stooped to put the key in the door, and fell, a heavy mass, right across the threshold.

Gilbert turned the key at once. But he hesitated to step over the prostrate man, who was not unconscious and was struggling to arise. He knew that Luna's feet, dangling within a few inches of the ground, must brush the jailer's nether limbs, and might be perceptible, even to senses fuddled with drink. Accordingly, he held out his hand, with a friendly smile, and encouraged the man to rise, Twice in vain he essayed to gain his feet, and twice fell back, while Gilbert gasped and staggered with the strain. At the third attempt up he came, and fell upon the young man with such force as to cause him to stagger back with violence against the wall. It was quite unavoidable; he could do nothing to break the force of the impact. If the girl let forth a sound they were undone.

She remained perfectly silent, though he felt a shudder run through her limbs. He hardly knew what he said to the tipsy fool, who now, melted by the gift of the coin, flung himself upon him to embrace him.

That must be the end—discovery was now inevitable. In anguish Gilbert held up his arms—"Man, stop, stop! My rheumatism! Have a little pity. Here, sit down on this stool—another mouthful of this will strengthen you."

He held the glass of steaming spirits which stood on the table to the sot's lips; and in the succeeding moment had opened the door and staggered out.

Mizpah folks were early abed, and he found an empty street. He hastened along, reeling and staggering, the burden on his back seeming, like Christopher's, to grow heavier each moment. Suppose she should relax the clasp of her hands and slip to the ground? The strain must be awful. He stopped a moment to give a hoist, but the immediate slipping back which followed warned him that she was near the end of her resource. He pushed on, wild with apprehension, believing that, should he meet anyone upon the road, he must be detected. The sight of his shadow, cast by the firelight on the wall, had told him how mad a risk he ran.

His own door, with the glimmering lantern above, seemed like a ray from heaven. He lived alone, a woman coming in each day to do his "chores," as it was called. His supper would be laid, he knew. They must eat and then flee. What was he to do for clothes for the girl?

He almost hurled himself within, drew the great bar behind him, and, stooping under the dead weight of an apparently inert burden, found his tinder-box, made a light, and, with frantic fingers, flung away his wrappings.

The girl fell, limp and senseless, into his big chair, and lay there, in the light of his lamp, so reduced by cruelty and privation that he was inclined to think his rescue of her was too late.

The drops stood upon his forehead as he began to realize what he had done. He had broken the law, made himself responsible for a girl from nobody knew where. Flight was imperative; and how was flight possible?

His nerves were jarred with the strain of what he had undergone; but he set his teeth to the completing of his adventure, took the boiling kettle from the hot coals, made drink, and held it to her lips. By degrees she came back to consciousness. His clock told him that it was barely eight o'clock. The whole night lay before the fugitives.

When Luna was sitting up, drinking her milk and gazing timidly about, he also set to work to eat, while he tried to collect his wits and decide what he must take with him and whither shape his course. So far he had succeeded, so far they were free. But——

He started, and his face froze. There were steps and voices in the silent street without—hurried steps, coming from the direction of the prison. And as he sat, counting the hammer strokes of his heart, there was a loud and peremptory knocking upon his door.

He raised his head and looked at the fragile waif-girl who sat as if paralysed. He rose, and stood, a picture of perplexity. Then he was himself again. He crossed the room and looked at her a moment with a gaze half of command, half of appeal. She answered it as if he had spoken, rising to her feet and taking his hand. He led her across to the door of his bedroom, opened it, and said under his breath, "In— in——"

She obeyed without words, without hesitation, and he shut and locked the door behind her, putting the key in his pocket as the knocking without was repeated, and more loudly.

He threw his cloak over his damaged cassock and went to meet Fate.

Without, in the snowy night, stood three men. They seemed to be a gentleman and his two servants. The gentleman wore a costly and much-be-furred travelling suit, and his voice and courtly bow at once proclaimed him English.

"Pardon this intrusion. Do I speak to Master Gilbert Caton, the parson here?"

Gilbert admitted it.

"Dare I beg for a few minutes of your valuable time, sir? I come merely to ask a question. I am here to trace my mother and my young niece. My name is Clare—Leonard Clare, of Clare Hall, in the County of Devon. My father had a large estate west of this, which was attacked by Indians, and many of my family murdered. But I am told that my mother, with one child of my brother, escaped, and I have traced them with tolerable certainty, to this district. The town authorities, however, tell me nothing is known of them here. As they are of the Episcopal faith, I deemed that you might know something; and before leaving the place I venture to importune you."

A sudden trembling of the limbs assailed Gilbert as he stood. With a motion to his guests to enter he turned away, and sank down into a chair, covering his face with his hands.

Then, looking up with a dawn of hope and illumination, "Have you horses?" he eagerly demanded.

"We have horses—yes."

"Then it will be best to fly," said Gilbert, huskily.

Mr Clare stood, majestic and astonished, in the small room, looking doubtfully at the young parson, whose sanity seemed questionable. "To fly?" he echoed.

"The people of Mizpah," said Gilbert, hoarsely, "burnt your mother as a witch. I saw her burn, without there, in the market. They have fixed the burning of your neice for to-morrow—to-morrow. There is a holiday, that the folks may see the sight."

Mr Clare let forth a kind of bellow. "To burn my niece! And you urge me to fly?"

Gilbert nodded. He rose and went to his bedroom door. He threw it wide and called to the girl within. She came and stood in the doorway in her ragged petticoat—hunted, wild, shrinking, her great eyes dilated to their utmost. For one moment she stood poised there, then darted to Gilbert and clung to him with all her might.

"Don't! Don't!" she shrieked. "Don't let them take me! Kill me —kill me yourself! Don't let me burn!"

She was so overwrought that it was long before Gilbert could make her understand that she was saved. Now that the way to act was plain to him all his energy and resource returned. He explained the situation as clearly as he could to Mr Clare.

He felt sure that it would be unwise to wait till morning and tackle the authorities. The people, baulked of their prey, would very likely break out and riot. Moreover, the inhabitants of all other villages in the district had the same blind fear and hatred of a witch, and so were potential enemies. The safest plan was to dress the girl in boy's clothes and to ride away there and then. The night lay before them clear and fine, though cold. They must travel straight through till they gained the coast, and there take ship for England. He could find something for Luna to wear, and they could lend a spare cloak.

Leonard Clare listened, with wrath in his heart, yet knowing that the advice was good. It was arranged that he should send his servants back to the inn to pay his reckoning and bring his horses and his baggage. There was a spare horse for the carriage of such things as were necessary for travel, and until they were clear of the district and could buy another horse Luna could ride that.

There was need of urgent haste, and in the stress of the proposed flight Leonard Clare had hardly time to realize the desperate part played by the young parson.

But when Luna had been shut once more into the bedroom to wash and dress herself the two men faced each other, and, noting the blue marks under the younger man's eyes, Clare's heart smote him for an ingrate. He spoke then in a fine, dignified way of his indebtedness. He dared not insult the young man by offer of reward, but if there were anything he could do——

Gilbert thanked him quietly. He said simply that he could not leave the girl to be murdered. He had done what he could, and God had done the rest.

He cut protestations short by sketching a map of the route he advised and giving minute directions.

In the midst of it the bedroom door softly opened, and there slipped out a slim figure in knee-breeches, and shirt with hair all gathered away under a riding-hat.

Luna's timidity was gone. Her eyes were full of a new terrible idea. Going straight up to Gilbert, she said, in her low, wondrous voice:—

"And what will you do?"

He leaned across the table and looked her in the eyes.

"Stay here and do my work," he said, quietly.

"And when they find I am gone they will seize you."

He shrugged his shoulders. "They may not. They may think the devil ran off with you in the night."

"If they do *not* think so, the mob will tear you in pieces."

"I can't help that. I have done my duty."

The girl turned slowly from him, as if she could not tear her eyes from the dominion of his. She looked at her uncle.

"I cannot leave here unless Master Caton comes too."

"I must humbly beg to be forgiven. I had not realized the danger that you have run by your heroic rescue of my niece," stammered Mr Clare. "The events of this night—I think my wits are too weak, sir. But let me repair this. Come with us tonight, and your future career shall be my care."

Gilbert hesitated, his face aflame. Luna went close to him and took his hand. "If he stays, I stay with him," she said clearly.

The sound of the horses at the door was heard. Voices mingled with the tramplings. The mayor had come to express regret that Mr Clare was leaving the village with his inquiries unanswered.

They came out and spoke with him. Gilbert explained that he was going a stage with Mr Clare, who was not certain of the first ten miles before striking the main road. He mounted the spare horse, and they put the page-boy up before him.

"Mind you get back in time for the burning," said the mayor, anxiously. "We shall want you to say the final prayers."

"There will be plenty of time for that," said Gilbert, tranquilly.

A WATER WITCH

Mrs H. D. Everett

Mrs H. D. Everett (1855-1905) was another of the Victorian
ladies who found ghostly phenomena fascinating and belonged to
several of the renowned London 'Ghost Circles'. She wrote quite
extensively on the cases she helped investigate and also used
material culled from enquiries for her fiction. Probably her best
collection is that which appeared under the title *The Death Mask*,
and it is from this that I have selected "A Water Witch". Published in the very early years of this century, it is typical of so
much Victorian fiction: gently paced, moral and full of people to
whom taxing public demands were an unknown quality, protected
as they were from such things by position, money and their up-
bringing.

~~~~~~

We were disappointed when Robert married. We had for long wanted
him to marry, as he is our only brother and head of the family since
my father died, as well as of the business firm; but we should have
liked his wife to be a different sort of person. We, his sisters, could
have chosen much better for him than he did for himself. Indeed we
had our eye on just the right girl—bright-tempered and sensibly
brought up, who would not have said No: of that I am assured, had
Robert on his side shown signs of liking. But he took a holiday abroad
the spring of 1872, and the next thing we heard was that he had made
up his mind to marry Frederica. Frederica, indeed! We Larcombs
have been plain Susans and Annes and Marys and Elizabeths for

generations (I am Mary), and the fantastic name was an annoyance. The wedding took place at Mentone in a great hurry, because the stepmother was marrying again, and Frederica was unhappy. Was not that weak of Robert?—he did not give himself time to think. We may perhaps take that as some excuse for a departure from Larcomb traditions: on consideration, the match would very likely have been broken off.

Frederica had some money of her own, though not much: all the Larcomb brides have had money up to now. And her dead father was a General and a K.C.B., which did not look amiss in the announcement; but there our satisfaction ended. He brought her to make our acquaintance three weeks after the marriage, a delicate little shrinking thing well matched to her fanciful name, and desperately afraid of mother and of us girls, so the introductory visit was hardly a success. Then Robert took her off to London, and when the baby was born—a son, but too weakly to live beyond a day or two—she had a severe illness, and was slow in recovering strength. And there is little doubt that by this time he was conscious of having made a mistake.

I used to be his favourite sister, being next to him in age, and when he found himself in a difficulty at Roscawen he appealed to me. Roscawen was a moor Robert had lately rented on the Scotch side of the Border, and we were given to understand that a bracing air, and the complete change of scene, were expected to benefit Frederica, who was pleased by the arrangement. So his letter took me by surprise. "Dear Mary," he wrote, and, characteristically, he did not beat about the bush. "Pack up your things as soon as you get this, and come off here the day after to-morrow. You will have to travel *via* York, and I will meet you at Draycott Halt, where the afternoon train stops by signal. Freda is a bit nervous, and doesn't like staying alone here, so I am in a fix. I want you to keep her company the weeks I am at Shepstow. I know you'll do as much as this for—Your affectionate brother, Robert Larcomb."

This abrupt call upon me, making sure of response and help, recalled bygone times when we were much to each other, and Frederica still in the unknown. A bit nervous, was she, and Robert in a fix because of it: here again was evidence of the mistake. It was not very easy then to break off from work, and for an indefinite time; but I resolved to satisfy the family curiosity, to say nothing of my own, by doing as I was bid.

When I got out of the train at Draycott Halt, Robert was waiting for me with his car. My luggage was put in at the back, and I mounted to the seat beside him; and again it reminded me of old times, for he seemed genuinely pleased to see me.

"Good girl," he said, "to make no fuss, and come at once."

"We Larcombs are not apt to fuss, are we?"—and as I said this, it occurred to me that probably he was in these days well acquainted with fuss—Frederica's fuss. Then I asked: "What is the matter?"

I only had a sideways glimpse of him as he answered, for he was busy with the driving-gear.

"Why, I told you, didn't I, that it was arranged for me to be here and at Shepstow week and week about. Falkner and I together, for it is better than taking either moor with a single gun. And I can't take Freda there, for the Shepstow cottage has no accommodation for a lady—only the one room that Falkner and I share. Freda is nervous, poor girl, since her illness, and somehow she has taken a dislike to Roscawen. It is nothing but a fancy, of course, but something had to be done."

"Why, you wrote to mother that you had both fallen in love with the place, and thought it quite ideal."

"Oh, the place is right enough, it is just my poor girl's fancy. She'll tell you I daresay, but don't let her dwell on it more than you can help. You will have Falkner's room, and the week he is over here I've arranged for Vickers to put him up, though I daresay he will come in to meals. Vickers?—oh, he's a neighbour on the opposite side of the water, Roscawen Water, the stream that overflows from the lake in the hills. He's a doctor of science as well as medicine, and has written some awfully clever books. I understand he's at work on another, and comes here for the sake of quiet. But he's a very good sort though not a sportsman, does not mind taking in Falkner, and he is by way of being a friend of Freda's—they read Italian together. No, he isn't married, neither is the parson, worse luck; and there isn't another woman of her own sort within miles. It's desperately lonely for her, I allow, when I'm not here. So there was no help for it. I was bound to send for you or for the mater, and I thought you would be best!"

We were passing through wild scenery of barren broken hills, following the course of the river up-stream. It came racing down a rocky course, full and turbulent from recent rains. Presently the road divided, crossing a narrow bridge; and there we came in sight of the leap the water makes over a shelf of rock, plunging into a deep pool below with a swirl of foam and spray. I would have liked to linger and look, but the car carried us forward quickly, allowing only a glimpse in passing. And, directly after, Robert called my attention to a stone-built small house high up on the hill-side—a bare place it looked, flanked by a clump of firs, but with no surrounding garden-ground; the wild moor and the heather came close under the windows.

"That's Roscawen," he said. "Just a shooting-box, you see. A new-built place, raw, with no history behind it later than yesterday. I was in treaty for Corby, seventeenth century that was, with a ghost in the gallery, but the arrangement fell through. And I'm jolly glad it did,"—and here he laughed; an uncomfortable laugh, not of the Larcomb sort, or like himself. And in another minute we were at the door.

Freda welcomed me, and I thought her improved; she was indeed pretty—as pretty as such a frail little thing could be, who looked as if a puff of wind would blow her away. She was very well dressed—of course Robert would take care of that—and her one thought appeared to be of him. She was constantly turning to him with appeal of one sort or another, and seemed nervous and ill at ease when he was out of her sight. "Must you really go to-morrow?" I caught her whisper later, and heard his answer: "Needs must, but you will not mind now you have Mary." I could plainly see that she did mind, and that my companionship was no fair exchange for the loss of his. But was not all this exaction the very way to tire out love?

The ground-floor of the house was divided into a sitting-hall, upon which the front door opened without division, and to the right you entered a fair-sized dining-room. Each of these apartments had the offshoot of a smaller room, one being Freda's snuggery, and the other the gun-room where the gentlemen smoked. Above there were two good bedrooms, a dressing-room and a bathroom, but no higher floor: the gable-space was not utilised, and the servants slept over the kitchen at the back. The room allotted to me, from which Captain

Falkner had been ejected, had a wide window and a pleasant aspect. As I was hurriedly dressing for dinner, I could hear the murmur of the river close at hand, but the actual water was not visible, as it flowed too far below the over-hanging bank.

I could not see the flowing water, but as I glanced from the window, a wreath of white mist or spray floated up from it, stretched itself out before the wind, and disappeared after the fashion of a puff of steam. Probably there was at that point another fall (so I thought) churning the river into foam. But I had no time to waste in speculation, for we Larcombs adhere to the good ways of punctuality. I fastened a final hook and eye, and ran downstairs.

Captain Falkner came to dinner and made a fourth at table, but the fifth place which had been laid remained vacant. The two men were full of plans for the morrow, and there was to be an early setting out: Shepstow, the other moor, was some thirty miles away.

"I am afraid you will be dull, Mary," Robert said to me in a sort of apology. "I am forced to keep the car at Shepstow, as I am my own chauffeur. But you and Freda will have her cart to jog about in, so you will be able to look round the nearer country while I am away. You will have to put up with the old mare. I know you like spirit in a horse, but this quiet gee suits Freda, as she can drive her going alone. Then Vickers will look in on you most days. I do not know what is keeping him away to-night."

Freda was in low spirits next morning, and she hung about Robert up to the time of his departure, in a way that I should have found supremely irritating had I been her husband. And I will not be sure that she did not beg him again not to leave her—to my tender mercies I supposed—though I did not hear the request. When the two men had set out with their guns and baggage, the cart was ordered round, and my sister-in-law took me for a drive.

Robert had done well to prepare me for the "quiet gee": a meek old creature named Grey Madam, that had whitened in the snows of many winters, and expected to progress at a walk whenever the road inclined uphill. And all the roads inclined uphill or down about Roscawen; I do not remember anywhere a level quarter of a mile. It was truly a dull progress, and Freda did not find much to say; perhaps she still was fretting after Robert. But the moors and the swelling hills were beautiful to look at in their crimson flush of heather. "I

(*above left*) An exciting moment from the Hon. Mrs Greene's werewolf story, "Bound by a Spell". (*above right*) Not all witchcraft stories were full of evil and hatred: there was the occasional light, almost romantic tale, as exemplified here in "The Witch of the Alps"

(*above left*) George Cruikshank illustrated a number of Victorian witch-craft stories and is seen at his best in this picture of an old witch and her beautiful neophyte. (*above right*) A humorous illustration entitled "Meeting

think Roscawen is lovely," I was prompted to exclaim; and when she agreed in my admiration I added: "You liked it when you first came here, did you not?"

"Yes, I liked it when first I came," she assented, repeating my words, but did not go on to say why she disliked Roscawen now.

She had an errand to discharge at one of the upland farms which supplied them with milk and butter. She drew rein at the gate, and was about to alight, but the woman of the house came forward, and so I heard what passed. Freda gave her order, and then made an inquiry.

"I hope you have found your young cow, Mrs Elliott? I was sorry to hear it had strayed."

"We've found her, ma'am, but she was dead in the river, and a sad loss it has been to us. A fine young beast as ever we reared, and coming on with her second calf. My husband has been rarely put about, and I'll own I was fit to cry over her myself. This is the fifth loss we have had within the year—a sheep and two lambs in March, and the cart-foal in July."

Freda expressed sympathy.

"You need better fences, is that it, to keep your cattle from the river?"

Mrs Elliott pursed up her lips and shook her head.

"I won't say, ma'am, but that our fences might be bettered if the landlord would give us material; as it is, we do our best. But when the creatures take that madness for the water, nought but deer-palings would keep them in. I've seen enough in my time here to be sure of that. What makes it come over them I don't take upon myself to say. They make up fine tales in the district about the white woman, but I know nothing of any white women. I only know that when the madness takes them they make for the river, and then they get swept into the deeps."

When we were driving away, I asked Freda what the farmer's wife meant about a white woman and the drowning of her stock.

"I believe there is some story about a woman who was drowned, whose spirit calls the creatures to the river. If you ask Dr Vickers he will tell you. He makes a study of folk-lore and local superstitions, and—and that sort of thing. Robert thinks it is all nonsense, and no doubt you will think it nonsense too."

N

What her own opinion was, Freda did not say. She had a transparent complexion, and a trifling matter made her change colour; a blush rose unaccountably as she answered me, and for a full minute her cheek burned. Why should she blush about Roscawen superstitions and a drowned cow? Then the attention of both of us was suddenly diverted, because Grey Madam took it into her head to shy.

She had mended her pace appreciably since Freda turned her head towards home, trotting now without needing to be urged. We were close upon a cross-roads where three ways met, a triangular green centred by a fingerpost. There was in our direction a bank and hedge (hedges here and there replaced the stone walls of the district) and the right wheel went up that bank, giving the cart a dangerous tilt; it recovered balance, however, and went on. Freda, a timid driver, was holding on desperately to the reins.

"Does she often do this sort of thing?" I asked. "I thought Robert said she was quiet."

"So she is—so we thought her. I never knew her do it before," gasped my sister-in-law, still out of breath with her fright.

"And I cannot think what made her shy. There was nothing—absolutely nothing; not even a heap of stones."

Freda did not answer, but I was to hear more about that cross-roads in the course of the day.

II

After lunch Freda did not seem willing to go out again, so, as I was there to companion her, we both settled down to needlework and a book for alternate reading aloud. The reading, however, languished; when it came to Freda's turn she tired quickly, lost her place twice and again, and seemed unable to fix her attention on the printed page. Was she listening, I wondered later. When silence fell between us, I became aware of a sound recurring at irregular intervals, the sound of water dropping. I looked up at the ceiling expecting to see a stain of wet, for the drop seemed to fall within the room, and close beside me.

"Do you hear that?" I asked. "Has anything gone wrong in the bathroom, do you think?" For we were in Freda's snuggery, and the bathroom was overhead.

But my suggestion of overflowing taps and broken water-pipes left her cold.

"I don't think it is from the bathroom," she replied. "I hear it often. We cannot find out what it is."

Directly she ceased speaking the drop fell again, apparently between us as we sat, and plump upon the carpet. I looked up at the ceiling again, but Freda did not raise her eyes from her embroidery.

"It is very odd," I remarked, and this time she assented, repeating my words, and I saw a shiver pass over her. "I shall go upstairs to the bathroom," I said decidedly, putting down my work. "I am sure those taps must be wrong."

"She did not object, or offer to accompany me, she only shivered again.

"Don't be long away, Mary," she said, and I noticed she had grown pale.

There was nothing wrong with the bathroom, or with any part of the water supply; and when I returned to the snuggery the drip had ceased. The next event was a ring at the door bell, and again Freda changed colour, much as she had done when we were driving. In that quiet place, where comers and goers are few, a visitor is an event. But I think this visitor must have been expected. The servant announced Dr Vickers.

Freda gave him her hand, and made the necessary introduction. This was the friend Robert said would come often to see us, but he was not at all the snuffy old scientist my fancy had pictured. He was old certainly, if it is a sign of age to be grey-haired, and I daresay there were crowsfeet about those piercing eyes of his; but when you met the eyes, the wrinkles were forgotten. They, at least, were full of youth and fire, and his figure was still upright and flat-shouldered.

We exchanged a few remarks; he asked me if I was familiar with that part of Scotland; and when I answered that I was making its acquaintance for the first time, he praised Roscawen and its neighbourhood. It suited him well, he said, when his object was to seek quiet; and I should find, as he did, that it possessed many attractions. Then he asked me if I was an Italian scholar, and showed a book in his hand, the *Vita Nuova*. Mrs Larcomb was forgetting her Italian, and he had promised to brush it up for her. So, if I did not find it to great a bore to sit by, he proposed to read aloud. And, should I not know the book, he would give me a sketch of its purport, so that I could follow.

I had, of course, heard of the *Vita Nuova*, who has not! but my knowledge of the language in which it was written went no further than a few modern phrases, of use to a traveller. I disclaimed my ability to follow, and I imagine Dr Vickers was not ill-pleased to find me ignorant. He took his seat at one end of the Chesterfield sofa, Freda occupying the other, still with that flush on her cheek; and after an observation or two in Italian, he opened his book and began to read.

I imagine he read well. The crisp, flowing syllables sounded very foreign to my ear, and he gave his author the advantage of dramatic expression and emphasis. Now and then he remarked in English on some difficulty in the text, or slipped in a question in Italian which Freda answered, usually by a monosyllable. She kept her eyes fixed upon her work. It was as if she would not look at him, even when he was most impassioned; but I was watching them both, although I never thought—but of course I never thought!

Presently I remember how time was passing, and the place where letters should be laid ready for the post-bag going out. I had left an unfinished one upstairs, so I slipped away to complete and seal. This done, I re-entered softly (the entrance was behind a screen) and found the Italian lesson over, and a conversation going on in English. Freda was speaking with some animation.

"It cannot any more be called my fancy, for Mary heard it too."

"And you had not told her beforehand? There was no suggestion?"

"I had not said a word to her. Had I, Mary?"—appealing to me as I advanced into sight.

"About what?" I asked, for I had forgotten the water incident.

"About the drops falling. You remarked on them first: I had told you nothing. And you went to look at the taps."

"No, certainly you had not told me. What is the matter? Is there any mystery?"

Dr Vickers answered:

"The mystery is that Mrs Larcomb heard these droppings when everyone else was deaf to them. It was supposed to be auto-suggestion on her part. You have disproved that, Miss Larcomb, as your ears are open to them too. That will go far to convince your brother; and now we must seriously seek for cause. This Roscawen district has many legends of strange happenings. We do not want to add one more to the list, and give this modern shooting-box the reputation of a haunted house."

"And it would be an odd sort of ghost, would it not—the sound of dropping water! But—you speak of legends of the district; do you know anything of a white woman who is said to drown cattle? Mrs Elliott mentioned her this morning at the farm, when she told us she had lost her cow in the river."

"Ay, I heard a cow had been found floating dead in the Pool. I am sorry it belonged to the Elliotts. Nobody lives here for long without hearing that story, and, though the wrath of Roscawen is roused against her, I cannot help being sorry for the white woman. She was young and beautiful once, and well-to-do, for she owned land in her own right, and flocks and herds. But she became very unhappy——"

He was speaking to me, but he looked at Freda. She had taken up her work again, but with inexpert hands, dropping first cotton, and then her thimble.

"She was unhappy, because her husband neglected her. He had—other things to attend to, and the charm she once possessed for him was lost and gone. He left her too much alone. She lost her health, they say, through fretting, and so fell into a melancholy way, spending her time in weeping, and in wandering up and down on the banks of Roscawen Water. She may have fallen in by accident, it was not exactly known; but her death was thought to be suicide, and she was buried at the cross-roads."

"That was where Grey Madam shied this morning," Freda put in.

"And—people suppose—that on the other side of death, finding herself lonely (too guilty, perhaps, for Heaven, but at the same time too innocent for Hell) she wants companions to join her; wants sheep and cows and horses such as used to stock her farms. So she puts madness upon the creatures, and also upon some humans, so that they go down to the river. They see her, so it is said, or they receive a sign which in some way points to the manner of her death. If they see her, she comes for them once, twice, thrice, and the third time they are bound to follow."

This was a gruesome story, I thought as I listened, though not of the sort I could believe. I hoped Freda did not believe it, but of this I was not sure.

"What does she look like?" I asked. "If human beings see her as you say, do they give any account?"

"The story goes that they see foam rising from the water, floating away and dissolving, vaguely in form at first, but afterwards more like the woman she was once; and some say there is a hand that beckons. But I have never seen her, Miss Larcomb, nor spoken to one who has: first hand evidence of this sort is rare, as I daresay you know. So I can tell you no more."

And I was glad there was no more for me to hear, for the story was too tragic for my liking. The happenings of that afternoon left me discomforted—annoyed with Dr Vickers, which perhaps was unreasonable—with poor Freda, whose fancies had thus proved contagious—annoyed, and here more justly, with myself. Somehow, with such tales going about, Roscawen seemed a far from desirable residence for a nervous invalid; and I was also vaguely conscious of an undercurrent I did not understand. It gave me the feeling you have when you stumble against something unexpected blindfold, or in the dark, and cannot define its shape.

Dr Vickers accepted a cup of tea when the tray was brought to us, and then he took his departure, which was as well, seeing we had no gentleman at home to entertain him.

"So Larcomb is away again for a whole week? Is that so?" he said to Freda as he made his adieux.

There was no need for the question, I thought impatiently, as he must very well have known when he was required again to put up Captain Falkner.

"Yes, for a whole week," Freda answered, with again that flush on her cheek; and as soon as we were alone she put up her hand, as if the hot colour burned.

III

I did not like Dr Vickers and his Italian lessons, and I had the impression Freda would have been better pleased by their intermission. On the third day she had a headache and charged me to make her excuses, so it fell to me to receive this friend of Robert's, who seemed quite unruffled by her absence. He took advantage of the opportunity to cross-examine me about the water-dropping: had I heard it again since that first occasion, and what explanation of the sounds appeared satisfactory to myself?

The fact was, I had heard it again, twice when I was sitting with Freda. Then we both sat listening—listening, such small nothings as we had to say to each other dying away, waiting to see which of us would first admit it to the other, and this went on for more than an hour. At last Freda broke out into hysterical crying, the result of over-strained nerves, and with her outburst the sounds ceased. I had been inclined to entertain a notion of the spiritist order, that they might be connected with her presence as medium; but I suppose that must be held disproved, as I also heard them when alone in my own room.

I admitted as little as possible to Dr Vickers, and was stout in asserting that a natural cause would and must be found, if the explanation were diligently sought for. But I confess I was posed when confronted with the fact that these sounds heard by Freda were inaudible to her husband, also present—to Robert, who has excellent hearing, in common with all our family. Until I came, and was also an auditor, no one in the house but Freda had noticed the dropping, so there was reason for assuming it to be hallucination. Yes, I was sorry for her trouble (answering a question pressed on me), but I maintained that, pending discovery, the best course was to take no notice of drops that wet nothing and left no stain, and did not proceed from overflowing cisterns or faulty pipes.

"They will leave off doing it if not noticed; is that what you think, Miss Larcomb?" And when I rashly assented—"Now perhaps you will define for me what you mean by *they*? Is it the 'natural cause'?"

Here again was a poser: I had formulated no idea that I cared to define. Probably the visitor divined the subject was unwelcome, for he turned to others, conversing agreeably enough for another quarter of an hour. Then he departed, leaving a message of concern for Freda's headache. He hoped it would have amended by next day, when he would call to inquire.

He did call on the following day, when the Italian lesson was mainly conversational, and I had again a feeling Freda was distressed by what was said, though I could only guess at what passed between them under the disguise of a foreign tongue. But at the end I recognised the words "not to-morrow" as spoken by her, and when some protest appeared to follow, she dumbly shook her head.

Dr Vickers did not stay on for tea as before. Did Freda think she had offended him, for some time later I noticed she had been crying?

That night I had an odd dream that the Roscawen house was sliding down from its foundations into the river at the call of the white woman, and I woke suddenly with the fright.

The next day was the last of Robert's stay at Shepstow. In the evening he and Captain Falkner returned, and at once a different atmosphere seemed to pervade the house. Freda recovered cheerfulness, I heard no more dropping water, and except at dinner on the second evening we saw nothing of Dr Vickers. But he sent an Italian book with many scored passages, and a note in it, also in Italian, which I saw her open and read, and then immediately tear up into the minutest pieces. I supposed he wished her to keep up her studies, though the lessons were for a while suspended; I heard him say at dinner that he was busy correcting proofs.

So passed four days out of the seven Robert should have spent at Roscawen. But on the fourth evening came a telegraphic summons: his presence was needed in London, at the office, and he was bound to go up to town by the early express next day. And the arrangement was that in returning he should go straight to Shepstow and join Captain Falkner there; this distant moor was to be reached from a station on another line.

Freda must have known that Robert could not help himself, but it was easy to see how her temporarily restored spirits fell again to zero. I hope I shall never be so dependent on another person's society as she seemed to be on Robert's. I got up to give him his early breakfast, but Freda did not appear; she had a headache, he said, and had passed a restless night. She would not rise till later: perhaps I would go up and see her by-and-bye.

I did go later in the morning, to find her lying like a child that had sobbed itself to sleep, her eyelashes still wet, and a tear sliding down her cheek. So I took a book, and drew a chair to the bedside, waiting for her to wake.

It was a long waiting; she slept on, and slept heavily. And so I sat and watched, there began again the dropping of water, and, for the first time in my experience of them, the drops were wet.

I could find traces now on the carpet of where they fell, and on the spread linen of the sheet; were they made, I wondered fantastically, out of Freda's tears? But they had ceased before she woke, and I did not remark on them to her. Yes, she had a headache, she said, answering my question: it was better, but not gone: she would lie quietly where she was for the present. The servants might bring her a cup of tea when I had luncheon, and she would get up later in the afternoon.

So, as I was not needed, I went out after lunch for a solitary walk. Not being governed by Freda's choice of direction, I determined to explore the course of the river, and especially how it flowed under the steep bank below the house, where I saw the wreath of foam rise in the air on my first evening at Roscawen. I expected to find a fall at this spot, but there was only broken water and rapids, alternating with smoother reaches and deep pools, one of which, I concluded, had been the death-trap of the Elliott's cow. It was a still, perfect autumn day, warm, but not with the oppression of summer heat, and I walked with enjoyment, following the stream upward to where it issued from the miniature lake among the hills, in which it slept for a while in mid-course. Then I turned homewards, and was within sight of our dwelling when I again beheld the phenomenon of the pillar of foam.

It rose above the rapids, as nearly as I could guess in the same spot as before; and as there was now little or no wind, it did not so quickly spread out and dissipate. I could imagine that at early morning, or in the dimness of evening, it might be taken for a figure of the ghostly sort, especially as, in dissolving, it seemed to move and beckon. I smiled to myself to think that, according to local superstition, I too had seen the white woman; but I felt no least inclination to rush to the river and precipitate myself into its depths. Nor would I gratify Dr Vickers by telling him what had been my experience, or confide in Freda lest she should tell again.

On reaching home, I turned into the snuggery to see if Freda was downstairs; it must, I thought, be nearly tea-time. She was there; and, as I pushed the door open and was still behind the screen, I heard Dr Vickers' voice. "Mind," he was saying in English, "I do not press you to decide at once. Wait till you are convinced he does not care. To my thinking he has already made it plain."

I stood arrested, not intending to play eavesdropper, but stricken with surprise. As I moved into sight, the two were standing face to face, and the doctor's figure hid Freda from me. I think his hands were on her shoulders, holding her before him, but of this I am not sure. He was quick of hearing as a cat, and he turned on me at once.

"Ah, how do you do, Miss Larcomb? I was just bidding adieu to your sister-in-law, for I do not think she is well enough to-day to take her lesson. In fact, I think she is very far from well. These headaches spell slow progress with our study, but we must put up with delay."

He took up the slim book from the table and bestowed it in his pocket, bowed over my hand and was gone.

If Freda had been agitated she concealed any disturbance, and we talked as usual over tea, of my walk, and even of Robert's journey. But she surprised me later in the evening by an unexpected proposition.

"Do you think Mrs Larcomb would have me to stay at Aston Bury? It would be very kind of her if she would take me in while Robert has these shootings. I do not like Roscawen, and I am not well here. Will you ask her, Mary?"

I answered that I was sure mother would have her if she wished to come to us; but what would Robert say when he had asked me to companion her here? If Robert was willing, I would write—of course. Did he know what she proposed?

No, she said, and there would be no time to consult him. She would like to go as soon as to-morrow. Could we send a telegram, and set out in the morning, staying the night in York, to receive an answer there? That she was very much in earnest about this wish of hers there could be no doubt. She was trembling visibly, and a red fever-spot burned on her cheek.

I wish I had done as she asked. But my Larcomb common-sense was up in arms, and I required to know the reason why. Mother would think it strange if we rushed off to her so, and Robert might not like it; but, given time to make the arrangement, she could certainly pay the visit, and would be received as a welcome guest. I would write to mother and post on the morrow, and she could write to Robert and send the letter by Captain Falkner. Then I said: "Are you nervous here, Freda? Is it because these water-droppings are unexplained?" And when she made a sort of dumb assent, I went on: "You ought not to dwell on anything so trivial; it isn't fair to Robert. It cannot be only this. Surely there is something more?"

The question seemed to increase her distress.

"I want to be a good wife to Robert; oh, I want that, Mary. I can do my duty if I go away; if you will keep me safe at Aston Bury for only a little while. Robert does not understand; he thinks me crazed with delusions. I tried to tell him—I did indeed; hard as it was to tell." While this was spoken she was torn with sobs. "I am terrified to be alone. What is compelling me is too strong. Oh Mary, take me away."

I could get no fuller explanation than this of what was at the root of the trouble. We agreed at last that the two letters should be written and sent on the morrow, and we would hold ourselves in readiness to set out as soon as answers were received. It might be no more than an hysterical fancy on Freda's part, but I was not without suspicion of another sort. But she never mentioned their neighbour's name, and I could not insult her by the suggestion.

The letters were written early on that Thursday morrow, and then Grey Madam was brought round for Freda's drive. The direction chosen took us past the cross-roads in the outward going, and also in return. I remember Freda talked more cheerfully and freely than usual, asking questions about Aston Bury, as if relieved at the prospect of taking refuge there with us. As we went, Grey Madam shied badly at the same spot as before, though there was no visible cause for her terror. I suggested we had better go home a different way; but this appeared impracticable, as the other direction involved an added distance of several miles, and the crossing of a bridge which was thought to be unsafe. In returning, the mare went unwillingly, and, though our pace had been a sober one and the day was not warm, I could see she had broken out into a lather of sweat. As we came to the cross-roads for the second time, the poor creature again shied away from the invisible object which terrified her, and then, seizing bit between her teeth, she set off at a furious gallop.

Freda was tugging at the reins, but it was beyond her power to stop that mad career, or even guide it; but the mare kept by instinct to the middle of the road. The home gate was open, and I expected she would turn in stablewards; but instead she dashed on to the open moor, making for the river.

We might possibly have jumped out, but there was no time even for thought before we were swaying on the edge of the steep bank. The next moment there was a plunge, a crash, and I remember no more.

The accident was witnessed from the further side—so I heard later. A man left his digging and ran, and it was he who dragged me out, stunned, but not suffocated by the immersion. I came to myself quickly on the bank, and my instant thought was of Freda, but she, entangled with the reins, had been swept down with the mare into the deeper pool. When I staggered up, dizzy and half-blind, begging she might be sought for, he ran on down stream, and there he and Dr Vickers and another man drew her from the water—lifeless it seemed at first, and it was long before any spark of animation repaid their utmost efforts.

That was a strange return to Roscawen house, she tenderly carried, I able to walk thither; both of us dripping water, real drops, of which the ghostly ones may have been some mysterious forecast, if that is not too fantastic for belief!

It was impossible to shut Dr Vickers out, and of course he accompanied us; for all my doubt of him, I welcomed the service of his skill when Freda's life was hanging in the balance, and she herself was too remote from this world to recognise who was beside her. But I would have preferred to owe that debt of service to any other; and the feeling I had against him deepened as I witnessed his anguished concern, and caught some unguarded expressions he let fall.

I wired to Robert to acquaint him with what had happened, and he replied "I am coming." And upon that I resolved to speak out, and tell him what I had guessed as the true cause of Freda's trouble, and why she must be removed, not so much from a haunted house, as from an overmastering influence which she dreaded.

Did the risk of loss—the peril barely surmounted, restore the old tenderness between these two? I think it did, at any rate for the time, when Robert found her lying white as a broken lily, and when her weak hands clung about his neck. Perhaps this made him more patient than he would have been otherwise with what I had to say.

He could hardly tax me with being fancy-ridden, but he was aghast—angry—incredulous, all in one. Vickers, of all people in the world; and Freda so worked upon as to be afraid to tell him—afraid to claim the protection that was hers by right. And now the situation was complicated by the fact that Vickers had saved her life, so that thanks were due to him as well as a kicking out of doors. And there was dignity to be thought of too: Freda's dignity as well as his own. Any open scandal must be avoided; she must neither be shamed nor pained.

I do not know what passed between him and Dr Vickers when they met, but the latter came no more to Roscawen, and after a while I heard incidentally that he had gone abroad. As soon as Freda could be moved, her wish was fulfilled, and I took her to Aston Bury. Mother was very gentle with her, and I think before the end a genuine affection grew up between the two.

The end was not long delayed; a few months passed, and then she faded out of life in a sort of decline; the shock to the system, so they said, had been greater than her vitality could repair. Robert was a free man again, war had been declared, and he was one of the earliest volunteers for service.

That service won distinction, as everybody knows; and now he is convalescent from his second wound, and here at Aston Bury on leave. And I think the wiser choice his sisters made for him in the first place is now likely to be his own. A much more suitable person than Frederica, and her name is quite a plain one—a real Larcomb name: it is Mary, like my own. I am glad; but in spite of all, poor Freda has a soft place in my memory and my heart. Whatever were her faults and failings, I believe she strove hard to be loyal. And I am sure that she loved Robert well.

THE DEVIL STONE

Beatrice Heron-Maxwell

Beatrice Heron-Maxwell (1863-1920) introduces us to a different aspect of witchcraft in this intriguing story which made its debut in print in *Pall Mall Magazine* at the turn of the century. It could be described as a story of possession—echoing the report by Mrs Catherine Crowe earlier in the book—but is probably better defined as a tale of lurking evil. The Victorians—certainly a great many of them—had a very real fear of evil influences, and in her story Miss Heron-Maxwell describes the occult power of an ancient Indian ring and how it tragically affects the lives of two people. The authoress travelled extensively throughout Europe and the Far East during her youth and wrote a considerable amount of fiction set against foreign backgrounds.

∞∞∞∞∞∞∞∞∞∞∞∞∞∞∞∞∞∞∞∞∞∞∞∞∞∞∞∞∞∞∞∞∞∞

It was in the dusky, tepid twilight of a particularly hot, vaporous, drowsy day at Aix-les-bains, in Savoy, that I passed through the hotel garden, and prepared to take a languid stroll through the streets of the little town. I was tired of having nothing to do and no one to talk to; the other people staying at the Hotel de l'Europe were mostly foreigners, and, apart from that, entirely uninteresting; and as to my father, he was almost a nonentity to me at present, till his "course" was completed. From early morn to dewy eve he was immersed in the waters, either outwardly or inwardly, or both; and beyond occasional glimpses of him, arrayed in a costume resembling that of an Arab sheikh, being conveyed in pomp and a sedan chair to or from the baths, I was, figuratively speaking, an orphan until *table d' hôte*.

As I crossed the verandah some one rose from a long chair, and, throwing his book down, said, "Where are you going, Miss Durant? May I come too?"

"If you like," I answered, politely but indifferently; "I am only going to look for spoons."

"For——?"

"Spoons. I am collecting, you know; it is something to do—and one can always give them away when one is tired of them."

So we sauntered along, side by side; and as we did so I began to feel less bored, and more reconciled to the trouble of existence, and finally amused and interested and flattered.

For this quiet-looking middle-aged man—to whom my father had introduced me two days before, as an old friend of his, and whom I had mentally summed up as "Rather handsome, clever perhaps, conceited possibly, and married probably"—was making himself agreeable as only a cultivated, polished man of the world, who wishes to make a favourable impression, can; and gradually I found myself acknowledging that his dark, intellectual face, with its crown of waving, iron-grey hair, was something more than handsome, and that his cleverness was sufficient to carry him beyond conceit, while apparently it did not set him above a very evident enjoyment of a girl's society and conversation. He had already learnt most of my tastes and occupations, and drawn from me, by a magnetic sympathy, some confessions as to my inmost thoughts and aspirations, telling me in return that he was travelling wearily in search of rest, authoritatively ordered by his doctor; and he was deploring his lonely bachelorhood, when my attention was attracted by some quaint spoons half hidden amongst other dull silver things in a forsaken-looking little shop to which our wanderings had led us through narrow, dingy byways. "I wonder how much they are," I said; and, asking me to wait outside, Colonel Haughton disappeared into the obscure interior. I remained gazing through the window for a moment, then, impelled by what idle impulse I know not, I walked slowly on.

The sound of a casement opening just over my head and a feminine laugh arrested me, and I looked up. It was a curious laugh, low and controlled, but with a malicious mockery in it that seemed a fit ending to some scathing speech; and just inside the open lattice, her arms resting on the sill and chin dropped lightly on her clasped hands, leant the most beautiful woman I have ever seen. It was but a glimpse of auburn hair on a white forehead, of eyes like brown pansies, and parted lips that looked like scarlet petals against the perfect pallor of her rounded cheeks, but it is photographed for ever on my brain. For, as I looked, a man's hand and arm, brown, lean, and very supple, with nervous fingers, on one of which a green stone flashed, clutching a poniard, came round her neck, and plunged the dagger, slanting-wise, deep down into her heart. The smile on the beautiful lips quivered and fixed, but no sound came from them, and the eyes turned up and closed; and as she swayed towards the open window, the spell that was upon me broke, and with a shuddering cry I fled. On, on—blindly, madly, desperately—with no sense or thought or feeling save an overwhelming horror. A red mist seemed to close round me and wall me in, and as I fought against it I felt my strength fail, and all was dark and still.

Somewhere in the darkness a voice speaking, the touch of a hand on my face, a glimpse of light, a sense of pain that some one was suffering, then consciousness and memory. My father's anxious face bent over me, and his voice, as though from a distance, said, "Theo, are you better, dear? No, don't get up—rest, and take this." And, sinking back, I vaguely understood that I was in my own room at the hotel, and that a stranger, a doctor no doubt, was present. He enjoined absolute quiet till he saw me again, and asked that he should be informed at once if there was any recurrence of fainting. Later, when I was in a condition to explain the origin of this attack, he would be able to prescribe for me. The light of dawn was struggling through the curtains, and I knew that I must have been unconscious for many hours. With the effort to banish all recollections of the terrible scene I had witnessed, came lethargy, and later, deep and dreamless sleep.

Some days of seclusion and rest partially restored my health and spirits, and I began to feel that what had passed had been a sort of evil dream, a terror that were best forgotten. My father when he heard my story was at first incredulous; then, impressed in spite of himself by my earnestness, he gave an unwilling belief to it, but he

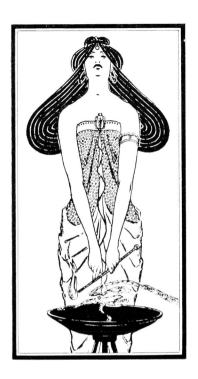

(*left*) An artist's rather unusual impression of a witch from *Uncanny Tales*, a collection of occult stories by Mrs Molesworth

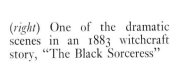

(*right*) One of the dramatic scenes in an 1883 witchcraft story, "The Black Sorceress"

The arrest of a witch at Salem, taken from *Ye Little Salem Maide* by Pauline Mackie

entreated me to mention it to no one save himself. He could find no account of a murder in the local papers, nor could he ascertain whether the tragedy I saw was known to have taken place, and as he did not wish my name to be introduced in any inquiry he allowed the matter to drop. To him I spoke of it no more, but the remembrance of it would not be wholly banished. I was haunted by the sight of that lovely face, and the sound of that laugh with its dreadful sequel. And a strange fancy had come to me also that the face was in some way familiar to me; I would lie with closed eyes for hours, seeking in vain to recall the resemblance that just eluded me. One day meditating thus I roused myself from my reverie, and met my own reflection in a mirror that hung opposite. Breathless I gazed, while a new terror took possession of me. There was the resemblance I had sought: there were the auburn hair, the deep dark eyes, the colourless face with scarlet lips just parted. Not so beautiful, perhaps, as the one I had seen at the window; indeed, as I gradually comprehended it was myself I gazed upon, I could see no beauty in the familiar features; but so like—so wonderfully, terribly like! And then for the first time I began to doubt the reality of my vision, and to long eagerly for the power to put it from me. I determined to rest and dream no longer, and that afternoon I descended to the garden.

"At last!" said Colonel Haughton, taking both my hands. "I thought we were never going to see you again. I have been reproaching myself with having overtired you that day—with having left you: I had no intention of remaining away from you for more than a moment, and I want to explain what detained me. When I came out and found you gone, I concluded you had returned here, and hurrying on I was fortunate enough to reach you just before you fainted. Your father tells me you have had a touch of malaria, and I hope—— But I distress you, Miss Durant; I am tiring you. Let me find you a comfortable chair and leave you to rest."

"No, no," I cried eagerly; "stay;—I will sit here. Tell me, where did you get that ring?"

On his finger shone a curious green stone, that seemed the counterpart of the one I had noticed on the hand that held the dagger.

"That is exactly what I want to tell you," he said. "After getting your spoons for you, I noticed, resting on a carved bracket, this ring. It is a very curious stone. You see it looks quite dull now, yet it can

o

sparkle with all the brilliancy of a diamond. And on the back of it is cut part of the head of a snake. I have only seen a ring like this once before, and that was long ago in a hill temple in India. They called it the Devil Stone, and worshipped it, and they told me the tradition of it. Centuries before, this stone had been discovered by a holy man, embedded in a sacred relic, and he made a shrine for it, whence it was stolen by robbers. The next stage in its history was its division into two equal parts by a Maharajah, who had them set into rings, one of which he wore always himself, and the other he bestowed on his Maharanee, whom he loved greatly. One day he found it missing from her finger, and in a fit of jealousy he killed her, afterwards destroying himself. His ring passed into the possession of the Brahmins, but hers could never be traced. They say that eventually the two will be reunited, and that until this happens the lost ring will fufil its mission. It is supposed to impel its wearer to deeds of violence, and to his own destruction; and when the evil spirit within it is gratified, it flashes and sparkles. They say, too, that if you cast it from you, you throw away with it the greatest happiness of your life and lose the chance of it for ever. Yet, if you wear it, it dominates your fate. The instant I saw it, I recognised the lost ring, and asked the man his price for it. He refused to tell me—said it was not for sale; and I left the shop, because I did not wish to keep you waiting longer; but I returned next day, and succeeded in obtaining it. The old man, a curious old Italian, was very reticent about it, but he seemed to have gathered some knowledge of the tradition, and said it had the "evil eye," and was neither good to sell nor to wear. It had been sold to him by a compatriot, he said, who had a dark history—a man who was ever too ready with his knife, and who had come to a bad end. I told him I would steal it, and he might charge me what he liked for some other purchases, so we settled it that way."

"Are you not afraid to wear it?" I asked. "It makes me shudder to look at it. There is some deadly fascination about it, I am sure."

"I am afraid of nothing," he said lightly, "except your displeasure, Miss Theo. If it annoys you I will not wear it, but I confess it has a very great fascination for me. I do not believe in superstition, but I like the stone for its antiquity and strange history. Some day I will send it to my friends the Brahmins; meanwhile it inspires me with no evil propensity, and since it has interested you I am grateful to it so far."

So I resolved to put the ring and its story out of my mind, and to occupy myself only with the new interest that had dawned upon my life. The next few days went by so happily, and it seemed so natural to me that Lionel Haughton should be always at my side, that I did not stay to ask myself the reason for our close companionship—yet I think within my heart of hearts I knew. And each day, each hour I spent with him, was bringing us nearer together and binding us with ties that would not easily be broken.

"Haughton is very much improved," said my father one day, "since I knew him many years ago—his brother was my great friend, and I did not see much of this one—he seems to have spent a good deal of his life in India, and I fancy it has affected his health. I suppose he won't return there. I must persuade him to come and pay us a visit when we go home, eh, Theo?"

One evening, when our stay was drawing to a close, we proposed to go to the Casino, where I wished to try my luck at gambling. "I am always lucky if things go by chance," I said, "and I have neglected my opportunity here sadly. Let us go and gamble to-night, and I will win fortunes for all of us." Colonel Haughton did not, however, join us as usual at *table d'hôte* that evening, and a note handed to me afterwards from him told me that he had been feeling ill, but was now better, and would meet us later at the Casino. It was the first time I had ever played, and before long it became apparent that my prophecy about my luck was being fulfilled: I won, and won, and won again, till a heap of gold and notes was in front of me, and I was the centre of all eyes at the table. I played recklessly, and yet I could not lose, till suddenly my attention was distracted by the arrival of Colonel Haughton, who leant over my shoulder and placed his stake next to mine. As he did so the ring seemed me to emit a faint sparkle, and I felt as if my careless good fortune had deserted me. I *wanted* to win now, whereas before I had played for the excitement only, with the true gambler spirit. And yet from that moment I lost. He also lost, heavily—so heavily that I wondered if he were rich enough to take it as philosophically as he appeared to. Nevertheless so large a sum had I won at first that, though much diminished, it was still a small fortune that I gathered up when we left the tables.

"You brought me bad luck," I said to Colonel Haughton, as we walked back to the hotel. "Do you know, I think it was your ring."

"I would never wear it again if I thought that," he answered. Then as we reached the garden, and my father passed on to the salon, "Theo," he continued, "stay a moment. I have something to tell you My darling, I love you; I love you more than life: will you try to care for me a little in return? I want you for my wife. I worship you!"

Ah, Lionel! beloved! it scarcely needed the assurance of your love for me to bring me the certainty of mine for you! If ever the gates of Heaven open to mortal eyes, they stood ajar for us that night; the starlit garden was changed into a veritable Eden, and we walked with wondering joy therein, and thought not of an angel with flaming sword, who waited silently to drive us from our Paradise into outer darkness.

It was scarcely noon, the following day, when we began the ascent of the Dent du Chat, one of the mountain peaks that tower above Aix.

"I feel as if I had wings, and must soar into a higher atmosphere," I had said gaily; "and since we cannot fly, let us climb. I want to reach the top of that mountain with you, and leave the world behind us. Let us go."

We were to ride up to a certain distance, and then dismount and gain the highest point on foot. Three guides accompanied us, following leisurely, talking and gesticulating to each other, and paying little heed to us, save an occasional frantic rush at the mules when we approached an awkward corner of the zigzag pathway, which had the effect of adding a momentary uncertainity and danger to our otherwise tranquil ascent. We were not sorry when, after two or three hours of this progress, the guides told us we must halt, and that they would remain in charge of the mules till we returned to them. It was rather a toilsome climb, and the sun was beating fiercely down upon us; but we felt rewarded when, not far from the top, we reached a plateau where we could rest, while a cool breeze from the distant snowy peaks revived us.

"Here is an arm-chair all ready for you," Lionel said, leading me to where a soft couch of mossy turf lay beneath the shadow of an upright, projecting piece of rock. A yard or two farther on, the precipitous side of the mountain descended, sheer and impassable down almost to its foot, terminating in a dark and narrow gorge between two ridges. Away on the left far below us nestled Aix, and by its side the Lac du Bourget, with its island monastery surrounded by water as blue as Geneva's own.

"How lovely it is!" I exclaimed; "I never knew before how beautiful life could be."

"Nor I," he answered; "I have been waiting for my wife to teach me." And then he told me of his life in India, and of many adventures he had had, and finally we spoke again of the ring and of my strange and sudden illness on that day.

"Some day I will tell you all about it," I said, "and why I have such a curious feeling against the ring. I wish you would not wear it; yet now that you possess it I have a sort of superstitious dread that, if you part from it, it will revenge itself upon you in some way. I am sure I saw it sparkle last night when the cards went against us. You were so terribly unlucky."

"Unlucky at cards, lucky in love," he quoted; but I noticed a shadow on his face. "What have you done with all your wealth, little gambler?—you have not had time to spend it yet."

"Here it is," I answered, drawing out my pocket-book, in which I had stuffed the notes; "but I have taken a dislike to it—I shall give it away, I think. I would rather be lucky in another way," and I laid it down beside me on the grass.

"I will send the ring to India on my wedding day," Lionel exclaimed; "till then will you wear it for me?" and, drawing it from his finger, he was about to place it upon mine.

But I would not allow him to do so, and laying it on the bank notes I said, "There's a contradiction! Good luck and bad luck side by side! Let us leave them there," I added, half laughing, half in earnest, "and start again fresh."

He turned suddenly away, and, fearing he was vexed, I laid my hand upon his arm; but he shook it gently off, and then I saw he was singularly pale, and that his breathing was quick and short, and his eyes had a strangely troubled and intent look. "Lionel, you are ill," I cried. "Oh, what is it, love? what can I do for you?"

"It is nothing," he said faintly, but his voice was changed: "it will pass off. I will return to the guides and get some water. Wait here till I come back."

"Let me come with you," I entreated, but he shook his head, and said he was better and would be quite well if I would do as he wished; then he began the descent. I watched him for a few moments, till he was lost to view at a bend of the mountain, before returning to my seat. But the sun had gone in, and it seemed cold and dark, and a dull heavy weight rested on my heart. I was lonely there without him, and the moments dragged on slowly and drearily, till I felt the suspense and stillness unendurable.

I decided I would wait only five minutes more and then I would follow him, and, leaning back wearily, I closed my eyes. A sort of faintness came over me—for I was tired, and the sudden change from perfect happiness to this anxiety, this vague alarm, had chilled and stupefied me.

It may have been a few moments after, or longer (I cannot tell), but I became aware suddenly that, although no sound of footsteps had reached me, there was some one near. I remained absolutely still and listened intently, and though there was no tangible movement or sound, there was an impalpable stir in the stillness round me, some vague breath that seemed to speak of danger. I felt paralysed with the same powerlessness that had seized me when the tragedy at the window was enacted before my eyes. It flashed into my mind that perhaps it was a thief, attracted by the notes and ring lying beside me, who had crept behind believing that I slept. My hand was almost touching them, and as I glanced down to see if I could reach them without moving, I noticed with a thrill of indescribable horror that the green stone was sparkling brilliantly with a thousand rays of scintillating light.

And then—something stirred behind me, and round my neck crept a hand, holding a short sharp knife such as Indians carry, and poised it over my heart as if to strike. With an instantaneous desperate throb of agonised revolt against my impending fate, I grasped the ring and flung it towards the precipice. As it flashed through the air the knife dropped, and the murderer sprang to the edge in a vain effort to catch the stone ere it fell. He stumbled, missed his footing, and, with one terrible cry and his hands grasping the air wildly, he fell backwards into the abyss.

And it was Lionel—my beloved!

When the guides came to look for us I told them smilingly that the English gentleman had dropped his ring and in trying to find it had slipped and fallen over the precipice.

They led me dow the mountain with reverent care and hushed steps and voices; for they said to each other, "Figure to yourself this English colonel was in love with the beautiful young lady, and he has perished before her eyes,—it is a terrible thing, and it has turned her brain."

And when my father told me gently, some days after, that they had found *him* and he was to be buried that day in the little cemetery, I laughed outright.

But I have never smiled since—and I am quite sane now—only I think I have done with laughter for the rest of my life. And I sometimes wonder why these things should have been; and if there is any explanation of them, save one.

BLACK MAGIC
A Story of The East

Jessie Adelaide Middleton

Jessie Adelaide Middleton (1861-1921) was certainly one of the most famous Victorian ghost-lore collectors and her two major works, *The Grey Ghost Book* and *Another Grey Ghost Book* are much sought-after items today. Her tales were collected from all over the world and in "Black Magic" she takes us to India and a story from Army life. The British Empire was still at its greatest when this story was written and the imperious attitude of the characters is so typical of the British ruling class abroad. It is a tale doubly evocative: of an age and of a type of dark magic.

~~~~~~

The lady who has kindly authenticated this story from her own personal knowledge had a cousin who married an officer in the Indian Army and went out to India about the year 19—. As I am not permitted to mention their names, though they have allowed me to use the story, I will call them Captain and Mrs Ross. Mrs Ross had beautiful red-gold hair, which is much admired by the native races.

On arriving at Calcutta they went up-country, where Captain Ross was stationed, and Mrs Ross, who had never been in India before, was charmed with all she saw.

When they arrived at his bungalow, Mrs Ross noticed an old native who was squatting outside the compound. He was a particularly repulsive-looking old man, ragged, dirty and evil-looking, who, although he salaamed very humbly as the new mem-sahib passed by, gave her a most sinister look which made her shiver.

She asked her husband about him, telling him her experience, and Captain Ross said calmly—

"Oh, he has been there for ages; nobody takes any notice of him."

"But I don't like the look of him," persisted his wife. "Can't you send him away?"

"Certainly not," said Captain Ross, laughing. "It doesn't do to offend these fellows. He is a very important old chap in his way—that is to say, in the eyes of the natives. They say he is a wise man, and they are all afraid of him."

Of course, Mrs Ross said no more, being unwilling to do anything of which her husband disapproved. The old man came every day and sat at the gate. Every time she passed him he salaamed most respectfully, but looked at her in a horrid way. It was quite evident that he had seen from the first that she disliked him and wanted him to be turned away from the bungalow.

After a few weeks her husband was called away on duty, and before going he recommended his wife not to go near the native bazaars; but Mrs Ross, strangely enough, had kept on feeling that she wanted to go to the native part of the town. Her head ached ceaselessly, and she felt a strange, restless feeling that she did not want to stay in the bungalow. She spoke of this to her husband over and over again.

"All I want is to go out there!" was her cry; and he soothed her and told her that it was all "nerves" and that she should have a change of air as soon as it could possibly be managed.

One day Mrs Ross was sitting under the verandah, when she felt that some one was near her. Looking round, she had a shock, for there, close behind her, was the old native, his eyes fixed on her with a malevolent stare. Captain Ross was still away on duty, and there was nobody except the native servants within call. Mrs Ross was terribly nervous, but, summoning all her courage, she got up and faced the man and told him sharply to go away at once.

He made no sign of moving, but stood looking at her with the same malignant look she had already noticed. A second time she told him to go, saying she would have him turned out by the servants. She was about to call them, when he said very slowly and impressively—

"Me not go till have one of your hairs out of head."

His eyes had a most peculiar power, and Mrs Ross was too frightened to move or call for help. He fascinated her as a cat does a mouse under its paws, and she realized that at all cost she must not show the white feather.

"All right," she said, as kindly as she could. "If you want one you shall have it. I'll go and let down my hair and bring you one."

He let her go so calmly and quietly that the awful thought seized her that the native servants might be in the plot against her. She was new to India, and had read dreadful stories of native treachery; so, instead of raising an alarm, she went into the bedroom and sat down to think.

"What am I going to do?" was her agonized thought. "I am not going to give him the hair. He wants it for some devilish reason. I mustn't put myself in his power. What shall I do?"

While she was wondering what she could do, her eyes suddenly lighted on a mat which was on the floor next her bed. It was one of her wedding presents, and was woven out of hair. In a trice she thought to herself, "I know! I'll give him a hair out of the mat. It is sufficiently like mine to deceive him." Stooping down, she carefully extracted a long hair out of the mat; then she rang the bell, and when the servant answered it, she gave him the hair and told him to give it to the old man out on the verandah.

The servant remonstrated with her, and was evidently horrified at the idea.

"Must no give hair," he said. "Him mustn't have hair."

"Do as I tell you," said Mrs Ross. And the native withdrew.

Presently he returned and said the old man was gone.

Mrs Ross breathed a sigh of deep relief.

When Captain Ross came home that evening his wife told him the whole episode, and he was exceedingly angry, and scolded the servants soundly for letting the old Hindoo come into the verandah. He said she had done quite right, and had now better let the matter drop.

One night, about a week later, they were both sitting in the dining-room after dinner. It was about eleven o'clock. Captain Ross was smoking, and Mrs Ross was sitting in an easy-chair. It was about a week after the incident of the hair. The servants had brought in coffee, and retired to their own quarters. Captain Ross was smoking a cigarette and stirring his coffee slowly, very worried about his wife, who had been feeling very ill all through dinner. He was puzzled as to what was the matter with her, as he had never known her to be like this before. Suddenly she pushed back her chair, and her husband saw her rise slowly, take a step towards the window, stretch out her arms, sway slightly and moan faintly.

Just at this moment he heard a noise in their bedroom above—a kind of muffled flap! flap! flap! which seemed to move across the floor. He looked at his wife, and saw her give a startled glance upwards.

Seizing his revolver, which lay near, he jumped up and listened. Still the noise went on—flap! flap! flap! He went to the door and opened it softly. The noise grew more distinct. Presently he heard it coming to the top of the stairs and then down—flap! flap! flap!

Captain Ross rushed out, and in the dim light saw something coming downstairs. He fired where the noise was, but it still went on. Then he fired again, and again a third time. Still the noise passed on and out over the verandah, and was heard crossing the compound.

The sound of the shots roused the servants, who rushed in with lights. Mrs Ross staggered blindly out on to the verandah, and her husband sprang forward to grapple with the expected thief, but, to his amazement, there was no one there.

As they stood looking, his wife gave a loud exclamation and clutched him by the arm, crying, "Good God! Look there!"

Crossing the compound was the Chinese mat from the bedroom above, with three burnt holes where the bullets had passed through it.

THE SATANIST

Mrs Hugh Fraser

Mrs Hugh Fraser (1864-1925). With the death of Queen Victoria
and the end of her long and restrictive reign, a great many aspects
of the social climate changed: not the least of these being in the
world of literature. Of course, there had been the occasional out-
spoken writer and artist (though I am taking no cognisance of the
underground pornographic publishing industry which flourished
during the nineteenth century), but by and large books had con-
formed rigorously to all social and moral strictures. To say the
flood-gates of permissive writing were opened with the old
queen's death would certainly not be accurate, but the atmosphere undoubtedly became one in which the publication of more
radical views and more explicit fiction became possible. In the
area in which this book is covering we find suddenly more detailed
stories of horrible black magic practises and accounts of nude
witchcraft ceremonies. To close, then, I have selected the following story of Satanism with its quite chilling scenes and vivid
descriptions of a black mass. "The Satanist", along with several
other stories of the same period set the standards for today's
occult fiction and can be seen mirrored in the tales of August
Derleth, Dennis Wheatley and, more particularly still, Ira
Levin's exciting macabre novel, *Rosemary's Baby*. Like them,
too, it is a story without an ending—for the practice of Satanism
itself is unending.

~~~~~~

The message which Léonie received from her friend Yolanda had
not been very explicit, but something in its tone caused her to shudder
as she hurried to her friend's house. Almost immediately on entering

Léonie was hurried into the sitting-room, the door was locked and she was hustled onto the couch.

"Do not think me insane, Léonie," Yolande began briskly, "but the time has come for me to pay you a debt of confidence for all your dear friendship to me. And I am going to do it now. Now——" she repeated, turning away and going over to a tall standard lamp. "Will you come here to the lamp, please? I want you to unfasten my bodice for me. Do not be afraid, but do as I ask you."

And Léonie rose and followed, in the trance-like passivity imposed upon her by the strange fatefulness of the girl's action and request.

"Yolanda, dear, is it absolutely necessary?"—was all she asked. "Then it shall be as you wish."

Only once, when the silk dinner-blouse divided, showing a splash of white undergarment beneath, did she waver, in nightmare despondency, and find force to look away.

"Yolanda, are you quite sure?" she entreated. "Perhaps there are things—things that you might be sorry for afterwards?"

"No——" with a desperate determination to which Léonie had no option but to defer. The nape of the girl's neck, bowed with an indomitable meekness, as to meet a mortal stroke, as well as the two hands of her that had clenched themselves into her skirt on either side in a passion of resolve, conveyed a command that was not to be disregarded. "Go on, Léonie—why do you make it harder for me?"

Léonie obeyed. Loosening the edges of the embroidered cambric, she parted them, laying bare the skin to below the milky shoulder-blades; and then, carried beyond herself at something else that the movement of her fingers had disclosed, she leaned forward under the lamp with a scream of horror.

"Ah, you have seen?" sighed Yolanda, her rigidity relaxing. "Then cover it up, please. Now I can tell you what I hope never to have to tell again to anyone—except to a priest, some day, when I have had my full share of this world's happiness, and am tired of love—if that can ever be. Come, say, do you still wonder that I am jealous of my womanhood, Léonie—that I would rather keep my life for a man's whole love and belief than lose it, perhaps, and his love, too, for the sake of my salvation?"

Léonie, too full of sickened bewilderment at what she had seen to speak at any length, could only utter a few disjointed words of pitying tenderness, as she replaced the dainty coverings over the sight that had thrust a knife-blade into her imagination.

"Oh, you poor little girl—you poor little girl!" she stammered, the tears blinding her so that she could scarcely see for them. "My own gentle Yolanda—who could have done you such a wickedness?"

And when she had done with closing the blouse she placed her lips to it, impelled by a rush of reparatory tenderness for that which it concealed.

Yolanda, when it was over, came round, disengaging the train of her skirt that was coiled about her ankles, looked up and smiled dazzlingly, as might a soul on its release from the gyves of physical pain and weariness.

"Take comfort, my Léonie—all the pain has gone now," she said. "It will never torture or shame me again. Let us go back to the sofa and I will tell you what I have never told you before—how I came to be what I am to-night. It will not take so very long, perhaps."

Her chin supported by her hands, her elbows resting on her crossed knees, Yolanda was staring into the fire, seeking to trace in it the scattered mosaic-fragments of memory in order to piece them together anew, before beginning upon her story. Presently, without altering her position, she said:

"Do you know, Léonie, now that I come to think of it, this is going to be the first time that you and I have ever spoken of my life before I met you. That was five years ago. Why have you never asked me any questions about myself?"

"What right had I, Yolanda? If you were willing to take me for granted, how could I do otherwise by you in return? I was drawn to you from the first—that night when we were the only two people to leave the meeting of the Roman Lodge before the—the unthinkable part of the ceremonial. I knew at once that you were only there as I was myself, through fear of *Them*, and my heart went out to you. I did not even know your name—do you remember?—and I told you mine as we came away together. You never asked me how it was that I first joined *Them*, and I never dreamed of asking you why you did. We were both suffering the same horrible shame and self-loathing, and that was enough for me."

Yolanda touched the other's knee, as she might have done something holy, lingeringly, very lightly.

"Thank you for all you have been to me ever since," she went on. "And thank you for never having asked me the reason of my being where you first saw me, that night, Leonie. But now, as I say, the time has come to tell you. If it is possible, I should like you always to think of me a little compassionately—even if I *should* seem to deserve only condemnation. God knows!—I would give anything to be reconciled to Him—

"Well, it all dates from the day that I was born," she proceeded. "I ought to have been a boy, you see, and I was not. I was only a girl. So that everything was against me from the start. And the fact of my not having any brothers or sisters did not help to make it any better for me.

"I sometimes think that if children could be taken away from their parents altogether, in certain cases, and brought up by people who had no personal interest at stake in them, until they were old enough to have a moral armour of their own, it would be better for all concerned, the parents as well as the children themselves.

"You never met my mother, because I did not intend that you should. I was afraid that she might teach even you, in those last years of her life, to look upon me as though I had been something never to be touched without gloves.

"Yolanda! Your own mother? But——"

"Try not to interrupt me if you can help it, Léonie—although what you have got to hear will be enough to make you. But I want to be as perfectly just as I can in speaking of my mother. I did her an injury, and it was not in her nature to forgive injuries. She was unfortunate, too, in many ways. She had no practical religion left at all when I knew her, and the mention of another life was quite enough to send her into a passion, because it entailed the idea of death, and—of surrender to a Providence with which she would never willingly consent to be reconciled—in revenge for what she considered the cruelty of its dealings with her. I have never known anyone with such an awful bitterness of hatred for the thought of dying as she; it was a monomania, an obsession.

"I spoke just now of an injury I had done her. It was very simple. In the first place, as I say, my being a girl and not a boy was a dreadful disappointment to her, because she had set her heart on having a son to reap the benefit of my father's career in politics; and, secondly, because after I was born she lost all her health and good looks. Before then she had been one of the most beautiful women of her day; when her strength and beauty fell away from her, she had nothing left, as she thought, to live for any more. I daresay her mind became just the least bit affected by brooding over it, too, as time went on. At any rate, I prefer to think so now, in charity to her memory. She was too terribly unhappy and humiliated and embittered to be perfectly sane.

"I only wish I had been able to see it in that light while she was still alive.

"She never once spoke pleasantly to me if she could help it. Of course, she had to keep up appearances in public; but she never kissed me in her life, nor did she ever once come into my room, when I was still a little girl, to say 'Good night' to me. Oh, but if ever I am allowed the chance of saying 'Good night' to a child of mine——"

She paused before continuing:

"When I was about twelve, and she saw that I was going to be nice-looking, the thing became so monstrous that people were beginning to notice it, until, at last, papa sent me away for a couple of years to a convent school in the South, in Milan. I think he was afraid she might do something to me and that there would be a scandal. At any rate, he kept me away from home as long as he decently could. He would not even let me go back for the holidays until he thought, I suppose, that she had had time in which to get over her dislike of me—although he made a point of travelling up to Milan himself twice a year, to take me for a month or six weeks to Cadennabia or Mentone. He was always kind to me. After I began to grow pretty he used to amuse himself by showing me off to any men friends of his that we met in the hotels. They used to pay me the silliest compliments to please him—not always in the best of taste, perhaps —but I was grateful for them.

"Until I went to the convent, religion had not been to me, in any sense, what it is to most children, a sort of spiritual play-room or kindergarten. It was nothing but a matter of half an hour in church once a week—papa always insisted on my going, although he never went near one himself—and of four or five minutes alone on my knees every morning—praying to I scarcely knew what. I had no one to stimulate me, to see, as other children have, towards things religious, by hearing me say my prayers and telling me about God and my Guardian Angel.

"The nuns in Milan did all they could to interest me in what meant so much to them. But the time was past to do any real good with me by their methods; there was no foundation for them to build upon, although, as I say, they did their best. They had me confirmed and saw to it that I made my First Communion properly, after which they could only treat me as they did the other girls, by keeping me out of harm as long as I was in their hands. All I got from my stay with them, apart from a very fair education, was an unalterable conviction of the agency of God in the affairs of everyday life. It was not love for God at all, because there was no room in me for love of anything except admiration; but just that—an abiding, haunting conviction that was more rebellious than submissive. You can understand it, can you not, that I should have thought the nuns took it all rather too seriously, when I used to hear papa talk of his friends about what he called 'the regrettable lack of broadmindedness and generosity of the present Church system,' before me? I saw that he was a great man, an important man, and that they were only women without anything like his knowledge of the world or his strength or cleverness.

"After my return with him to home, things really went a little better, at first, than they had before. It seemed to me, and I was quite sharp enough by then to notice it, that my mother was rather afraid of me—although I was wrong in that, because it was not of me but of papa—and I could see that she tried hard, when we were all together, to make him believe that she had changed towards me. But I took care not to be left alone with her. I knew perfectly well that her dislike for me was ever so much stronger than she, and that, given the slightest chance, it would get the upper hand of her. Then it was that I really began to hate her in return—her slyness and the underlying ugliness of everything she said or did to me as long as papa had his eye on us both.

"For those first few weeks I kept up my religious duties in a sort of mechanical way, although I grudged them what I felt was their intolerable interference with my hatred for my mother. One night, I remember, when I came to the 'Forgive us our trespasses as we forgive,' and so on, I simply could not say it. I could not go on. I had to get up and stand there while I stormed against the unfairness of it. I said, 'You have no right to ask it of me—I am not the offender. Why should I tell lies about it? I will not, I will not! Why are You on *her* side? What harm have I ever done to You or to her?' "

The resentful peal that rang in her accents, even now, as she passed through that dread hour again in vivid recollection, was more than Léonie could endure unmoved.

"Yolanda—don't!" she cried. "It was all so long ago—and you were only a child! Let it stay in its grave. Think of what you have to tell me and go on!"

"You are right, Léonie," the magic voice replied. "It shall rest in its grave decently enough after to-night. But for this once you must consent to look at it. From that moment until four years ago, when my mother left us, I never prayed again. As I say, I could not. I have prayed, since then, for her and for myself—not often, I am afraid, or well, but still I have prayed. And you know that I have never been able to lose my faith.

"After that night, it seemed as if my own words had let loose the Powers of Darkness in the house. Not a day, not a waking hour went by without my feeling that the spirit of hatred was getting ready to escape from my mother's control; the very air felt stagnant and poisoned with it, and at night I never went to bed without locking my door. So I learned to know what fear is. But the fact of my fear only stiffened me in my obstinacy against submitting and forgiving; against asking for forgiveness and grace to get the victory over myself. It was then that I began—quite unconsciously, for I had never yet even heard of such things—to wander over the border into the dominion of *Them*.

"I must tell you about that time, a maid, Rosina Delré, was told to look after me and see that my clothes were properly kept."

"That creature!" broke out Léonie.

"Well, she is dead now, so let us try not to think too hardly of her— and she was sincerely penitent at the end. Until then I had seen no more than a little of her. She was very quick and unobtrusive in doing what she had to do; but I caught her watching me once or twice as though she had something she wanted to say, but was undecided as to how I might take it. I fancied she must be sorry for me, and was almost inclined to confide in her for want of sympathy and an ally— the loneliness was getting to be too much for me—but I could not quite bring myself to it, and held my tongue until, at last, circumstances drove me to telling her everything."

Again she paused, in order to make sure of her own courage before continuing.

"One morning, towards the end of that summer, I was in the garden with papa when a telegram came for him, to say that he was to go at once to Monza.

"There had been heavy floods there, and he was wanted to help in organizing the relief measures. The rivers had overflowed their banks after heavy rains, although we had not had a drop for weeks at home, and the heat was terrific.

"He caught the first train he could, starting at midday, and I was left alone with my mother and the servants; you can imagine what I felt at the prospect before me!

"How we got through lunch, my mother and I, is more than I can tell you. It was like eating one's food with some great crafty cat; her eyes, although they were never directly on me, were never quite off me. She seemed to be all the time calculating her strength and my own. Yet she only spoke once, to tell the butler that she would not be at home that afternoon to anyone.

"By the time that lunch was nearly over, my nerves were strung to such a pitch of expectancy and anger that I could have struck her. I remember so well longing for her to do or say something that should goad me into forgetting myself altogether. But she only went on eating and drinking in the same deliberate, cruel way; eating really very little, but drinking—yes, until something that was hardly human seemed to be peeping at me out of her eyes.

"I knew that it must be close upon me, that moment I had been dreading so all those three weeks and which I had come by then to long for so impatiently.

"After lunch my mother left the dining-room and went towards the study, across the hall; I meant to have left her by going to my own room, when she turned and stopped me.

" 'Where are you going?' she asked. We were by ourselves and the door of the dining-room was shut. 'To my bedroom,' I said. I could hear how my voice shook with anger and nervousness, and I saw that she had heard it too—and that she had been hoping for something of the sort, because she swallowed once or twice in her throat and then began to laugh in a kind of glee at my helplessness.

"At that laugh of hers everything seemed to me to go round and round in a reddish mist. I could only stand there, holding on to the stair-rail, until the dizziness cleared away again, and I realized that she was ordering me to do something.

" 'Do you hear me?' she said, without raising her voice above a whisper, and when I shook my head she took me by the shoulders and pushed me in front of her to the study door. I was so dazed, so unprepared for that dreadful hatred that had suddenly come over me, that I let her do as she liked—I could scarcely keep on my feet, much less find my wits enough to resist her.

"She threw open the study door and then twisted away from behind me so quickly that in trying to recover myself, I tripped and fell forwards by papa's big table that stands in the middle of the room. My head came against the edge of it and the blow stunned me a little—I think so because I have never had any but the very haziest idea of what actually happened next.

"I must have lain there on my face some minutes, before I began to wonder, stupidly, why I should be lying on the study carpet of all places in the world, with my blouse hanging to my wrists, in broad daylight. At first I thought it must be a bad dream and decided to wake up from it. So I tried to raise myself, when I was thrown down again to the floor and heard my mother's voice saying over and over again, 'You *shall* cry out! You *shall* cry out!' Then it all came back to me, and—Léonie, try to put yourself in my place—I bit my hand to keep myself from satisfying her. Physical sensation was returning to me—but I am not going to speak of that. You know what you have seen, but to this day I have never found out for certain what it was that she used upon me. I think it must have been something of metal —until then she had always worn a chatelaine upon a long chain, neither of which I ever saw again. At length I managed to stand up, but she was too spent to do anything but tumble into the nearest chair, giggling and crooning to herself like a madwoman.

"I left her there; and then, just as I was, went out into the hall and up to my bedroom. As it happened, I met no one, but I do not think I should have cared if I had. I was only impatient for the time to come when I might dare to let myself think without the feeling that my mind would go from me if I did. I was barely fourteen, remember, a baby in years, but I had become a woman in heart and purpose—and not a good one.

"As I reached my room and went in, I saw that someone was bending over the chest of drawers putting away some linen. It was Rosina. Before I knew where I was I had thrown myself into her arms and was clinging to her, my face over her shoulder, so that she should not see how I was trying not to give way to pain and shock. She did not say anything, but just let me hold her, without attempting to interfere in my struggle for breath—for something seemed to be choking me—until, when I began to tell her what had happened, she made me sit down on the bed, and then locked the door.

"Bad as I know her to have been, Léonie, I shall never forget what she did for me—if I had been her own daughter she could not have handled me more sensitively; all the time that she was bathing and dressing me she kept on trying to console, me calling me pet names and crying over me.

"Soon the whole wretched story was out. When I came to telling her of the last three weeks, and of how I found it impossible to say my prayers, Rosina seemed to become suddenly full of a sort of eagerness, so to speak—I cannot call it by any other name—and began to kiss me as though she were relieved about something.

" 'I know what you feel,' she said. 'But you are not alone in that. Did you think you were the only one who had learned the injustice, the cruelty of life? No, indeed; there are thousands of us, an army. You shall join us and we will comfort you. Like all the rest, you, too, have been fed upon lies, the old lies of the priests, who hate that anyone should be free from them and their God, their Jehovah. Would you like to be happy, to be free, free to love and to hate? To be able to laugh at the tyranny of what is called Religion, to be what Nature meant you to be, true to her laws and yourself only?'

"She said this, it struck me, as if she had learnt it by heart from a book, which gave it to my ears a weight and an authority that it could never have had if it had come only from an ill-educated peasant-woman like herself. As you must know, I was right in thinking so.

" 'Yes,' I said, as eagerly as she. 'That is what I want—freedom to be myself and to do as I like. But how is it to be done? I am only a girl still, and have to do as I am told; to go to church and pretend that I like it.'

"Of course, it is impossible for me to remember, word by word, exactly what passed between us. But I will try to reconstruct it as well as I can.

" 'True,' she answered; 'you have to pretend, but then, so do many of us. It cannot be helped. You must take it as part of your revenge upon everything that has hurt you and deceived you—the priests and their God who compel you to it, in trying to extort from you by force and fraud a worship at which your whole being revolts. But, if you will promise to keep it a secret, I will show you how you can defeat them.'

"I promised to do anything she pleased, and then she went on:

" 'First of all,' she asked, 'do you believe in Lucifer, the archangel who preferred the loss of Heaven to that of his pride?'

" 'Yes,' I said, 'I suppose I do.'

"Then she put the elements of the scheme before me; put them fairly ably, always with the same peculiar glibness, as though she were repeating a lesson—the scheme of *Them* and their creed of the ultimate triumph of Lucifer over God, and of how they held that Lucifer was all-powerful and all-willing to reward his servants—not by the promises of any vague joys of the Christian Heaven, but in solid value of this world. 'The priests themselves,' she said, 'acknowledge this much in their Bible. Read where it tells how Lucifer took their Christ " . . . and led him into a high mountain, and showed him all the kingdoms of the world in a moment of time; And he said to him: To thee will I give all this power and the glory of them; *for to me they are delivered, and to whom I will I give them.* If thou wilt, therefore, adore before me, all shall be thine." ' "

"Ah, how often have I heard *Them* quote it!" Léonie exclaimed. "The old story—without the context!"

"Yes, now one knows how to read it truly; but it was different then. I was thunderstruck at the possibilities it suggested. Although something in me seemed to hold out for a time against receiving and availing myself of it, yet, at length, it began gradually to take hold of me. When Rosina saw that I was wavering, she left me for a minute and came back with a book in her hand, a copy of Carducci's poems, which she opened and showed me that hideous pæan of his—you know it, I expect:

> " 'Salute, O Satana, O Ribellione,
> O Forza vindice della Ragione,
> Sacri à te salgano gli incensi ei voti,
> Hai vinto il Geova dei Sacerdoti!' "

"Yes, I know them," said Léonie. "Poor little Yolanda! What chance had you?"

"I had met Carducci, once, when I was with papa, and had heard them talk of 'Humanity' and 'Progress' and the 'Universal Brotherhood of Man.' I had heard papa agree with him, and the recollection seemed to place a seal of authority on Carducci's abominable lines that endowed them for me with a power they might not have had otherwise.

"I read them again and again. Although I could not help being terrified by their blasphemy, yet I saw that my only choice lay between subscribing to it or else taking up my burden again where I had left it—my burden of allegiance to Christianity. As I still hesitated, Rosina pretended to be angry with me and snatched the book out of my hands.

" 'If you are afraid of the priests, then go back to them,' she said. 'Since you are coward enough to let yourself be punished like an animal, it is no affair of mine. I am sorry I offered to help you!'

"And so she went away and left me to my own thoughts.

"Hours passed, and no one came near me. Not a sound reached me from anywhere, except, now and then, a rumble of thunder through the open windows of my room—the same room that I am still using at home, and that looks over the gardens. As time went by, it grew so dark that I could hardly make out the dressing-table between the windows. I give you these details to show you just what I was going through there by myself—the twilight and the loneliness about me were so exactly the same as those within me.

"The darker it got, the darker my mind became, until the last glimmer of good seemed to go out of it. As it did, and I told myself that nothing should deprive me of my hatred, and that I would rather lose my soul than forgive my mother for what she had done to me, the room was suddenly lit up by a light that danced and hovered between the bed and the window and then disappeared, leaving it all blacker than before.

"It was only sheet lightning, of course, but to me it seemed as if my choice had been noted and registered beyond all recall. But although I felt sure of it, yet the idea had no effect upon me—beyond hardening my determination to let nothing rob me of my hatred. I was too proud of it even to get up and shut the windows against the storm that was beginning to roar in at me from the sky. Besides, I could not stir without feeling as though my body were on fire.

"It was not long after that, that I heard the door open again. Rosina had come back, and was bringing me some food.

" 'Here is something to eat,' she said, 'You must be hungry. I will close the windows and light the candles. Shall we talk while you have your supper? Your mother will not disturb us—I have seen to that. She is too much afraid of your father's getting to hear of it to do anything more.'

"But all I wanted was something to drink, for my throat was burning. Rosina saw at once how feverish I was and took advantage of it. She gave me some wine and water and told me only to sip it a little at a time. Then she asked if I were still afraid to be free?

"From then on I had no more will of my own left me any longer, and Rosina seemed to do what she liked with me.

"There was nothing that she left unsaid; when I think of how really extraordinarily cleverly she managed the whole thing, it still astonishes me—she did not neglect a single point that could strengthen her argument and make me her slave.

"She began by flattering me about my prettiness. She talked of love—I refuse even to think of how she spoke about it—and said that the priests and the Church were its enemies and that, as long as I was a Christian, it would be forbidden to me. After that she spent a long time in working on my hatred towards my mother for her cruelty to me, and in stirring up all my resentment against God, until at last she saw that I was ripe for anything and that nothing, however unnatural or repulsive, would be too much for me to consider. She made me repeat Carducci's hymn after her—by then I found it quite easy—and then told me to say that I belonged to Lucifer. Somehow, I did not want to—but she made me. 'Say it,' she said. 'Say, "I belong to Lucifer, not to the priests any longer." Let me hear you say it.'

"When I had said it, she told me that I should have to prove myself by doing a certain paltry service for my new master.

"'What is it?' I asked.

"'Nothing dangerous or difficult,' she answered. 'It only has to do with the bit of wafer that the priests give you at "Communion," as they call it. Instead of swallowing it, as you have been in the habit of doing, you must keep it, the next time, and give it to me.'

"As she said this, she bent over me and brought her eyes so close to mine that I could not even shut them, but had to look into hers. I had lost all wish to think for myself. I only wanted what she wanted, and I said 'Yes,' because there was nothing else that I could think of to say."

Yolanda paused to glance at a small clock on the mantelpiece. It was growing late, and she made haste to bring her tale to an end.

"About ten days later, when I was well enough to go to Communion again," she continued, "I went to the Cathedral with Rosina. She kept close to me, even at the altar-rails. After Mass we went home together and up to my room, where I took what she wanted from my handkerchief and gave it to her, without letting my eyes rest on it—*that* was still impossible for me.

"It was nearly a month later, however, before I could persuade her to take me to make friends with the other people—*Them*—that she had told me so much about. All that time, whenever she could get me to herself, she used to talk to me of the happiness of the Satanists, and of their splendid freedom to enjoy themselves as they pleased. She gave me some books, too—horrible books with pictures—that she made me lock up in my room. At first I could not bring myself to do more than look at them—the very touch of them made me want to wash my hands! For days I was ashamed to look at myself in the glass.

"But, gradually, I became accustomed to the idea of wanting to read them—I was only fourteen, remember, Léonie—and my curiosity got the better of me. So I read them. Ever since then I have had to fight against the consequences to my mind.

"The marvel seems to me that I am not worse than I am, and that those books did not kill my soul altogether. But they did something that Rosina wanted of them—they ploughed my imagination and prepared it to receive the reality of *Them* and their insane atrocities—the Black Mass and all the rest of it—in a way that she knew she could never have dared attempt to do in words. That was my noviate!

"At last, when she thought that I was hardened enough to stand it, she took me with her, one Friday night, to that awful house that you and I know so well—to our cost!

"Imagine my amazement when, after Rosina had given the countersign, we were let in, and I found myself standing in front of Botti—the man I had known all my life as our old doctor! He seemed quite at his ease, though, and led the way to the upper room—you know it—where he talked for some time about what would happen to me if I ever betrayed *Them*, even to my father. Then he made me take the oath and sign my name, and we all went down again to the hall, where he opened the door into the chapel—the door into Hell.

"There is no call for me to try and give you any description of what followed, Léonie. The first poisonous breath of the braziers; the stench of burning weeds; the abominable caricature-crucifix; the grotesque monstrosity of Botti in his biretta with the red buffalo-horns, and his vestments with the vile embroidery on the back of them; the terrific blow, to one's intelligence, of that first Black Mass.

"When it came to the part where Botti had consecrated and had thrown the Host down among the miserable mad men and women who were scrambling for It, I turned sick—literally—and Rosina had to get me out of the place.

"I think she was frightened, even then, that I might not be able to keep the thing to myself without seeking comfort from it from my father or a priest, and she repeated Botti's threats until she was sure of me again, sure that I was far more frightened of him than of anything else.

"But I have never once been able to be present at a Black Mass without having to shut my eyes when it comes to that hideous consecration. And, when it is over, never once, thank God, have I let myself be kept there for so much as a single moment—if anyone had ever tried to hold me back, I would have killed him or her, rather than endure it. Since I grew up, I have never been to that house without a weapon—you believe that of me, do you not, Léonie?"

Léonie looked up quickly.

"I have never believed anything else, Yolanda."

Léonie's eyes travelled to the white face and over the shapely form that shook with the energy of the girl's appeal. Then they fell again, and she was silent.

"Besides," continued Yolanda, "there is something that I have not told you. I—I have found a compromise——"

"*A compromise?*"

"A middle way, so that I no longer do the sin that I did. For months past I have been——"

"Yes, well, and what have you been doing, Yolanda? How have you avoided the one particular sin? That is to say, if you have been trafficking with *Them* all this time?"

"I do not know what you will say when I tell you," replied the girl. "It is simply this—not a single wafer that I have given Botti lately has been consecrated. Do you not see? I have stolen the unconsecrated ones at night from where they are kept in the sacristy of the Cathedral——"

"What can I say to you, Yolanda? It is all frightful—hateful!"

"And yet I do not see what else I can do. At least it is not so bad as stealing the consecrated Hosts at Communion or from the tabernacle."

To Yolanda's surprise, however, Léonie made no effort to argue with her, but was silent again for a while as though communing within herself upon some other matter.

"Yolanda, dear," she said at last, "I want to say that whatever help I can afford you, I will gladly. Yet we are faced by the forces of evil and our task will not be easy. I tremble for the future."

With that Léonie fell to her knees and began to pray that they might be given wisdom and strength sufficient to bring them safely through what lay before them, and past what lay in wait for them, out there in the darkness and the night . . .

Witchs are not evil people
We do not worship the Devil That's a
Anti Witch bllet our Rede is,
    "An't hurt none, do thou wit t" And uxe
eIIeP that any thing that you do will come back 3 fold